TRACK TWO DIPLOMACY
IN THEORY AND PRACTICE

TRACK TWO DIPLOMACY IN THEORY AND PRACTICE

Peter Jones

with a Foreword by George P. Shultz

Stanford University Press
Stanford, California

Stanford University Press
Stanford, California

© 2015 by the Board of Trustees of the Leland Stanford Junior University.
All rights reserved.

No part of this book may be reproduced or transmitted in any form or by any
means, electronic or mechanical, including photocopying and recording, or in any
information storage or retrieval system without the prior written permission of
Stanford University Press.

Printed in the United States of America on acid-free, archival-quality paper

Library of Congress Cataloging-in-Publication Data

Jones, Peter L. (Peter Leslie), 1961– author.
  Track two diplomacy in theory and practice / Peter Jones ; with a foreword
by George Shultz.
    pages cm
  Includes bibliographical references and index.
  ISBN 978-0-8047-9406-0 (cloth : alk. paper)
  ISBN 978-0-8047-9624-8 (pbk. : alk. paper)
  1. Track two diplomacy. I. Title.
JZ1323.7.J66 2015
327.2—dc23

                                                              2015002257

ISBN 978-0-8047-9632-3 (electronic)

To Emma and William

Contents

Foreword

George P. Shultz

TRACK TWO DIPLOMACY IS SOMETHING I HEARD OF frequently during my years as Secretary of State. To be honest, I was often somewhat leery of it. I did not question the motives or the integrity of *most* who were engaged in it. Rather, my concern was that it would get in the way of our official diplomatic efforts and confuse others as to where the United States stood on various matters. More than once, I gave instructions to State Department officials to inform a foreign government in no uncertain terms that the US Government had nothing to do with this or that Track Two initiative and did not endorse it.

Since leaving office, I have had a deeper association with Track Two and have taken part in some of these discussions. My views have evolved now that I am no longer charged with the day-to-day management of foreign policy (which can be largely a matter of rushing from one crisis to another, but must be transformed and informed always by a sense of strategy) and have time to reflect more on things. In particular, I now realize that properly done Track Two does not seek to "get in the way" of Track One diplomacy, as those in office sometimes fear, but rather to complement it, often by going to places where Track One is unable to tread and by tackling subjects it cannot approach.

To my mind, this is the essence of useful Track Two. It achieves its greatest contributions when it provides a forum for the kinds of discussions which are vitally necessary if a thorny problem is to be dealt with. In this sense, Track

Two provides a mechanism to explore new ways forward without committing anyone to anything. When it is carefully and well done, that is extraordinarily useful. Most importantly, Track Two provides a space whereby serious people can consider and develop alternate and creative ways of viewing things—something governments mired in conflict are notoriously bad at doing, I have generally found.

To be successful at this challenging task, it seems to me that a few key considerations need to be borne in mind. First, these dialogues must involve influential people who can sway opinion at home. These are not "academic" discussions; they are meant to generate ideas which can have a real-world impact. Often, those taking part will be retired leaders or retired senior officials, but they can also be civil society leaders, depending on what audience the particular Track Two is trying to reach. What matters is that they should be people to whom others will listen when they come home with new and controversial ideas. Second, it is critical that the mood around the table allow for a far-reaching and no-holds-barred discussion. At the same time, the discussion must have a basis in reality in terms of what can work. The creation of a conversation which is at once far-reaching but also grounded in reality is a difficult balancing act. I particularly like the fact that this technique is referred to in the field as a "problem solving" approach, which I think is exactly right; it is not about defending positions but about mutually and collaboratively trying to understand and then resolve a problem. Which brings me to my third observation: the role of the convener and facilitator of the dialogue, the so-called third party, is crucial in creating an atmosphere in which the right kind of discussion can take place, and in gently nurturing and steering the process over time. It is a complex role which is often underappreciated and misunderstood. One of the greatest contributions of this book is to explore the role of the third party and to demystify it.

This book is the result of a challenge. In 2011, I sponsored Peter Jones to bring to the Hoover Institution at Stanford University a meeting of an ongoing India–Pakistan Track Two project he has been running called "The Ottawa Dialogue." It was a meeting about the difficult nuclear relationship between these two countries, and it was part of a series which had quietly been underway for some time and which has continued since. That meeting, and the others in the series, brought together retired people from the two countries who had held very senior positions of leadership on these issues just a short time before, as well as subject-matter experts from academe and civil society in the two countries. The discussions were tough, even brutal at times, but productive. The mood was informal, even though it was not always comfortable, and the participants seemed willing, even eager, to explore ideas that they had not been able to when they had been in office.

Sitting in on these meetings, and talking with Peter about his ongoing Track Two work in this region and others, caused me to wonder if anyone had ever written a book which presented and analyzed the current state of thinking about Track Two and its place in international relations. This would not be a theoretical book, although it should be informed by theory, but rather a book that would make the subject accessible to officials and students. When Peter told me that there had been some books which tried to tackle this in years past, though with mixed results, and that there was nothing recent which covered this ground, I challenged him to write the book. You hold in your hands the result.

What makes for successful Track Two? As Peter shows us in these pages, much depends on what a given project seeks to achieve—there are many different definitions of Track Two and each has its particular set of objectives and methods. Indeed, one of the most useful elements of this book is its careful and rigorous unpacking of the term "Track Two," which is too often casually used to cover a myriad of different kinds of dialogues. By showing us that dialogues held under the rubric "Track Two" can have very different methods, participants, and objectives, this book provides a critical guide to those who intersect with Track Two, whether as officials, scholars, or students, as to how to approach the subject and understand its potential contributions.

I also appreciate the fact that the book does not shy away from discussing the limitations of Track Two. These are important. There is a tendency for enthusiasts to believe that their favored method is applicable in all cases, when it is not. People who are active in the field, and those who study it, must be aware when Track Two is *not* appropriate to a situation or problem. In my experience, cases where Track Two projects overstepped their ability to be helpful were the ones which did damage and brought disrepute to the field as a whole. As in so many things, really well-done Track Two is often quiet and few know of it, while badly done Track Two generates considerable notoriety.

I am excited about this book. I wish it had been around when I was Secretary of State. It brings together in a clear and readable way the theory of

Track Two, but tempers it critically with real-world insights and observations. Peter's background as an official who has negotiated important international agreements, as an academic who brings scholarly rigor to his subject, and as someone who both practices and studies Track Two at the highest level shines through on every page.

I challenged Peter to write the book on Track Two. He has met my challenge.

George P. Shultz
Hoover Institution
Stanford University

Preface

THIS BOOK HAS BEEN OVER TWENTY YEARS IN THE making. In the early 1990s, while working on arms control issues in Canada's Department of Foreign Affairs, then known as "External Affairs," I was assigned to work on the Middle East peace process. I had no particular Middle East background, having spent my academic training on arms control and my years in government service working on East–West, Cold War arms control issues, primarily at the United Nations and in Europe. But the Cold War had recently ended and Canada had been asked to play a facilitating role in one of the multilateral working groups of the Middle East peace process, the one dealing with arms control and regional security.

It was a fascinating experience but ultimately a frustrating one, as the working group fell apart after some years over a series of issues it was not equipped to tackle. In particular, the diplomatic realities of the moment were such that certain countries, including Iran, Iraq, and Syria, were either not invited or not willing to take part, and it was not possible to have a serious discussion of regional security or arms control without them at the table. It also proved impossible to discuss certain issues, such as Israel's ambiguous nuclear status, in these official talks. Finally, although the multilateral working groups of the peace process were supposed to work outside of the central issue of that process, namely the Israeli–Palestinian dispute, it proved impossible to insulate the multilaterals from the corrosive effects of that all-encompassing conflict.

I left government service in 1995 and began four years as the leader of a new project on Middle East security and arms control at the Stockholm International Peace Research Institute (SIPRI). My first thought on arriving at SIPRI was to gather up some of my former colleagues and other noted experts on Middle East regional security to discuss what had happened in the peace-process working group, and what might be done to further the work we had tried to accomplish there. Key to this, I felt, was to create a process which would include those who had not been part of the official talks (the Iranians, for example), and also to tackle the issues the official talks had not been able to address because they were too sensitive for some governments in the region to discuss.

After some soundings in the region, it became clear to me that the only way to do this was to hold the discussions informally and unofficially, even though many present would be officials and even though we would be talking about issues that had been very much on the agenda of official negotiations. It further became clear that critical to this definition of informal and unofficial discussions there would have to be a very clear and explicit understanding that we would not actually be negotiating, as only governments can do that. Rather, we would be exploring some of the underlying questions surrounding these issues, which had proved impossible to do in the formal negotiations, in order to see if we could come up with some ideas that might make progress possible should formal talks ever resume. Thus began a four-year project which saw multiple meetings across the region and eventually produced a small book outlining proposals for a Middle East regional cooperation system, as developed by regional officials and experts[1]—an idea that the official discussions I had been part of were never able to come to grips with.

At one point during this SIPRI process one of my Middle Eastern colleagues said to me, "You know, you are running quite a good Track Two here." I had no idea what he meant; the term was quite new to me. His comment spurred me to look into the term "Track Two." The literature at that time was very limited, much more so than today, but it still fascinated me. The idea of bringing together small groups of influential people to quietly discuss things that could not be discussed officially, and including in those discussions people from countries that did not officially recognize each other and thus had few if any other means of communicating, struck a chord in me; it was something I had instinctively known was often missing from the way important problems were dealt with by official diplomacy. All too often

I had seen situations where an official negotiation had become stuck over an issue which the diplomats around the table were not able to discuss because of "instructions" not to do so, but which clearly needed to be addressed if the larger negotiation was to move forward. Sometimes this was intentional, as one country simply wanted to slow the talks. In such cases no amount of creativity would provide a way forward. Sometimes, however, it was not intentional but rather a case of wider issues and differences getting in the way of the discussion of a particular problem. In yet other cases, it was clear that representatives of two countries needed to talk to each other but could not do so in an official diplomatic process because of the lack of formal "recognition" between their countries.

In cases where I had seen negotiations succeed under very difficult circumstances, it was often because creative diplomats were able to develop informal paths of discussion whereby questions could be explored in a "brainstorming" format rather than argued or bargained over around the negotiating table. Such talks are sometimes referred to as "walks in the woods"—informal discussions on the margins of negotiations but still very much over the issues on the table. The phrase "a walk in the woods" refers to an attempt on the part of negotiators to quietly explore possibilities for compromise which go beyond their strict instructions. It is most famously attributed to an incident in 1982 when the US and Soviet chiefs of delegation to the strategic arms limitation talks in Geneva (Paul Nitze and Yuli Kvitsinski, respectively) quietly left the negotiating room for a walk in the woods on the outskirts of the city to see if they could work out a way to overcome the significant differences in their formal instructions. They were able to do so, but their compromise formula was subsequently shot down by the bureaucracies in Washington and Moscow—leading some to wonder if either government was really serious about arms control at that time.[2]

At other times, a "prenegotiation" is held. This is a structured process whereby officials meet somewhat informally to identify and explore the issues likely to be in play, should negotiations ever commence formally, in order to develop a structure of concepts and trade-offs that will then be bargained over once formal negotiations proceed.[3] Walks in the woods and prenegotiation can be critical to diplomacy and share elements in common with Track Two. But they are also activities where the participants are still bargaining over national positions—perhaps also using the informality of the talks to develop those positions, but bargaining over official positions nonetheless.

Useful as these methods are, what is often missing from official diplomacy is a process whereby those dealing with a complex problem can completely step back from their official roles and enter a realm where their objective is not to develop and then defend a national position within a bargaining process, but to work together to fundamentally reassess their mutual understanding of the basic issues in play and then to see if they can jointly reconceptualize their fundamental differences and discover what the problem is really about. Such a discussion would, by definition, involve exploring the deeper psychological or subjective aspects of the issue and redefining what those aspects mean to each side.

Might it be possible to develop other means of having such informal discussions as a way of getting beyond the limitations of official diplomacy? During my time at SIPRI, I began researching Track Two as a discrete method, and also became involved in other Track Two projects in the Middle East and Asia. After leaving SIPRI in 1999, I returned to government service in Canada, spending seven years with the Prime Minister's Department, known as the "Privy Council Office," working on national security affairs. For much of this time I was immensely fortunate to have a series of superiors who encouraged me to continue to work on Track Two projects in the Middle East even while serving as an official—something which would likely not happen today and was, even then, regarded suspiciously by some in the Canadian bureaucracy (often by those who felt that their real or, more often, their desired "turf" might be compromised). I also continued my exploration of Track Two as a subject in its own right, and began thinking that it was a generally misunderstood and underappreciated element of foreign affairs and foreign policy. By definition, much of what happens in Track Two takes place away from the limelight, and officials are sometimes skeptical of it.

My research and practice in the field led me to the view that a university course on the subject might be of interest to those studying international affairs, especially the subjects of diplomacy and the resolution of disputes. Looking around the world, I could find no other example of such a course, and so I developed one and pitched it to the Politics Department at Queen's University in Kingston, Ontario. They accepted, somewhat to my surprise, and so I began a two-year stint as an adjunct professor there while still working in the Privy Council Office. The response of the students was extremely enthusiastic. Like me a few years earlier, most of them had never heard of

Track Two but saw it as a novel method for coming to grips with persistent conflicts that will not yield to traditional diplomatic methods.

The combination of my growing involvement in Track Two activities, my research interests, and my teaching on the subject eventually led me to leave government service once again in 2007 and to seek a position which would allow me to concentrate full time on Track Two. Around this time I was extremely fortunate that the University of Ottawa was launching a new Graduate School of Public and International Affairs and, as a basic part of the philosophy of the new school, was looking for faculty having backgrounds which straddled the academic and policy worlds. I was also fortunate that those launching the graduate school came to view Track Two as an area that could be a good fit for the school's activities and research. I have been at the University of Ottawa ever since, and it has proved a very supportive home for this work.

The primary catalyst for this book, however, occurred in 2011, when I had the good fortune to meet former US Secretary of State George P. Shultz. A meeting of an India–Pakistan Track Two project I had been running for some years, called "The Ottawa Dialogue," held a session at the Hoover Institution on War and Peace at Stanford University, where Mr. Shultz is the Thomas W. and Susan B. Ford Distinguished Fellow. Mr. Shultz was very supportive of the meeting, and also expressed an interest in learning more about Track Two—something he had heard of often, particularly during his tenure as secretary of state. Mr. Shultz challenged me to write this book and made possible an Annenberg Distinguished Visiting Fellowship at Hoover for this purpose. I have used my periods in residence at Stanford to complete the bulk of the writing, and have benefited enormously from the experience. In particular, Mr. Shultz's penetrating, incisive, and always supportive comments and criticisms have made the book far better. His is a very rare combination of decades of practical experience at the very highest levels of statecraft and a constant willingness to subject "common knowledge" to the withering scrutiny of an enormous intellectual curiosity.

Many people have kindly read various drafts, and the book has been greatly improved by their comments. Ron Fisher and Esra Çuhadar served as the two "anonymous" readers who reviewed the book for Stanford University Press, though both identified themselves to me after they had submitted their reviews and both made numerous and highly thoughtful comments on it. Others who read the book and gave me valuable insights include Ian Anderson,

Byron Bland, Poul-Erik Christiansen, Craig Dunkerley, Jim Goodby, Happymon Jacob, Karin Jones, Shoshana Lucich, Andrea Magahey, Ifat Maoz, Adam Moscoe (who also helped format the book for Stanford University Press), T.V. Paul, Brenna Marea Powell, Katherine Tice, and Nicole Waintraub (who has also served as my assistant and colleague in many Track Two projects).

At the University of Ottawa, I wish to thank President Allan Rock, who has always seen Track Two as an example of the kind of thing a university should be deeply engaged with; Francois Houle, the Dean of Social Sciences when I joined the faculty and a great supporter of my Track Two work; his successor as Dean, Marcelle Merette, who has enthusiastically continued this support; Luc Juillet, the first Director of the Graduate School of Public and International Affairs; and his successor, Catherine Liston-Hayes, both of whom see Track Two as an activity very much in keeping with the mission of the school. I also wish to thank the students who have taken my course on Track Two over the years, at the University of Ottawa and at Queen's University, for constantly challenging me to think of the subject in new ways.

Finally, I would like to thank all those at the Stanford University Press who worked so diligently and professionally to realize this book, including Geoffrey Burn, James Holt, and Tim Roberts.

Introduction: Why This Book, What Is It About, and Who Is It For?

A S MY OWN EXPERIENCE HAS STRADDLED THE TRACK One, Track Two, and academic worlds, this book will attempt to do the same. At various times in my career I have been active in all three, sometimes in overlapping ways. This overlap strikes me as a critical nexus where greater understanding could be forged. I have often observed that those involved in official diplomacy have little understanding and appreciation for the complex and nuanced role that Track Two can play, and also for its limitations. But the reverse is also true: many of those active in the world of Track Two are ignorant of the realities and pressures of the diplomatic world and not particularly adept at framing their efforts to make them accessible to hard-pressed officials. Further, those whose primary interest in Track Two is academic, say as part of their study of international affairs, sometimes fail to sufficiently understand the realities of either.

This book is thus aimed at multiple audiences. The first audience is officials who perhaps want to understand more deeply what Track Two is and isn't, and what roles it can and cannot realistically be expected to play. The second audience is practitioners of the various forms of Track Two—for there are many kinds of Track Two, often existing in isolation from each other. A need exists to bridge the divides between these practitioners and officials, and between the different types of Track Two itself. The final audience is students of international affairs who are interested in the role that this generally little-understood form of interaction can play in helping to resolve conflicts, increasing regional cooperation, or developing new international norms. The book thus deliberately crosses disciplines and traditions, and it makes no apologies for this. Purists in any one of these three areas, and perhaps especially theorists, may well be disappointed, but so be it. The book is not aimed at them; it is intended for those who want to explore the territory where the three come together.

The book also borrows from different theoretical and empirical traditions to construct an eclectic approach, whose primary purpose is to explain and analyze its subject rather than to further a particular theoretical approach or argument. Scholars of international affairs who are looking for primarily theoretical discussions will thus be disappointed, as will officials looking for hard and fast answers. Practitioners of Track Two who believe that their particular method of practice is the only type of activity that can legitimately bear the name Track Two will also be disappointed—but I hope they will also be curious to learn what others are doing under that name.

So much for what the book isn't. What I hope readers *will* find is an exploration of the various dimensions and guises of Track Two; how they work in theory and in practice; and how Track Two could more profitably be assessed, both by officials and by academics. These are not small questions. In studying and practicing Track Two in many regions of the world over two decades, not only have I been impressed by the sheer diversity of activities that go on under the title "Track Two," but I have noted significant differences between how it is practiced and understood in different places. While it may be too ambitious to try to produce an all-encompassing typology of Track Two, this book will have made its contribution if it provides a fuller picture than has heretofore existed of the range of activities which go on under this title, and provokes some new thinking as to how these activities relate to each other, to official diplomacy, and to academe.

The book is divided into two sections. The first section, on theory, opens with a chapter which explores the definition of Track Two, or more precisely, tries to give the reader a more sophisticated and fulsome explanation of the different definitions which have evolved over the years and how they relate to each other. Many people have tried to define Track Two, and the differences between the definitions are indicative of widely varying conceptions of what it is, what its objectives are, and how it relates to official diplomacy, or does not.

The second chapter in this section situates Track Two in terms of prevailing theories and schools which are used to describe and analyze international affairs. I contend that one of the key problems various groups and individuals have had in assessing Track Two is that they have come at it from very different starting points depending on their conception of international relations (IR). Realists, liberals, and constructivists see the world in different terms and assess the character and utility of Track Two quite differently. It is thus necessary to discuss how Track Two relates to the prevailing schools of IR. Beyond that, this chapter explores how at least some practitioners of mediation generally, and Track Two in particular, have tried—with mixed results—to fit their work into the prevailing paradigms of IR in coming to grips with what Track Two is and where it fits. Many of those who actually work in the field of Track Two do not conceive of debates over IR theory as being especially relevant to what they do, though they borrow from them in an eclectic fashion to better understand what they are doing.

The third chapter explores some of the ways in which specific theoretical concepts apply to those who are engaged in Track Two. One of these is the question of "theories of change," the way a Track Two practitioner believes that his or her work will have an impact on the conflict. A related question is whether a Track Two practitioner is seeking to manage, resolve, or transform a conflict; each of these goals is different and will bring different basic assumptions and techniques into play. Another issue is when to launch a Track Two project. Some are influenced by an idea known as "ripeness," while others believe that ripeness is too limiting. Finally, the chapter also explores several matters relating to culture and ethics.

The second section of the book addresses a series of questions relating to the broad theme of practice. Issues explored in these chapters include the ongoing debate over the characteristics and roles of the "third party" in convening and running a Track Two process; an analysis of the methods, objectives, and limitations of the "problem-solving workshop," regarded by many as the prototypical technique whereby many Track Two processes bring together those in conflict; how the results of Track Two projects are "transferred" to the official track, or to other destinations, depending on the intent of the project; how the results of Track Two projects might be measured; and practical issues about ethics within the field. I explore these questions by examining the literature in the field, but I also make extensive use of my own experience as to how they play out in practice. The Conclusion brings together main themes and suggests areas for consideration by those interested in developing the field.

SECTION I
IN THEORY

1 What Is Track Two Diplomacy?

FOR A TERM WHICH IS WIDELY AND OFTEN USED IN THE field of international relations, "Track Two diplomacy" defies easy definition. This is, in some ways, a source of strength. A loosely defined concept is one which can be applicable in many situations and can evolve quickly to meet the needs of different parties in different circumstances. Those who look at Track Two through a primarily operational lens would urge us not to seek specificity at the expense of flexibility. One is after all dealing with a process which is profoundly about the interactions between people, and firm definitions which attempt to cover all aspects of such situations are likely to be constraining and therefore not useful in the real world.[1] Others argue that the lack of a firm understanding of what Track Two is can be a potential source of weakness; absent a widely accepted definition and, more importantly, absent the rigorous empirical and intellectual standards which often accompany efforts to develop such a definition, one can struggle to understand and communicate the boundaries of accepted practice. This means that the field can be open to unrestricted experimentation and even amateurish and destructive practices. Critics and skeptics can lambaste Track Two, critiquing certain cases which may not be representative of the field in the eyes of its proponents. And it becomes difficult to further establish the credibility of the field through research and analysis when different people are studying different things.[2]

Over the years many attempts have been made to define Track Two; the main ones will be explored in this chapter. Some attempts have focused on the specifics of the activity itself, developing from various case studies an outline of what happens in a "typical" Track Two event as a means of defining the field more generally. The problem is that no two Track Two processes are the same, and some are wildly different. Such definitions therefore may capture a specific case or two but rarely capture the array of activities which go on under this name.

Others have focused on defining who the actors in a Track Two process are as the key to defining what is happening in a larger sense. They have tried to define the roles of those who are in conflict and the roles of those who take on the task of the so-called third party which brings the protagonists together. They also study the types of people who do this. Once again, however, this approach does not yield a satisfactory, much less an all-encompassing definition of Track Two. Different Track Two processes can have very different kinds of actors. These can range from those who are entirely removed from official life, to those who are not officials but are very close to their governments, to officials themselves who are "acting in their private capacity." Moreover, the backgrounds of these individuals can vary widely in their approaches to international affairs and to world politics.

Still others have sought to define Track Two by reference to its place within the larger negotiation process, most often seeing Track Two as a form of "prenegotiation"—a set of informal talks which help the two sides get to the formal negotiating table. While useful in some ways, this definition can limit views as to when and how Track Two is useful in that it conceives of Track Two as necessarily a tool to help parties get to an official negotiating table. Often Track Two is precisely this, but sometimes it is not; sometimes Track Two projects can be underway in parallel with official negotiations. But they can also be undertaken not to complement official talks, or the prospect of them, but rather to develop alternatives to official negotiation, often at the so-called grassroots level. Finally, some have tried to define Track Two by breaking it into a variety of categories, depending on what is going on, and then speaking about each in specific terms. While satisfying to some, no typology can ever really capture the large multiplicity of cases.

With so many, often conflicting, dimensions in play, it is probably impossible to come up with a concrete explanation or definition of Track Two which will adequately cover all cases. Attempts to do so quickly degenerate into largely frustrating theoretical debates over the application of certain terms and concepts to circumstances they were never meant to cover. Moreover, the question of defining Track Two is, for some, part of broader debates over the evolution of the field of conflict resolution. What this chapter will attempt to do, therefore, is to give the reader a sense of the array of activities which go on under the rubric of "Track Two diplomacy," and also a sense of the attempts which have been made in the past to explain and define it. Such a baseline is critical for the chapters that follow, which delve into specific issues confronting the field.

The First Use of the Term

Many are surprised to learn that the term "Track Two diplomacy" was not coined until relatively recently. It is generally agreed that the term was first used by Joseph Montville, an American foreign service officer.[3] In 1981 Montville used the term to denote unofficial conflict resolution dialogues. He defined Track Two as

> unofficial, informal interaction between members of adversarial groups or nations with the goals of developing strategies, influencing public opinion, and organizing human and material resources in ways that might help resolve the conflict.[4]

Montville was keen to persuade his diplomatic colleagues that such dialogues should be better understood by diplomatic "professionals." In looking at the growing field of conflict resolution, and the growing number of such initiatives that were going on outside the realm of official diplomacy, Montville was concerned that his fellow diplomats were in danger of missing an important development in the field of international relations. He was particularly concerned that a long-standing professional bias against nonofficial involvement in international affairs was leading his colleagues to dismiss something which was subtly changing the landscape of their profession, whether they liked it or not.

Indeed, official suspicion of individuals trying to insert themselves into "diplomacy" has a long history. One of the earliest attempts by a government to formally prevent individuals from inserting themselves into foreign relations was the Logan Act of 1799, passed by the US Congress after a private citizen, Dr. Logan, had traveled to Paris on his own to discuss US-French relations with the French government. The Logan Act reads, in part,

> Any citizen of the United States, wherever he may be, who, without authority of the United States, directly or indirectly commences or carries on any

correspondence or intercourse with any foreign government or any officer or agent thereof, with intent to influence the measures or conduct of any foreign government or of any officer or agent thereof, in relation to any disputes or controversies with the United States, or to defeat the measures of the United States, shall be fined under this title or imprisoned not more than three years, or both.[5]

Almost two hundred years later, many of Montville's diplomatic colleagues still viewed unofficial dialogues as, at best, an irrelevance, while others actively viewed them as a nuisance and believed that such processes should stay out of the way of officials. This view had still not changed significantly almost twenty years after Montville's early work when Cynthia Chataway undertook a study of the attitudes of US officials towards Track Two.[6] Montville wanted diplomats to recognize that government has no monopoly on creativity in the face of difficult international problems and that a relationship between officials and Track Two could generate positive outcomes if properly structured and utilized. But that message has been slow to find widespread acceptance.

Initially there was no magic about the term "Track Two diplomacy." Montville merely noted that if official diplomacy might be called "Track One," then unofficial attempts to resolve differences might be called "Track Two." There is an undeniably elegant simplicity to this term. But it also unfortunately implies that such discussions could be construed as a form of "diplomacy." With very rare exceptions they are not: practitioners of Track Two diplomacy are not diplomats. That title belongs only to those who officially represent their countries.[7] While some Track Two processes may be closely related to, and even sponsored by, official diplomacy and while officials may take part in various Track Two processes in their "private capacities," such processes cannot substitute for official interactions between states and should not try to do so.

It is thus probably unfortunate that the word "diplomacy" found its way into the lexicon surrounding unofficial dialogue and peacemaking, as it has created the potential for misunderstandings as to what is going on here. As we shall see, many of those who have subsequently tried to refine the definition have deliberately dropped the word "diplomacy" from their formulations. While their efforts have found favor with specialists in the field, the broader term "Track Two diplomacy" has caught on in the popular mind and in official circles, and is most often used in the vernacular to describe these efforts. We are thus stuck with it; but we should try to better understand it.

The Conflict Resolution Field

While the bulk of this chapter is dedicated to an exploration of the evolution of the idea and practice of Track Two, it is necessary to situate the discussion within the development of the broader field of conflict resolution. Indeed, for some people, Track Two is best understood as a subfield of the broader area of conflict resolution. This is true for much of Track Two, but not all; there are variants of Track Two that are not dedicated to the resolution of conflict. These include Track Two processes aimed at promoting regional security in various parts of the world, and these need to be understood in their own terms. They will be discussed later in this chapter. Within the conflict resolution stream of Track Two, which is the bulk of the field, there are differing understandings as to what "conflict resolution" actually means in practice, as we shall see when we explore this question in greater detail in Chapter 3.

The field of conflict resolution, as we presently know it in terms of international conflicts, emerged in the middle of the twentieth century when a small group of social scientists, influenced by both interwar theorists of international affairs and the development of new theories of labor relations and other means of settling domestic disputes,[8] began to wonder if these ideas might not be applicable to international relations as well. At the time, the emerging field of international relations theory was heavily influenced by "realist" ideas, and the pioneers of what would become conflict resolution were not generally well received by the mainstream in either academe or official circles.[9]

Nevertheless, these pioneers carried on and began to develop sets of theories as to how conflicts originated, developed, and might be resolved. Over the years, the field has witnessed a significant evolution in its understandings and debates. The earliest days of the field, at its international level of analysis, tended to focus on state-to-state conflicts and the problem of peace between nations. Through the 1960s and the 1970s and onwards, and particularly after the end of the Cold War, new thinking emerged on the question of "intractable" disputes between ethnic and other groups which went on beyond the state-to-state level of analysis, although such conflicts were often exacerbated by events at the state level. Concepts such as social justice, gender and conflict, and the impact of good governance on conflict resolution became much more widely understood and debated. One of the key documents which launched new thinking about conflict resolution in the post–Cold War world was the *Agenda for Peace* released by UN Secretary General Boutros Boutros-Gali in

1992.[10] At the same time, new approaches to negotiations, such as Harvard Law School's "principled negotiation" method, emerged.[11] Much more work was done to understand the complexity and the impact of culture and history on conflicts, beyond Cold War models of international affairs. As will be discussed later in this chapter, much of what would become Track Two as we presently understand it emerged and was refined at this time and was influenced by these wider developments and understandings of what conflict is, how it arises, and how it can be resolved peacefully.

The end of the Cold War saw significant advances in the field through the late 1980s and into the 1990s. As many conflicts which had been (apparently) suppressed by the superpower rivalry burst forth, a host of "scholar-practitioners" and nongovernmental organizations (NGOs) in the conflict resolution field emerged to tackle them at many levels.[12] This brought with it calls for a more professional approach, including techniques to evaluate the impact of interventions. There were also criticisms that the field was too dominated by Western concepts and traditions,[13] and a growing awareness that the wide array of issues that attend what came to be known as "fragile" states need to be understood and addressed. Also during this time, and since, debates have arisen in the field as to the proper relationship between conflict resolution efforts at the level of political and military elites, which seek to manage disputes, and efforts which focus on grassroots peacebuilding as the path to genuine reconciliation (this difference in objectives will be further discussed in Chapter 3).[14]

It would be far too time consuming to detail the evolution of the field of conflict resolution, and several studies already exist for those interested (see notes 9 and 12). Moreover, we shall be exploring various aspects of the field as they relate to Track Two as the book goes along. What matters here is that Track Two has not developed in an intellectual vacuum; it is part of a larger field and has been influenced by (and has influenced) that field over many years.

Track Two Background

Though the term was not coined until 1981, what we would today call Track Two emerged well before that. It is difficult, however, to pinpoint exactly when Track Two began. General discussions of international affairs by interested public elites began at least before World War One in the form of various "peace societies," which often met in The Hague. In retrospect, much of this activity was naïve and would not be considered Track Two by those active in the field today. Immediately following World War Two, a private group called "Moral Rearmament" convened a number of retreats involving prominent German, French, and later, British citizens with the aim of promoting reconciliation between these societies.[15] In the Asia-Pacific region an international NGO called the Institute of Pacific Relations (IPR) was "a pioneering channel of unofficial diplomatic dialogue" from 1928 to 1961.[16] The IPR disbanded following difficulties during the McCarthy era.

Intensive and ongoing Track Two took place between the superpowers during the Cold War. The unofficial Pugwash Conferences and the Dartmouth Conferences opened avenues for dialogue on matters of science, strategic stability, and security. Sometimes tacitly encouraged by the governments of the United States of America and the Union of Soviet Socialist Republics, and occasionally barely tolerated, these dialogues produced ideas which featured in later arms control agreements. These unofficial discussions also provided a mechanism whereby leading figures who were not officials but who often had the ear of their respective governments could meet to discuss issues of peace and security; these were sometimes the only venues where such discussions could take place during the darkest times of the Cold War.[17]

What is now widely regarded as the first example of modern Track Two arose in the mid-1960s when John Burton, a former Australian diplomat, and some of his colleagues at University College London and elsewhere sought to apply some of their emerging theories as to how conflicts should be understood and could be ended. Burton had left official diplomacy after his meteoric rise in the Australian Foreign Service, when he became disenchanted with what he regarded as its excessive focus on such "realist" concepts as "balances of power" as the determining factor in maintaining peace. He developed a view that human factors such as dialogue and communication could be equally important in avoiding and resolving conflicts. Burton therefore decided to test his theories by convening a new sort of process to help resolve a boundary dispute between the newly independent Southeast Asian countries of Malaysia, Singapore, and Indonesia. Interestingly, Burton and his colleagues acted in response to a challenge laid down by their associates at the University of London and elsewhere. They had drawn academic fire for arguing that dialogue, values, and relationships were as important in international affairs as power—a view which ran counter to the prevailing international relations theory of the day: realism. Thus, from the beginning, Track Two, like conflict resolution more generally, has struggled to establish credibility in the eyes of hard-nosed, realist-oriented officials and academics.

Drawing on contacts in the Southeast Asia region, and with support from the United Kingdom government, Burton invited small teams of influential people from each of these countries to London for a series of quiet workshops during 1965–66. Those invited were for the most part not officials but had close government connections in their countries. Using facilitation techniques designed to draw out the participants on the underlying aspects of the dispute rather than trading exchanges over their official positions, Burton and his colleagues assisted the participants in exploring the causes of the disputes and developing potential solutions. These ideas were quietly transmitted to the Malaysian, Singaporean, and Indonesian governments by the participants in the London workshops and were subsequently incorporated into agreements between the countries. Though the exact extent to which the process contributed to the resolution of the boundary disputes is debated, most believe that it played a role.[18] Burton and his colleagues labeled their method "controlled communication." They believed that it constituted a new method of dealing with international disputes consisting of informal, unofficial workshops, chaired by a neutral third party who facilitated the protagonists' mutual analysis of problems with the aim of helping them develop solutions that were not apparent through traditional diplomatic techniques.[19] This was perhaps the first attempt by social scientists to develop and label a specific technique of bringing together nonofficials for a dialogue intended to have an impact on a specific conflict.

Burton's pioneering efforts drew attention in the academic community, particularly among those searching for methods of resolving disputes other than the realist paradigm which dominated official relations during the Cold War. A small but active "scholar-practitioner" community arose, intent on further refining and developing Burton's ideas.[20] Herbert Kelman, a Harvard-based social psychologist who has been a leading figure in informal discussions between Israelis and Palestinians, organized one of the longest-running and best known such dialogues.[21] During the course of his work and research, which began when he met and worked with Burton in the 1960s, Kelman and his colleagues developed a refinement of Burton's "controlled communication," which they referred to as "interactive problem solving."[22] Some years later Kelman defined this model as

an academically based, unofficial third party approach, bringing together representatives of parties in conflict for direct communication. The third party typically consists of a panel of social scientists who, between them, possess expertise in group processes and international conflict, and at least some familiarity with the conflict region. The role of the third party . . . differs from that of the traditional mediator. Unlike many mediators, we do not propose (and certainly, unlike arbitrators, we do not impose) solutions. Rather, we try to facilitate a process whereby solutions will emerge out of the interaction between the parties themselves. The task of the third party is to provide the setting, create the atmosphere, establish the norms, and offer the occasional interventions that make it possible for such a process to evolve.[23]

Kelman's definition is notable for several reasons. Perhaps most importantly he delves into what the so-called third party, the convener of the process, actually does and how it does it. The third party in such a project is not a mediator, as traditionally understood. Rather, in some ways it plays the role of facilitator. Critical in this distinction is the idea that the third party is not there to propose his or her own solutions but to help those in the conflict examine the root causes of their differences and then jointly find their own solutions.[24] This is done through a process of ongoing interaction under controlled circumstances, which are set by the third party with the acceptance of the participants.

Key to these controlled circumstances are what have come to be known as the "rules" of the workshops, to which the participants agree as they are being recruited, and which will be discussed further in Chapter Five. The objective of the rules is to create an atmosphere whereby the participants in the dialogue can move beyond reciting and arguing over their official positions (and beyond trading accusations and recriminations over who "started it"), and towards a joint analysis aimed at uncovering and sharing their perceptions of the root causes of the dispute. The ultimate objective, though it usually takes several meetings over a period of time, is to move from this joint examination of the root causes to an exercise in jointly developing ideas as to how these root causes may be overcome. These ideas are then refined into proposals which are communicated to officials on the two sides of the dispute, or to the wider public—at whatever level the regional participants feel is appropriate to their agreed objectives—a phenomenon known as "transfer," which will be explored in Chapter 6.

It was while Burton and Kelman and others were engaged in such activities, and writing about them throughout the 1960s, 1970s, and 1980s, that these processes first came to the attention of Montville, who as noted coined the phrase "Track Two diplomacy" in 1981 in an effort to get his official colleagues to take notice. Also during this time, social psychologists, such as Leonard Doob and Edward Azar, were probing into how these sorts of small-group interactions actually work and more broadly asking how long-term, systemic, "intractable" conflicts should be best understood and approached. Doob's work, though based largely on trial and error and considered controversial at the time, is generally regarded as pioneering in understanding how small-group interactive peacemaking processes work.[25] Azar contributed greatly to the field through his understanding of protracted social conflicts as primarily taking place over deeply held ethnic and religious beliefs rather than as outcrops of the then prevailing superpower rivalry—though that rivalry had complicated those beliefs. As such, Azar held that these conflicts were best approached not through a Cold War realist paradigm but rather through a social-psychological one, a finding counter to the mainstream views of the day.[26] This work contributed greatly to the field's approach, both to the people who participate in such projects and to the way projects should be structured to best understand the root problems they are dealing with.

Also during this time, Vamik Volkan, a professor and a practitioner of psychiatry, pioneered his "psychodynamic approach," which differed from Kelman's more cognitive approach. Volkan developed techniques and practices which dealt primarily with emotions and psychoanalytical frameworks. He focused on large-group identities and "chosen traumas" and how these had become internalized in communities in conflict so as to prevent the consideration of reconciliation. Volkan explored concepts such as mourning and how they applied to communities in conflict. He explored how structured but unofficial dialogue and interaction could build bridges across group divides and how this strategy would ultimately allow societies and then leaders to reconceptualize the conflict and begin to explore alternate paths forward.[27]

Another individual who has contributed significantly to the development of the field and has also studied and discussed its origins is Ron Fisher, a social psychologist from Canada who has lived and taught in the United States for the latter part of his career. In 1993, Fisher produced a further refinement of the field under the term "interactive conflict resolution" (ICR).[28] Fisher's ICR has both a focused and a broad dimension:

> In a **focused** manner, Interactive Conflict Resolution is defined as involving small-group, problem-solving discussions between unofficial representatives

of identity groups or states engaged in destructive conflict that are facilitated by an impartial third party of social-scientist practitioners. In a **broader** manner, ICR can be defined as facilitated face-to-face activities in communication, training, education, or consultation that promote collaborative conflict analysis and problem solving among parties engaged in protracted conflict in a manner that addresses basic human needs and promotes the building of peace, justice and equality [emphasis added].[29]

Among Fisher's many contributions to the ongoing development of what is generally called Track Two was to point out that such processes can have different audiences and objectives, and need to be structured differently in each case. To this point, those writing about Track Two in various manifestations had been primarily developing the idea that it consisted of a process of small, quiet, ongoing dialogues between influential people which would seek to come up with specific proposals that could be transferred to the official realm as a possible basis for negotiation. Research and writing was thus oriented towards how to create such discussions between influential people, and how best to transfer the results of such interactions to the official realm.

Fisher pointed out, however, that there can be a broader level of interaction aimed at bringing together larger and more diverse groups of people from both sides of the conflict for background discussions aimed at preparing wider segments of society for engagement in conflict resolution activities. Fisher posited that real peace is not just made between elites, however important elite engagement must be, but that representatives of wider segments of societies which have been engaged in long-standing and bitter conflicts must also be prepared to participate in reconciliation efforts and to receive the outcome of such efforts.

This idea of a broader process composed of simultaneous engagement on multiple levels as the key to promoting real and lasting peace between societies, of which elite interactions are but a part, was taken up by Harold Saunders, a former US diplomat, with his concept of "circum-negotiation."[30] With this idea, Saunders sought to take the kind of small, elite-driven dialogues which had heretofore defined much of Track Two and situate them within a broader framework of dialogues aimed at promoting wider societal reconciliations. Like Fisher, Saunders argued that real and lasting peace cannot just be made between elites but must result from a much wider process involving all levels of societies in conflict. While those running elite-driven dialogues cannot necessarily be expected to also run much wider processes, they must be aware of the fact that these wider processes are going on, appreciate the need for them, and seek to find ways to place their efforts within this broader whole. Failure to do so could result in a series of small groups of influential elites who have explored the requirements for peace between themselves, and have even come up with proposals and ideas, but which find little acceptance of these ideas by their wider societies still mired in conflict. Saunders further contributed to the development of the field with his idea of "sustained dialogue," a notion that really deep-seated changes in people's fundamental perceptions regarding conflicts over ethnicity and identity take time and can only arise out of sustained dialogue processes that unfold over a lengthy period of repeated meetings.[31]

At about the same time, Diamond and McDonald were developing a complementary but somewhat different concept which they called "multi-track diplomacy."[32] They identified nine discrete "tracks" of peacemaking activity, which must all be engaged by a variety of processes if real change is to be affected in war-torn societies. Diamond and McDonald explored in detail the functions of each track and the relationship between them. They held that these nine tracks constitute a synergistic "system." They tried to develop ideas which would help those engaged in peace processes make connections between the nine tracks with a view to cross-fertilizing and stimulating the work of the different tracks into a more coherent and systematic set of reinforcing activities. Though their "systems-based approaches" are easier to study in theory than to consciously implement in practice, the efforts of Saunders and of Diamond and MacDonald remain among the more far-reaching theoretical attempts to place the kinds of dialogues generally associated with Track Two diplomacy into a broader framework of inter- and intrasocietal peacemaking. The multitrack model is represented in Figure 1.1.

As part of this idea of broader approaches to promoting peace, many have argued that Track Two interventions, in addition to bringing together individuals from societies involved in conflicts for mutual exploration of the underlying causes of their disputes, could also focus on *training* in conflict resolution techniques, or other mechanisms of living together. Such training can take place at the elite level—to train officials and those close to government in conflict resolution[33]—and also on the grassroots or local levels.[34] In both cases, the idea is to expose those in conflict to ways they can develop skills that give them alternatives to violence as a means of addressing their disputes. It is expected that the recipients of this training will apply their new learning to their own relations, and that they will also serve as a cadre of local

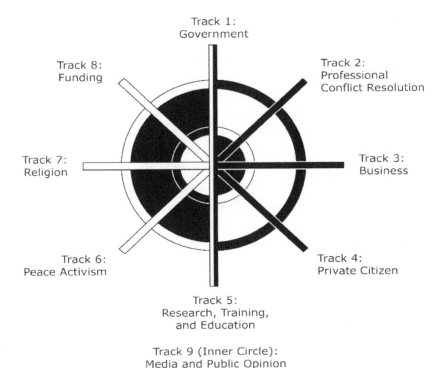

Track 1:
Government

Track 8:
Funding

Track 2:
Professional
Conflict Resolution

Track 7:
Religion

Track 3:
Business

Track 6:
Peace Activism

Track 4:
Private Citizen

Track 5:
Research, Training,
and Education

Track 9 (Inner Circle):
Media and Public Opinion

FIGURE 1.1 Multi-Track Diplomacy. Source: From L. Diamond and
J. McDonald, *Multi-track Diplomacy: A Systems Approach to Peace* (West
Hartford, Conn: Kumarian Press, 1996), 15.

conflict resolution experts who will fan out across their societies and be able
to lead future efforts at reconciliation.[35]

A further refinement of the general concept of Track Two came from Susan
Nan and others who in the 1990s defined a concept known as "Track One and
a Half."[36] This refers to unofficial dialogues within which all or most of the participants from the conflicting sides are officials, though they can also be nonofficials acting under something approaching "instructions" from their respective
governments. Despite this semiofficial status, they participate in dialogues in
their "private capacities," and often rely on an unofficial third party to facilitate the process as a nonofficial dialogue, often in strict secrecy. The essential
element of Track One and a Half, or "Track 1.5," is that it is very close to an
official process but one which the two parties do not wish to refer to as such,
often because of issues relating to "recognition." Track One and a Half is the

closest that unofficial dialogues get to official diplomacy, and it has been comparatively rare. The famous Oslo process for Israeli-Palestinian peacemaking, though it began as something that might be called Track Two, soon became Track One and a Half, as its participants—after the first few rounds of discussions—were Israeli and Palestinian officials who were negotiating on instructions from the leaders of their governments but who had to maintain the fiction of an unofficial process because their governments, especially the Israeli government, maintained strict laws at the time against meetings with officials from the other side.[37] Another name sometimes given to dialogues at the Track 1.5 level is "back-channel" communication or diplomacy, although some forms of back-channel discussions are not facilitated and therefore might not qualify.[38]

Interestingly, and as a little-known example of how Track Two as traditionally understood can ultimately influence official diplomacy, one of the reasons the Oslo meetings were able to succeed (though the Oslo process as a whole has not yet done so) was that many of its participants had been through the Israeli-Palestinian Track Two workshops run by Kelman over many years. There was thus a basis of familiarity on both personal and substantive terms between the participants before they got to Oslo, which helped them when Track One and a Half talks became possible.[39]

Another conceptual approach to the various kinds of Track Two emerged from a study of Track Two in the Middle East. Four authors (two Israelis and two Palestinians) divided Track Two into two broad categories: "hard" Track Two and "soft" Track Two.[40] Hard Track Two is in some ways similar to Nan's Track One and a Half, and Fisher's "focused" interactive conflict resolution. Its objective is to gather a small group of influential people to explore the background of the conflict and produce proposals which will lead to an official agreement. The Oslo process itself would be an example. Soft Track Two, somewhat like Fisher's "broad" interactive conflict resolution, is oriented towards broader discussions between representatives of civil society aimed at familiarizing the two sides with each other,[41] but without necessarily having an expectation of reaching an agreement—though some soft Track Two projects aim at a joint paper or book.

One of the recurring themes in attempts to define Track Two is how close any given activity is to official diplomacy and what the relationship of the field as a whole is to official diplomacy. Some have taken the view that Track Two's essential purpose must be to support Track One and to help participants in difficult conflicts get to a place where official negotiations can begin. For example, Burgess and Burgess, in the context of writing a handbook on how to undertake

Track Two processes, offer this definition: "Track I is used here to describe any activities that bring the parties to a conflict into direct negotiation to achieve an agreement or a resolution. Track II refers to any activities that support, directly or indirectly, Track I efforts."[42] Others, such as Kelman, Saunders, and Fisher, would argue that their ideas of interactive problem solving, interactive conflict resolution, and circum-negotiation can be quite different from what usually goes on in Track One, as they seek to get participants to move beyond the kind of bargaining that takes place in Track One and towards a process of reconceptualizing their conflict. While these scholars would certainly not be opposed to their work assisting Track One, and while they recognize that the results of their work will have to be taken up by Track One eventually if they are ever to be turned into formal agreements, these scholars do not set out consciously to assist Track One. Moreover, they foresee that the discussions which go on within their processes will likely require official diplomacy surrounding the conflict to change radically in response to the ideas they generate. Of course, the definitions advanced by Burgess and Burgess and the others are not mutually exclusive in practice. Thus Saunders writes, "My own inclination is not to be too precious in drawing lines. The main line is between official and unofficial."[43]

Still others argue that the field must focus instead on the grassroots level. In recent years, this has been a growth area in conflict resolution generally and Track Two more specifically, which sometimes goes by the name "Track Three" or "conflict transformation." Leading analysts of the conflict transformation field, such as Lederach, Curle, and Galtung, increasingly believe that excessive attention to elite levels has led to a field overwhelmingly oriented towards managing conflicts rather than transforming societies in conflict. Proponents of this view believe that a "bottom-up" approach is called for if real peace is to be achieved in war-torn societies.[44] To the extent that an outside intervener is active, it should be based on an *elicitive* approach, which promotes local empowerment and transformation by respecting people and their knowledge and helping them find answers within themselves and their context, rather than *prescriptive* approaches, within which, it is charged, much traditional conflict resolution activity takes place.[45] But these ideas have been around for some time. In the 1990s, for example, Vincent Kavaloski was writing about an idea he called "transnational citizen peacemaking." This view held that states and the elites who run them perpetuate ongoing conflicts. Kavaloski argued that real and lasting peace should be made by networks of informed and empowered citizens acting outside of the nation-state system.[46]

FIGURE 1.2 Source: Adapted from Figure 1 in Chigas, D., "Capacities and Limits of NGOs as Conflict Managers," in Crocker, C.A., F.O. Hampson and P. Aall (eds.), *Leashing the Dogs of War* (Washington DC: United States Institute of Peace, 2007), 553–81

In her analysis of the role of NGOs in the conflict field, Chigas represents unofficial third party interventions as a pyramid (adapted version in Figure 1.2), and notes that true peace in complex conflicts will only be achieved when all levels are being attended to, and the actors on various levels are working with each other. She thus comes back to the ideas expressed by Saunders in his circum-negotiation concept and Diamond and McDonald in their multi-track diplomacy idea.[47]

Yet another way to represent the various kinds of Track Two that have arisen in the literature and in practice is by laying them out in the context of their relationship to Track One. This might be represented as in Figure 1.3. According to this typology, Track 1.5, or "hard" Track Two (as defined by Agha *and colleagues*), is closest to official diplomacy, while the other kinds recede from it. As we shall see in variations of this chart that appear in subsequent chapters, as one moves along the scale toward such things as "soft" Track Two and multi-track diplomacy, the objectives and mechanisms that exist in association with these various forms of Track Two change substantially. Indeed, the far right of the scale is represented by a break and then such ideas as Kavaloski's concept of transnational citizen peacemaking, Chigas's

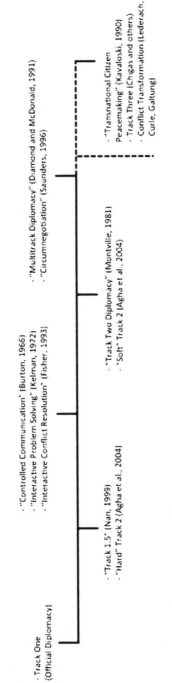

- Track One
(Official Diplomacy)

- "Track 1.5" (Nun, 1999)
- "Hard" Track 2 (Agha et al., 2004)

- "Controlled Communication" (Burton, 1966)
- "Interactive Problem Solving" (Kelman, 1972)
- "Interactive Conflict Resolution" (Fisher, 1993)

- "Track Two Diplomacy" (Montville, 1981)
- "Soft" Track 2 (Agha et al., 2004)

- "Multitrack Diplomacy" (Diamond and McDonald, 1991)
- "Circumnegotiation" (Saunders, 1996)

- "Transnational Citizen Peacemaking" (Kavaloski, 1990)
- Track Three (Chigas and others)
- Conflict Transformation (Lederach, Curle, Galtung)

FIGURE 1.3 Major Categories of Track Two

Track Three, and so on to convey the idea that these forms of Track Two are concerned with influencing civil society and grassroots actors rather than officials and governments.

As this brief exploration of various terms and concepts illustrates, the field of Track Two is multifaceted and fluid. The terminology is far from fixed, and the same terms can be used to mean quite different things. For my own purposes, I have come to define the term "Track Two" as *unofficial dialogues, generally between two antagonistic parties, and often facilitated by an impartial Third Party and involving individuals with some close connections to their respective official communities, focused on cooperative efforts to explore new ways to resolve differences over, or discuss new approaches to, policy-relevant issues.*

The core of this definition is an attempt to move away from conflict resolution as *necessarily* being the key to what is going on—though many of these efforts will have that as their goal—towards a notion of gathering influential people together to develop new ways to solve problems and then influence events. This formulation is deliberately chosen to create a wide scope of possible application for these efforts, which can include dialogues aimed at such objectives as building new norms, or discussions of regional issues. The definition, like others, also moves away from the word "diplomacy."

Of course, however one defines Track Two, there is a separate issue of whether and how Track One and Track Two processes should cooperate, or even collaborate. This is a very sensitive issue and should always be approached on a case-by-case basis. There are benefits to close cooperation, or even collaboration between the tracks, such as information sharing and more effective multilevel peacemaking, if it works. But there are also potential drawbacks, particularly if Track Two actors and Track One actors become confused in the minds of those in the conflict and these actors misunderstand which level they are dealing with at any given moment. The potential for loss of credibility and, for Track Two facilitators, the loss of their perceived independence, is great.[48]

Recurring Themes

Taken together, many of the definitions explored in this chapter have a set of characteristics which may be termed a "classic" approach to Track Two. While there are subtle differences between the definitions, they have some key characteristics in common:

- They emphasize small, informal dialogues, which the literature refers to as "problem-solving workshops," between people from the various sides of a conflict, which are usually facilitated by an impartial "third party."[49]
- Though the dialogues are unofficial, it is generally expected that the participants will have access to decision makers at home, or be able to influence the development of thinking in their societies.
- The dialogues are not meant to be meetings where the current positions of the conflicting sides are debated but rather workshops where the participants step back from official positions to jointly explore the underlying causes of the dispute in the hope of jointly developing alternative ideas.
- The dialogues are ongoing processes rather than "one-off" workshops.
- Practitioners tend to emphasize the value and importance of addressing the deep-seated, psychological aspects of disputes as being at least as important as discussing specific substantive differences.
- While not exactly secret, the dialogues are conducted quietly, and the so-called Chatham House Rule is applied.[50] This is done in order to create an atmosphere within which "outside-the-box" thinking can flourish and participants are not afraid to propose and explore ideas that could not be entertained by an official process or by one where exchanges might be repeated in the press. Importantly, it is not just in discussions *between* groups at the table that one seeks to encourage new approaches but also *within* each group. Indeed, some of the most dramatic and insightful discussions can take place when members of the same group begin to probe each other's assumptions and deeply held beliefs.

Such processes can lead to a number of results. Among these are

- Changed perceptions of the conflict and the "other"
- Opening new channels for communication between adversaries who had few other means of communicating (and in some cases no means of communicating)
- The identification and development of new options for future negotiation
- In the case of Track Two dialogues devoted to subjects other

than conflict resolution, such as regional security, the creation of communities of experts who have developed and are conversant with possible new approaches to issues

- Preparing the ground for the transition of ideas developed in Track Two to the official track
- The development of networks of influential people who can work to change views in their countries and regions

Regional Security and Track Two

Up to this point, the question of defining Track Two has been about understanding such processes when they are aimed at resolving conflicts. Indeed, the bulk of research on Track Two is about resolving conflicts. Thus, most of the terminological and analytical concepts with which we assess Track Two are rooted in the dynamics and traditions of this conflict resolution approach. While probably inevitable, this use of ideas developed in one context within another raises questions as to how much of the literature is relevant to the study of Track Two projects aimed at other objectives. For example, one field where Track Two has been underway is regional security, in which there is not necessarily a specific conflict to be addressed.

In the Middle East, a variety of Track Two projects and discussions have been held on regional security,[51] particularly since the official dialogue over regional security that was part of the peace process ended in 1995, through the so-called Arms Control and Regional Security working group (known as ACRS).[52] These dialogues, largely funded and run by groups from outside the region, have delved into issues of arms control and attempted to introduce discussion of broader concepts of security into the regional discourse. They have also been at the forefront of developing and maintaining an "epistemic community" of scholars and officials who are familiar with regional security and arms control concepts.[53]

In Southeast Asia a robust regional Track Two has developed a history and vocabulary of its own.[54] Curiously, the extensive literature on ASEAN (Association of Southeast Asian Nations) Track Two cites little if any of the conflict resolution Track Two literature, even though they are talking about similar things in at least some respects. Similarly, the leaders in the field of conflict resolution Track Two seldom, if ever, refer to work done by regional Track

Two experts in Southeast Asia. It is as if the two worlds exist in splendid isolation from each other. ASEAN Track Two features close interaction between governments and select think tanks. Indeed, much of what is referred to as "Track Two" in the Southeast Asian context might be called Track One and a Half in others.[55] This Track Two is closely aligned with official priorities of the countries of the region and is a venue within which select institutes and scholars with close connections to regional governments develop ideas before adopting them in the official discourse.[56] Indeed, it is often the case that the participants in discussions can actually be serving officials of the regional governments. An elaborate system has been worked out whereby these officials are present in what one observer of ASEAN Track Two has called the "polite fiction" of their "private capacities."[57]

In a major study of the role of Track Two in the region, Job has argued that it is primarily an "ideational" mechanism whereby elites with close ties to their governments develop and refine concepts for the consideration of those governments.[58] This degree of closeness, while a boon in many ways, has led to criticism that such efforts do not permit the examination of ideas "outside the box."[59] Defenders of the process argue that their closeness to official circles makes their work uniquely relevant to diplomacy. Largely in response to the perceived inability of regional Track Two to include civil society, a phenomenon referred to locally as "Track Three" has arisen; these are processes dealing with matters that civil society groups believe are neglected because the semiofficial process is not able or willing to address them.[60] In many respects, these dialogues are thus similar to the idea of Track Three as defined in Chigas's typology.

While there is an extensive literature devoted to this form of regional security Track Two in the ASEAN region, little attention is devoted by its champions to unofficial dialogues aimed at more conventional conflict resolution objectives for the region. Once again, one observes a kind of splendid isolation between the two forms of Track Two within the region itself, with unofficial dialogues aimed at resolving conflicts enjoying little if any recognition in the ASEAN Track Two literature. Thus, in the voluminous group of books and papers on Southeast Asian Track Two one rarely sees references to such things as the efforts of the Centre for Humanitarian Dialogue to end the conflict in the Indonesian region of Aceh[61], or those of other NGOs to address the ongoing conflict in the Philippines.[62] One wonders if ASEAN Track Two has consciously decided to stay away from conflicts due to its close association with ASEAN governments, who do not wish to deal with each other's internal conflicts as they are not part of established diplomatic tradition, sometimes known as the "ASEAN Way."[63]

In both the Middle East and ASEAN cases, the forms, methods, and objectives of these regional security Track Two projects are described through terms developed by the "conflict resolution" school of Track Two. And yet there is no cross-referencing between Track Two as conducted for regional security purposes and Track Two for conflict resolution. Clearly, there is a need for more research into the ways that different models of Track Two work.[64] Developing ways of understanding the role of regional security Track Two, and of measuring success, is difficult. This should not be surprising. Some of the most difficult questions in analyzing Track Two (even the more intensively studied bilateral dispute resolution model) are the roles and limitations of such processes, and how to assess effectiveness, a subject which will be tackled in the final chapter of this book.[65] This is even more the case for regional security Track Two, which is to some extent a form of ongoing conflict prevention.

As three scholars much involved in regional security Track Two processes in the Asia-Pacific region note, "many (if not most) of the benefits of Track 2 security dialogue are intangible and, therefore, not readily quantifiable."[66] Nevertheless, these scholars, in their analysis of regional security Track Two in the Asia-Pacific region, note four possible roles on which criteria for success can be developed and judged:

- Track Two processes can serve as a mechanism for the development of policy advice to governments, particularly as regards new issues or longer-term questions. In this sense, Track Two, if accepted by regional governments, can serve as a kind of reserve of intellectual capacity.

- Track Two processes provide a "laboratory" for the development and testing of ideas. New concepts or specific proposals can be debated in an atmosphere within which governments are not committed.

- Track Two offers an alternate route to the continuation of regional security discussions where official routes are blocked. This implies a high degree of confidence in (and probably control over) Track Two.

- Track Two performs a socialization role. At the most basic level, it permits participants to get to know each other. Beyond this, it is assumed that participants develop a keener appreciation of each other's perspectives and concerns. Ultimately, they can achieve shared understandings on difficult issues.

Ball *and colleagues* go on to note a number of limitations, some of which are specific to regional security Track Two in the Asia-Pacific. First, by developing a notion of regional Track Two that is closely linked to government, this region has developed a model whereby Track Two is often an extension of official diplomacy. While this heightens the likelihood that ideas will be transmitted, it can also mean that some of the problems of the official process are found in Track Two. A second perceived limitation of Asia-Pacific regional security Track Two is that it has, to date at any rate, largely ignored civil society. A final limitation appears to be its inability to move quickly in the face of pressing issues or a rapidly changed regional environment. This may be a function of the highly institutionalized nature of Asia-Pacific regional Track Two.

Turning to the Middle East, Kaye argues that regional security Track Two in that setting has displayed three roles.[67] She also posits that these roles usually run sequentially, a point not emphasized in the analysis of Ball and his colleagues:

- First, the "socialization" of the participating elites is a process whereby these elites are introduced, usually by Western experts, to various concepts relating to security, with much of the work taking place in informal workshops (this is a somewhat different socialization role from that described by Ball and colleagues).

- Second, the "filtering" of externally generated policy ideas into the local environment is a process whereby the regional participants take the ideas presented during the socialization period and re-form them in ways that are relevant to the participants' regional reality. If particularly successful, this role goes beyond straightforward reformulation of specific ideas and toward a broader reformulation of the conflict itself in ways which are more amenable to new approaches to regional security.

- Finally, the "transmission" to official policy involves a more formal process whereby the ideas developed in the other two roles are translated into official policies across the region. Two tangible indicators of success are lower defense budgets or arms control agreements.

Kaye notes three possible limitations of such processes: the difficulty of finding participants who have sufficient security credentials to be credible but
who are still open to new thinking; the fact that regional elites may simply
be unprepared to shift from realist thinking toward cooperative security concepts (in those cases where such a shift is necessary—that is, cooperative security projects); and the chance that regional elites may be unprepared to accept
that it is still in their interest to develop new approaches to regional security
when a basic difference (the Arab-Israeli dispute) has not been resolved.

Writing specifically about Track Two as a vehicle in the development of a
"weapons of mass destruction free zone" (WMDFZ) in the Middle East, Jones
notes four possible roles for Track Two[68]:

- The development of a cadre of regional experts who are conversant
  with the issues under discussion and with each other's views

- The provision of a forum in which people, including officials from
  countries that do not recognize each other, can meet to discuss the
  issues

- The development of a structured, ongoing process in which regional
  experts can tackle the complex issues that will arise if a WMDFZ is to
  be created

- The provision of a forum for the development of ideas for a broad
  regional security architecture, which will be a precondition for the
  creation of a WMDFZ

Conclusion

Track Two is complex and multifaceted. Its key concepts and ideas have
evolved over time, and many kinds of activities go on within the broad framework covered by the term. Much of the literature is concerned with Track Two
as a mechanism of conflict resolution, but there is also a literature on Track
Two as a mechanism for regional security; the two bodies of literature are
largely separate from each other. Those active in the field grapple with several
key issues, which are still not resolved and likely never will be to everyone's
satisfaction. All of this complexity is generally unappreciated by those who
simply use the term "Track Two diplomacy" to denote the general idea of unofficial dialogues intended to help resolve conflicts, or lead to better regional
relationships. Moreover, the field suffers generally from differences between

the basic paradigm of international affairs on which most Track Two efforts are based (constructivism) and the paradigm in which most official international diplomatic activities are generally understood to take place (realism).

While probably inevitable, this lack of consensus as to what Track Two is, and the different starting points in terms of basic approaches to international affairs, can have deleterious consequences. The term can be applied to very different kinds of processes, with very different objectives and methods, based on very different conceptions of the underlying causes of the dispute in question. Unless those using the term understand the differences between varying processes, they are likely to be confused and possibly frustrated by the multiplicity of methods and outcomes they will encounter, all under the single, all-encompassing term "Track Two."

A busy government official, for example, looking for policy relevance in the results of a Track Two project which utilizes a "circum-negotiation" approach to broader conflict resolution between societies in a larger sense, will be deeply disappointed if he or she understands the term "Track Two" to refer to what would actually be Track One and a Half, namely, exercises devoted to gathering influential actors in secrecy in order to develop a specific set of proposals which can subsequently be used by diplomats here and now. In such a case, the all-too-often response is to dismiss the entire field of Track Two as being well-meaning but rather "starry-eyed" and less than relevant to the operational needs of diplomacy. Conversely, a conflict resolution expert who is schooled in the need for "broad" dialogues to promote societal reconciliation, as the only path to a true and lasting peace, will likely dismiss the desire of officials to quickly create a Track One and a Half dialogue, by which to "solve" a pressing problem, as being ill-informed, lacking in sophistication, and likely to fail if it does not address the deeper causes of the conflict.

There may be no answer to these misunderstandings. But it is incumbent on those who are active in this field, including officials who deal with conflicts and are thus likely to run across various Track Two efforts as part of the landscape, to understand that different approaches and activities go on under the rubric of "Track Two," and to take account of these differences in designing and evaluating Track Two.

2   Theoretical Foundations of Track Two

IF TRACK TWO FINDS ITSELF SOMETIMES UNCOMFORT-
ably caught between official diplomacy and academe, and regarded
warily by some in both, part of the reason is that it also finds itself caught
between different traditions of international relations scholarship per se. Simply put, most who are involved in Track Two come at international relations
from perspectives which are often different from those of most officials and
many academics; they understand the causes of conflicts, and therefore view
what should be done to address them, somewhat differently.

On a diplomatic level, the tools and techniques of many Track Two projects—group explorations of deeper psychological issues surrounding the conflict, aimed at promoting new understandings of issues and possibilities—are
often somewhat different than those to which officials charged with resolving
international conflicts will avail themselves. These standard diplomatic tools
include incentives and penalties which appeal to cost-benefit calculations of
parties in a conflict and encourage them towards a different position. Track
Two projects also generally take a much longer time than most officials perceive to be available when they are in the middle of a crisis, or more generally,
than they expect to be in office.

In terms of academic explorations of Track Two, on the other hand, the
problem is that many practitioners of Track Two are more concerned with
what works than with how to define it in a scholarly sense. Some social scientists are suspicious or dismissive of an approach more concerned with getting

things done than explaining how activities fit into theoretical paradigms. Also, there is a sense that practice is biased towards the peaceful settlement of disputes and away from the realist idea that violence is sometimes necessary.

This difference is as old as Track Two itself, as we saw in the last chapter from Montville's attempts to interest his fellow diplomats, and Burton's experience in trying to convince academic skeptics that his new theories on how conflicts might be resolved had relevance to the "real world." This practice-vs.-theory debate may be one of the reasons Track Two has suffered at times from a sense of not being taken seriously by officials or by pure academics. Track Two's inability to explain or define itself in terms that can be measured and quantified has contributed to what one scholar has called its "double marginality"—suspected of irrelevance, or worse, by officials *and* by mainstream social science.[1] As Babbitt and Hampson note,

> CR [conflict resolution] studies are focused on applying the insights of theory and research to the resolution of actual conflict situations. Theory and research are drawn not only from political science but also from social psychology, sociology, economics and law. This has resulted in the field sitting somewhat uncomfortably alongside traditional international relations theory because its insights are filtered through many differing analytic lenses. . . . IR [international relations] scholars perceive a bias among CR scholars and practitioners toward peaceful methods of dispute settlement and resolution, one that deliberately and self-consciously eschews the use of force and violence. This translates unfairly to CR studies being seen as 'soft' theoretically, focusing more on praxis rather than contributing to innovation and advancement of our general understanding of conflict processes.[2]

In this chapter, we shall first look briefly at the major paradigms in the field of IR. We then look at instances where scholars and those active in the field have tried to configure various paradigms to fit with their conceptions of what they are doing; that is, we explore how various Track Two practitioners would place their activities in relation to the dominant schools of IR theory, and why. This exercise situates the forms of Track Two introduced in the previous chapter in terms of where they fit into IR from the point of view of practitioners and social scientists. Through such an effort, we can develop tools to assess different Track Two processes on their own terms instead of falling into the frustrating trap, described in the conclusion of Chapter 1, of trying to understand a given Track Two process that is based on one approach to IR, while using the tools and concepts of another.

The Schools

The dominant schools which seek to explain international conflict and peace are realism (and its variants), liberalism, and constructivism.[3] Track Two rarely follows any of these slavishly; rather, it is eclectic, drawing insights from the different theoretical schools in order to fashion analyses and approaches. Track Two is thus less concerned with "what works in theory" and more concerned with "what works in practice."

The realist school of international relations favors explanations of international affairs which stress interest-based bargaining, the competition for power between states, and zero-sum games as the keys to understanding how the world actually works. Liberalism places an emphasis on democratic development, economic interdependence, and participation in a web of international institutions which can lead countries to turn their backs on war as an instrument of statecraft. Constructivist theories stress interpersonal relations, community building, and the development of norms as keys to understanding how states and people interact, and how relationships can be changed over time.

While none of these schools are as definitive as they are presented here, much of Track Two is more comfortable in the constructivist tradition. Track Two tends to stress interpersonal, social-psychological dynamics to increase each side's understanding of the underlying factors motivating the other's position, and its own, as a tool to open up possibilities for cooperative problem solving. Almost by definition, it is difficult to quantify such processes according to traditional academic research criteria.

Realism

The oldest of the major schools, realism in its purest form posits that the world is an anarchic place, and that states seek to maximize their security through the acquisition of power—either by themselves or through alliances, or in some combination of the two. In some respects, realism grew as a response to what many postwar analysts of international affairs felt were the excessively idealistic approaches taken to the study of international relations in the interwar years.[4] Realists hold that the state is the key unit of international affairs; according to some realists, international order is best maintained when a few powerful states balance each other while other states play supporting roles within this structure.[5] Not all realists agree with this balance-of-power theory. Hegemonic stability theory argues that peace is most likely when there is only one really powerful state that can impose its views on the rest of the system in a way that cannot be challenged.[6] Realism is thus not a single theory but a multifaceted set of ideas, often competing with each other to try to explain the world.[7] For example, "classical" realists incorporate observations about human nature, often quite pessimistic ones, into their ideas as to why states seek power, while "neorealists" dismiss human nature and focus on what they believe are objective factors concerning balances of power—here the international "system" is seen as a constraining factor.[8]

Insofar as realists tend to view the Great Powers as key to the stability of the international system, they have not given much attention historically to conflicts surrounding specifically indigenous questions that are not linked to the currency of global power; there is a bias towards seeing conflict in the international system as an outgrowth of a struggle for power and particularly of Great Power rivalries. Merom, one of the few realists who has looked at how realist ideas can be used to explain regional cases,[9] has posited that stability in any given region is a function largely of the extent to which Great Powers are involved in that region. This involvement can be benign or aggressive and can take a variety of forms, such as diplomatic, economic, military, and so forth. The key is that regional stability is largely set by engagement from outside. Of course, the realities of power can also be replicated *within* regions as microcosms of the larger international system. Thus Lemke notes that regions can have their own "Great Powers," who on a regional level attempt to dominate through their own power and alliances. Regional conflict, in this view, is often the result of clashes between such regional hegemons, or between those who aspire to that status and outside powers who seek to restructure the region for their own purposes.[10]

Realist ideas are still powerful today, but were predominant during the Cold War. Realism began to be challenged by writers who were interested in the various forms of conflict resolution, many of which are today often lumped under the term "Track Two." Azar specifically argued that many of the most intractable conflicts in the developing world needed to be seen not primarily as realist outgrowths of the Cold War but as protracted conflicts over indigenous questions of ethnicity, identity, and religion. Of course, such conflicts could be exacerbated and distorted by the intervention of the Great Powers from outside the region, and frequently were, with disastrous consequences (especially for the local populations), but these conflicts were not caused by the kinds of Great Power rivalries at the heart of the Cold War. Therefore, in Azar's analysis, conflict resolution techniques needed to be based on different assumptions and approaches which stressed the development of indigenous dialogues on deep-seated issues rather than how outside interventions could "bring peace" to these troubled areas.[11]

Some realists have explored issues of ethnic conflict, but largely in terms of the implications, for regional balance, of the breakup of states along ethnic lines. Barry Posen argued that such circumstances would be inherently unstable as disadvantaged groups would be tempted to improve their situations through force, or by aligning themselves with other disadvantaged groups to take on those who had benefited most from any state breakup along ethnic lines.[12] While explaining well what happened in places like the former Yugoslavia, this work did not really explore the identity-based emotional factors which had led to the breakups and the fighting in the first place. Moreover, in terms of resolving such conflicts, realism can only argue that things will settle down when one side wins, or when a powerful external actor arrives to impose order. But what about situations of protracted ethnic and religious conflict where no one wins and where outside powers are not interested in intervening, or where multiple interventions cancel each other (or even make things worse)? Does conflict simply go on indefinitely? Realism would suggest that it does. But does that have to be so? Is there not another way to understand the problem, and search for possible solutions? These were the questions that Azar and other early writers in the field of conflict resolution were asking.

Other international activities which many realists regard dubiously are those of institution building or norm building as methods to achieving peace and stability. Though they recognize that institutions, such as those built around norms of conduct and regional frameworks, are an important part of the international scene, they do not generally believe that institutions create incentives or norms which are more powerful than the impulse of states to secure themselves through reliance on their own power or alliances.[13]

Once again, this idea that dialogue, institutions, and norms cannot lead to peace puts such theorists and practitioners squarely on the opposite side of many Track Two practitioners, who believe that a process of dialogue and norm building can, in itself, have the effect over time of changing the prevailing views between conflicts parties, and even in a region as a whole. In his study on the work of the Community of Sant'Egidio, a Catholic lay organization which has helped facilitate numerous Track Two processes, including one that contributed to ending the civil war in Mozambique, Bartoli accuses traditional realists of "underestimat[ing] the power of the mediation itself—the transforming power of the experience of adversaries talking with one another and with others in a setting that is conducive to constructive dialogue."[14] Similarly, on the regional level, Acharya argues that the ASEAN region has slowly been transformed through a process of interaction and dialogue leading to the development of new norms of conduct, with much of this dialogue taking place at the Track Two level.[15]

Much of realist theory was set out during the Cold War, and perhaps made most sense in that environment. International relations were, or at least were perceived to be, largely state-centric and dominated by the actions of a few Great Powers and their allies. Since the end of the Cold War, however, realism has had to contend with a world where Great Powers seem to be less able to unilaterally set the tone of global affairs; where substate conflicts and substate actors are seen as growing in importance; where regional powers, such as Israel and India, are no longer bystanders but are indeed more acting than acted upon (as in reality they were throughout the Cold War, even if realism could not adequately explain this); and where ideas are shaping international discourse to a much greater extent. One of realism's greatest weaknesses in this new environment has been its perceived inability to explain sudden and significant changes in the international order.

Various realists have tried to adapt the theory to account for the multipolar world they find themselves in, and for the fact that dialogue, ideas, and values do appear to matter in international relations. Neoclassical realism, for example, recognizes that ideas do shape perceptions of security, and that nonstate actors (particularly in combination with failed states) are significant players on the international security scene.[16] Neoclassical realists recognize that regional powers and substate actors can set the terms of regional security and peace to a much greater extent, and can do so in the face of Great Power involvement, or without such involvement, and that ideologies, religious beliefs, and ideas can be powerful motivators. It is a more complex world than previously imagined.[17] But the keys are still states and power, even if they are understood somewhat differently.

Liberalism

By contrast to realism, liberalism offers a theory or more precisely, a set of theories of international relations which is dynamic and explains well, in "big" terms, the phenomenon of change—or at least a particular kind of change.[18] However, "the liberal paradigm does not provide daily practical tools for managing the day-to-day business of diplomacy."[19] Liberalism holds that states and peoples can elect to pursue security and well-being through policies and actions designed around three key ideas, known to some as the "Kantian tripod": democracy; economic interdependence; and involvement in a web of international institutions which set the limits of what states can do.[20] The pursuit of more-democratic governments and ever deeper economic and trade links, and the creation of powerful and respected international institutions, are thus keys to developing and maintaining peace, both globally and regionally. In many ways, President Woodrow Wilson's famous Fourteen Points, which were elaborated at the close of World War One, were an expression of liberal theory.

Today much of this theory draws on the European postwar experience, and especially that of the establishment of the European Union. Liberals have set out to consider how a continent which had known centuries of war managed to transform itself into an island of peace and prosperity within the living memory of many of its citizens of the most bloody war in history. Liberals have then sought lessons for the rest of the world in that experience.[21] Much liberal research has gone into such ideas as the "democratic peace" theory (the idea that democracies generally don't go to war with each other), and also theories on the propensity for states in a situation of economic interdependence to avoid conflict with each other.[22]

But even these ideas are contested. In terms of the democratic peace, for example, Doyle notes that democracies may not fight each other but have shown a propensity to use the jargon of liberalism to justify fighting others, often in an effort to "make the world safe for democracy."[23] Moreover, the democratic peace may only really be applicable to a small number of mature democracies. Mansfield and Snyder have shown that what they call "emerging democracies" (those with still weak institutions and electoral politics largely based on tribal and ethnic realities) are perfectly capable of engaging in aggressive wars, and may even be more likely to do so than other types of regimes.[24] On liberal theories of enhanced economic interdependence as a key to peace, many argue that the current expression of that belief, the phenomenon of "globalization," is leaving in its wake as many losers as winners and setting the stage for conflicts as a result.[25]

Thus, while liberalism explains present-day Europe fairly well—though liberals do have to admit that Europe's early steps towards its liberal future were enabled by a thoroughly realist reality: the US security guarantee in the face of the perceived Soviet threat[26]—the question arises as to how well it travels to other regions. How are early steps towards the Kantian tripod begun and sustained in contested and violent regional environments? As with postwar Europe, it would seem that some sort of powerful actor needs to provide the environment which can incubate the emergence of a liberal situation. As Adler and Barnett note in their seminal work on "regional security communities," "The existence of powerful states that are able to project a sense of purpose, offer an idea of progress, and/or provide leadership around core issues can facilitate and stabilize this (nascent) phase (in the development of such communities)." They thus believe that the development of security communities is "not antagonistic to the language of power; indeed, it is dependent on it."[27] Does this powerful actor have to be an external great power, as realists might contend, or could it be ideas and norms which emerge from within the region itself?

Liberalism and realism have occupied an interesting if at times uneasy space within foreign policy, particularly in the United States. The commitment of President George W. Bush's administration towards democracy promotion, for example, was quite liberal and had a profound impact on that administration's policies in the Middle East. As the president admonished, skeptics of his policies, "who call themselves 'realists' . . . have lost contact with a fundamental reality" that "America is always more secure when freedom is on the march."[28] But this same administration was itself deeply skeptical of another fundamental part of the liberal creed: the creation and promotion of a web of binding international norms and institutions, especially those which might limit its own freedom to act unilaterally, up to and including preemptive attacks against those who might even be *considering* harming US interests as perceived by the administration. In reality, then, policymakers are rarely entirely bound by the strictures of one school; they pick and choose to suit what they perceive to be their needs and those of the moment.

Many proponents of Track Two, though in many cases somewhat more comfortable with liberalism than with realism on a conceptual level, would also have some concerns with this theory. In particular, the idea that mature democratic and economically interconnected states existing within a web of strong institutions do not fight each other may be all well and good, but how do peoples who are living in situations of strife and protracted identity conflicts come to realize these benefits? Liberalism does not really explain these things, beyond offering up some general nostrums (probably more applicable to states already on their way to representative, economically liberal economic situations) to do more and try harder with respect to democracy and free trade, and to hope that a benign external power will arrive to help establish the conditions within which a liberal order can take hold and thrive. Again, as with realism, this advice is perhaps not especially helpful in a situation like Azar's intractable ethnic conflict. Moreover, what if the transition to a liberal order itself leads to fighting between states undergoing this transition, or within states if certain groups, often minorities, feel that they have been disadvantaged by the transition?

Constructivism

Constructivists argue that realist ideas about "national interests," and liberal beliefs in the value of democracy, institutions, and free trade, miss the point. Constructivists believe that the key is the process whereby people and states come to hold the view that these things are either good or bad; it is the emergence of ideas and norms which themselves *construct* a new way of seeing reality, and therefore acting on it.[29] These processes can come from within a region just as easily as from outside it. Critical therefore are the efforts of actors who work to shape ideas and norms and to have them gain acceptance on the international stage. For those who are engaged in Track Two, and who believe in it, there is an element of faith, a belief that a community of experts and advocates, who have collectively mastered the complex questions of security and cooperation and who have developed concepts and proposals around specific problems and issues, is capable of transforming the international debate over such questions as human rights and security.[30] Measuring the specific manner in which these ideas may penetrate official policy is always a complex and inexact business. Key to the emergence of a constructivist order are "norm entrepreneurs," who develop and disseminate concepts and policy initiatives aimed at constructing a new and widely accepted narrative as to what is acceptable behavior and what is not.[31] An area where constructivists have difficulty, however, is in developing an encompassing theory of *how* the emergence of new norms and ideas can translate into concrete policy action leading to a more peaceful order.

In Southeast Asia, constructivist ideas emerging from a Track Two dialogue are held to have had a significant impact in the creation of a peaceful order in the region. Job has discussed the role of norm entrepreneurs, including those coming from Track Two, in the emergence of new thinking about regional security in the Asia-Pacific region.[32] Analysts, such as Acharya, see the creation and evolution of the Association of Southeast Asian Nations (ASEAN) as having been a multiyear process that created a regional security community based largely on constructivist theories of order and stability.[33] Job also argues that the primary role of Track Two in this process of regional change has been "ideational," that is, to provide a space for the development of the norms and ideas which have made the change possible, and for the creation of a regional network of respected advocates who have pushed for those ideas.[34] Of course, these views are contested by realists who argue that such transformation as has happened in the Asia-Pacific area is not as significant as Track Two advocates believe, and that it has come about through changes in realist calculations of the relative balance of interests and power. Typical of these was the passionate debate between Khoo, Peou, and Ba over Acharya's arguments as to whether ASEAN was actually a realist exercise in regional security or should be understood as a constructivist security community.[35] Key to this disagreement are debates, as between liberalism and realism, about whether a realist order must be established before constructivist norms can evolve.

Most constructivist studies do not adequately explore how the idea-centric, norm-building interactions they advocate can actually have negative impacts. Though the overwhelming number of constructivist studies have looked at the contributions of this school as a path to cooperation and peace, it is also true that the process can work the other way. Barnett's study of regional discussion of the idea of security in the Arab world has shown that a quite constructivist process of debating ideas and norms has led to a situation where radical religious ideas (which many Westerners find troubling) have, at least for the time being, gained greater currency in that region.[36] Snyder is therefore probably right when he notes that both Gandhi *and* Bin Laden were constructivists in their way.[37]

• • •

In briefly reviewing these schools, the intention has not been to provide anything like an exhaustive outline or critique of them, much less of the debates within and between them; indeed, other schools and subschools are also relevant.[38] Rather, the objective has been to show that IR theorists have looked in different ways at how to provide for stability and peace, and that these approaches have a profound impact not just on social science debates but on policy decisions. How one looks at these fundamental questions, and how one believes peace can best be achieved, will have a marked impact on one's conception of what a Track Two dialogue effort should look like, how it should be assessed, and even whether one should be attempted at all.

For example, for those for whom realism is the dominant conception of how things work, a dialogue based on a constructivist understanding may be seen as ineffective. For officials charged with understanding Track Two and how it might fit in with official diplomacy, evaluating a constructivist dialogue against the needs of traditional realist diplomacy can lead to misunderstanding, even dismissal of what is being attempted and has been achieved in the dialogue. Similarly, Track Two practitioners who are unable or who refuse to accept that the political realities of their intended audience are different from their own will find it difficult to get a hearing for the ideas which emerge from discussions. This does not mean that Track Two processes should slavishly follow the dominant school at work in the region of conflict—perhaps that school is itself part of the problem. But those running such processes should be aware that at least part of the audience needs to be addressed in terms it can understand and make use of. Of course, key to this is whom the results of the Track Two process are aimed at. Results aimed at officials stand a better chance of being accepted if they are couched in terms which are amenable to that audience. If the results are aimed at civil society, another approach will be more likely to succeed.

From a practical point of view, then, Track Two needs to combine elements of these schools in an eclectic manner if it is to be effective. While the process of meeting in small groups to jointly deconstruct the underlying elements of the conflict and then jointly construct a new understanding of it may be profoundly constructivist in its method, such a new understanding cannot by itself bring about change. It is the process of transferring the new understandings and ideas arising from Track Two discussions into the political realm on both sides that brings about the possibility of change, and that realm is often more influenced by realist or, less often, by liberal conceptions of the way power works. **In my own work, I take the view that Track Two is eclectic in method; often constructivist in process; and usually realist (more rarely, liberal) in the transfer of ideas to the official realm.**

Track Two Practitioners and Theory

How do those who are engaged in Track Two or even mediation more generally, whether practically or academically, see their work stacking up against these theoretical approaches to international affairs? More broadly, how do those who seek to end or transform conflicts see their work in relation to the IR schools? Few practitioners or scholars of Track Two have written specifically or extensively on where they believe their activities fit within traditional IR schools, or paradigms—a telling commentary perhaps on the perceived utility of those paradigms. Nevertheless, a few have explored the subject in sometimes tangential ways which are revealing.

Worldviews of Conflict

According to Davidheiser, worldviews "may be described as elaborate systems of understanding, expectations, and action that are continually reconstructed by individuals embedded in wider social systems. The interpretive maps are fluid; cognitive structures and filters evolve over time, undergoing continual iteration as they are re-forged in the cauldrons of life experience and social learning."[39] To some extent, the idea of a worldview is analogous to that of a culture, but proponents of the concept of worldviews as a tool for the exploration of conflict dynamics believe that it provides a wider scope for analyzing how deeply held belief systems influence peoples and groups in conflict.[40]

Bitter has proposed that approaches to conflict resolution generally fall into one of three distinct worldviews which influence how one approaches a conflict.[41] While not exactly congruent with the IR paradigms, these worldviews do overlap them. The mainstream worldview in the English-speaking world, in Bitter's view, focuses on the "specific interest" of those at the table. The objective is to see if a process can be developed whereby these interests can be reconciled. While there are different approaches to doing this, from competitive, or "zero-sum," bargaining to cooperative, or "sum-sum," bargaining, the focus is on developing a bargaining process to reconcile interests. As noted, these negotiations can take place on the basis of a realist paradigm of competition or be oriented to a constructivist approach toward the creation of a new and mutual understanding of the thing being bargained over which permits mutual gains.

The second of Bitter's worldviews of negotiation is "conflict transformation." This area features negotiation approaches and activities which see the differences behind the conflict as being socially constructed realities. The objective is thus to help the parties understand this and jointly construct a new reality amenable to a redefinition of their interests and to the possibility of compromise. This is obviously a constructivist approach to negotiation in terms of the IR paradigms.[42]

The third worldview concerns approaches to negotiation which focus on "human needs." This includes ways of conceiving of negotiation as an exercise in trying to address basic human fears, emotions, and needs, such as issues bound up with perceived threats to ethnicity and identity. This approach recognizes that not all issues can be negotiated in a traditional sense and argues that conflicts based on human needs require an approach which helps each party develop new understandings of its own narratives, and those of the other party, in order to find new ways forward.[43] This approach is closely related to much of the literature on Track Two as it has developed in the sense of conflict resolution. This worldview tends to fall outside the parameters of the IR paradigms, though specific formulas as to what might be done in any given case can be inspired by one of the paradigms even as a practitioner takes a "human needs" approach to understanding what the conflict is about.

Social Psychology

Fisher has stated that his method of interactive conflict resolution (ICR) is congruent with what he calls "an *eclectic model of intergroup conflict* which sees protracted conflict as rooted in discrepancies in interests, values, needs or power between groups that are exacerbated by cultural differences and history of antagonism."[44] He goes on to argue that ICR

> takes a social-psychological approach by asserting that relationship issues (misperceptions, unmet basic needs and so on) must be addressed and that the conflict will be resolved only by mutually acceptable solutions that are developed through joint interaction. . . . "Conflict resolution" therefore is not seen as a single or time-limited outcome but as a complex process of de-escalation and reconciliation that develops over time to the point where new qualities and mechanisms exist in the relationship to allow for the constructive settlement of disputes.[45]

The "social-psychological" approach Fisher refers to is based on an interdisciplinary field which has attempted to blend sociology and psychology to explain how people's thoughts, ideas, and feelings influence their approach to each other and to complex issues.[46] The social-psychological approach to conflict resolution "is designed to complement (and not to replace) approaches based on structural or strategic analysis by providing a special lens for viewing international conflict that brings some of its less explored dimensions into focus."[47] Fisher is thus saying that as a practitioner he takes an essentially eclectic approach to defining how groups came into conflict, and a social-psychological approach to interacting with the individuals who are taking part in his ICR workshops.

The field of social psychology has been concerned with conflict and conflict resolution almost since its beginnings in the nineteenth century.[48] At first the field tended to view conflict as a normal state of affairs, part of a competitive struggle that goes on between and within individuals over basic human needs and deep psychological impulses. By the middle of the twentieth century, scholars in the field were exploring the conditions in which people grow up, the roles they adopt within their societies, and economic and other factors to try to explain their propensity to violence and conflict. Regarding the idea of conflict resolution, early studies focused on why and how people in group settings decided to either cooperate or not and put forward theories which might explain this.[49]

Beginning in the 1940s, the field became heavily influenced by game theory, and for the next few decades a substantial subgroup within the discipline devoted itself to constructing ever more complex and mathematical game-theoretical experiments to demonstrate how individuals make choices to either fight or cooperate in given situations.[50] This activity had the effect of laying bare many of the hypotheses of the field, subjecting them to mathematical analysis based on units of measurement assigned, often quite arbitrarily, to certain choices or outcomes of the players in a game. Some of this work was very useful in demonstrating that the behavior of people in conflict situations is a complex mixture of cooperative and competitive tendencies, and that these nuances need to be appreciated.[51] But much of it was, in the words of the field's giants, "mindless."[52] Nevertheless, the method was influential in fields such as "strategic studies" and contributed to a public perception that many social scientists engaged in conflict analysis were members of a "Strangelovian" order. By 1977, it was estimated that over one thousand studies had been published in learned journals on aspects of conflict analysis based on game experiments of highly varying degrees of sophistication and validity.[53]

Others interested in social psychology turned away from game theory to explore the application of the field to the dynamics of conflict and bargaining in small-group and other settings, such as ethnic conflicts. This work has been largely evidence-based analyses drawn from the study of specific cases. Like game theory, it has sought to understand what determines cooperative versus competitive behavior in such settings.[54] The work which began in the 1960s by people such as Burton, Kelman, Fisher, and others (referred to in Chapter 1) around such methods as controlled communication, interactive problem solving, and interactive conflict resolution represents the efforts of social psychology practitioners in the field to develop a conceptual and theoretical basis to explain what they do.

In their study of the development of social psychology as it applies to intergroup conflicts, Çuhadar and Dayton note three theories which have sprung from the social-psychological tradition and have "guided scholarship on intergroup conflicts: social identity theory, stereotyping and prejudice, and contact theory."[55] Each of these has a lengthy and complex history marked by many debates, and Çuhadar and Dayton devote considerable space discussing how these theories have developed, the debates which characterize them, and how the theories have influenced the field of Track Two. Briefly, "social identity theory" takes as a basic premise that human beings naturally search for patterns as a survival mechanism in a complex world. In social terms, they search for categories of people; those who are "like us" (in-groups) and those who are "not like us" (out-groups). Researchers like Muzafer Sherif suggest that this is not enough to trigger conflict in itself; competition for resources or other valued objectives is necessary to add a dangerous layer to the in-group/out-group dynamic.[56] The *"stereotyping and prejudice"* approach is marked by studies into the nature of phenomena like prejudice and how they affect perceptions and conflict in divergent groups. Finally, "social contact theory," which may be the most influential of the three, holds that if a lack of knowledge about or exposure to the other side is a defining characteristic of such problems as prejudice, then the act of bringing people together in carefully structured and controlled circumstances can help them overcome these stereotypes and open up new possibilities for dealing with the causes of conflicts.

As noted (above) by Kelman, many in the field do not imagine that they can or should *replace* traditional paradigms of IR regarding how and why states and peoples come into conflict (though this was Burton's early claim, which so infuriated some of his colleagues at the University of London in the 1960s). Rather, there is a notion, as developed by Edward Azar, that such paradigms either do not fully explain intractable conflicts or do not provide adequate ways of assessing what should be done about them.

Structuralism and Social Psychology
Yet another view on the role of the IR paradigms in this field comes from the study on multiparty mediation in conflict settings, including Track Two,

by Crocker, Hampson, and Aall. They posited that all mediation takes place within one of two paradigms: structuralist (realist) or social-psychological (note that they mean something slightly different from the use of the term as described above).[57] Each of these paradigms "involve[s] alternate assessments about appropriate bargaining strategies and entry points, as well as. . . . A different set of conclusions about the possibilities for effective mediation . . . and the kinds of bargaining strategies that are likely to be most effective."[58] Importantly, they note that a mediation process will include different stages, during which some actors and paradigms will be more effective than others; a Track Two process based on a social-psychological paradigm may be most effective at the very beginning, but will at some point likely have to hand off to an official mediation, based on a structuralist paradigm, if a "deal" is to be "closed."

The "structuralist" school, as defined by Crocker, Hampson, and Aall, "is based on a belief that through the use of persuasion, incentives, and disincentives (i.e., a costing process), parties to a conflict can be led to and through a negotiated settlement. This paradigm, which is anchored in a rational choice view of the world, treats the causes of conflict as objective—as opposed to subjective—issues that can yield to negotiation."[59] Most effective in this type of mediation are officials, who have the backing of a state and can introduce incentives and disincentives to the process. The more powerful the state, the more powerful the mediator, provided the state in question is prepared to make good on its promises and threats and the parties in conflict perceive this to be the case. The activities of Richard Holbrooke at the Dayton peace talks in twisting the arms of the protagonists in the conflict within the former Yugoslavia are an example of Touval's concept of a "mediator with muscle."[60]

An important element of the structuralist approach is the idea that there are objectively identifiable moments when a mediation process is more likely to succeed, based on the willingness of the parties to endure pain and discomfort, often represented as a "conflict cycle" of rising and falling violence.[61] When the limits of tolerance are perceived to have been reached, parties in conflict are more likely to be willing to explore the idea of a settlement. The concept of "ripeness"—the idea that there are "ripe" moments when the protagonists have reached a "mutually hurting stalemate" and are looking for an acceptable "way out"—as developed by Zartman and others, is much discussed in the structuralist literature on mediation and will be further explored in the next chapter.[62] One criticism of this type of mediation is that it can lead to situations where a conflict is frozen, as opposed to being resolved. If the parties to the conflict perceive the costs of continued fighting to be greater than those of accepting the terms developed with the help of muscular mediator, they may agree to stop fighting, but they will not necessarily have "made peace": the fighting may erupt again in some years when unresolved underlying frictions have reached the boiling point again and calculations of cost and benefit have changed.

The social-psychological paradigm, as Crocker, Hampson, and Aall define it, focuses on "the processes of communication and exchange as a way to change perceptions and attitudes." Mediation efforts thus concentrate on "providing a forum in which parties can explore options and develop solutions, often outside the highly charged arena of a formal negotiating structure."[63] This paradigm thus focuses on facilitated discussions between representatives of the protagonists in conflict, aimed at helping them to get past the stereotypes and positions with which they characterize the conflict and to develop new understandings of the deeper issues of the conflict, of the "other side," and of their own attitudes towards the conflict. Out of these interactions are supposed to come new approaches to the conflict that are jointly developed. Much of this work is done in small, quiet workshops facilitated by a respected third party.

While many would consider this approach as primarily the domain of Track Two, it is also employed by official mediators, particularly those who represent international organizations which lack, in Touval's term, "muscle." The activities of the Organization for Security and Co-operation's High Commissioner on National Minorities are an example,[64] as are the many cases of the UN Secretary General's "Special Representatives" to various conflicts—particularly those cases where member states of the Security Council are clearly not willing to authorize the use of force, and where they, and other states who have the means to bring force to bear, are not prepared to do so.[65] These official, social-psychological mediators do not have the ability to impose rewards or penalties but can use the moral suasion of their positions to try to bring the parties to the table for discussions aimed at a peace agreement. Often this type of mediation will rely on the power of public opinion, both in the societies where the fighting is happening and more generally, to push protagonists in the direction of accommodation and peace. While it is often not as successful as "muscular mediators" in stopping the fighting where there is no stomach for an international intervention to stop it, in those cases where official mediators relying on social-psychological techniques do record successes they are often longer lasting than those of the structuralists, as they are based more on genuine reconciliation than on bringing about a ceasefire through the use of "carrots and sticks."

While the work by Crocker, Hampson, and Aall is not specifically related to Track Two but rather the broader question of multiparty mediation in a conflict setting, it does demonstrate that the choice of paradigm under which a mediator (or in the case of Track Two, a third party) works has considerable significance operationally. Mediators working under a social-psychological paradigm, for example, whether officials or Track Two facilitators, would be ill advised in the extreme to indulge in the realist strategy of making threats they cannot make good or promises they cannot keep, as their credibility would be lost in an instant. Moreover, in their use of terms to define what they feel are the two predominant paradigms governing mediation, the authors eschew the terms used in IR theory. Nevertheless, their descriptions of "structuralism" and "social psychology" (as used by them) bear some obvious relationships to realism and constructivism, respectively.

Four Approaches to the Israeli-Palestinian Case

In another groundbreaking work, Çuhadar and Dayton specifically related Track Two projects in the Israeli-Palestinian context to tailored derivatives of the various IR paradigms.[66] They looked at an inventory of seventy-nine such projects that have taken place since the Oslo breakthrough in the early 1990s. They then established a typology of Track Two projects, based on their relationship to the IR paradigms, and examined the characteristics and assumptions of each. Though their findings are primarily intended to be applicable to the Israeli-Palestinian case and their descriptions of the paradigms do not exactly accord with those in much of the IR literature, their findings are still an important contribution to our understanding of how different types of Track Two projects can be based on different conceptions of IR theory.

Çuhadar and Dayton posit the existence of four distinct theoretical approaches to Track Two as it relates to the Israeli-Palestinian case: the psychological approach, the constructivist approach, the capacity builder approach, and the realistic interest approach. Though they caution that the boundaries between the four were, in practice, sometimes artificial (most projects strayed across theoretical boundaries, as eclecticists would advise them to do), they nevertheless believe that these four approaches can between them explain all seventy-nine Track Two projects under study in terms of their founding assumptions, their working methods, and the strategies they adopted for the dissemination of their results.

Projects identified by Çuhadar and Dayton as having operated primarily under the *psychological* approach were based on the belief that the long legacy of negative, dehumanizing stereotypes and prejudicial images which each side holds of the other are a key factor in the continuation of the conflict. These projects therefore brought together various groups, such as teachers, for activities aimed at building trust and empathy and "rehumanizing" the other side. The primary means were small intergroup sessions in a nonthreatening environment, facilitated by experts skilled in intergroup dynamics who used structured discussions to help each side "get to know" the views and suffering of the other and to replace negative stereotypes with more genuine understanding of the hardships each side has endured in the conflict. This process is sometimes known as "social contact" (as discussed earlier) and relies on the theory that groups in long-standing, intractable conflicts have often developed very deep-seated views of the other side, based on negative stereotypes, which make them unwilling to take risks for peace. Much of this work draws on research into the use of "contact" as a method to reduce intergroup bias and prejudice.[67] The participants in such sessions are supposed to take their new understandings of the other side back to their respective communities and work to change stereotypes held within society at large. These projects would be examples of Fisher's "broad" ICR, or Agha and colleagues' "soft" Track Two, as discussed in Chapter 1. Of course, not all projects which take place within the *psychological* approach are examples of soft Track Two. The Turkish Armenian Reconciliation Commission was a Track Two project which took place at the Track 1.5 level.[68]

Projects operating under what Çuhadar and Dayton call the *constructivist* approach were often focused on the competing historical narratives each side has of the conflict. Borrowing from the emerging field of "narrative mediation," which sees it as necessary in intense conflict situations to help protagonists develop new and shared narratives of the conflict as a means to get beyond zero-sum positions which have grown out of diametrically opposed narratives,[69] Track Two projects within Çuhadar and Dayton's constructivist approach seek to help groups from the two sides jointly develop—indeed, jointly *construct*—new narratives which could be amenable to compromise on difficult issues. This is seen as particularly important in the Israeli-Palestinian conflict, as each side brings to the table well-developed narratives of victimhood which place the primary blame on the other for the suffering of the past and which support arguments that no peace is possible until "they" apologize and recognize that "they" must surrender their claims.[70] Projects initiated under this approach ranged from those aimed at bringing together scholars and historians with the objective of jointly exploring competing historical narratives and writing new and shared ones,[71] to projects which create new vehicles for the publication of research and opinion aimed at providing binational perspectives on issues,[72] to the creation of news services which make available to the public stories and analyses focusing on explanations of the conflict that do not subscribe to prevailing antagonistic narratives.[73]

These kinds of projects can be among the most emotionally difficult for participants, as they are required to leave behind their well-developed narratives (and thus their "comfort zones" in explaining and justifying their own actions and prejudices over many years) and to do so over critically important issues in the presence of people from the other side. This was something I learned when helping to facilitate a narrative Track Two project on the Palestinian refugee issue, which required the Israelis to admit that many thousands of Palestinians were forced out in 1948 (as opposed to having voluntarily fled) and that Israel would have to come to grips with this, apologize for it, and offer compensation, but which also required the Palestinian participants to explicitly accept that they would have to fully and finally renounce their claim to the "right of return" en masse as part of a final settlement.

In terms of our discussion of the definition of Track Two in the previous chapter, projects initiated under this paradigm can fall into both "focused" and "broad" (Fisher), or "hard" and "soft" (Agha *and colleagues*), depending on the specific circumstances. While an effort at providing a news service to the broader public is obviously a broad, or soft, one, an effort to bring together a small group of highly influential people to reexamine positions on a specific issue and then develop concrete policy proposals can be focused, or hard, in its methods and intended implications.

Projects initiated under the *capacity builder* approach address what is often felt to be a lack of experience and education in the fields of conflict resolution and peaceful coexistence. The theory is that by training conflict resolution experts, more and more people on each side will be able to work with the other side, and also within their own communities, to promote peace. These projects thus seek to empower individuals to become their own peacemakers, sometimes known in the literature as "agents of change," but also to create educational and other tools for promoting change on a societal level. Examples would include projects designed to bring together youth groups to better know each other and to develop conflict resolution ideas. One such project, the US-based "Seeds of Peace," has brought significant numbers of Israeli and Palestinian youth to the United States for annual summer camps, where they can meet each other—these sessions often being the first time these youth have ever met their opposite numbers—and develop conflict resolution skills.[74] Such projects are generally, though not always, examples of broad, or soft, Track Two, as identified by Agha and colleagues.

Finally, the *realistic interest* approach "often deals with the 'realistic interests' aspects of the conflict, such as resource conflicts and negotiable interests."[75] It thus focuses on the issues which dominate the conflict but also probes some of the deep-seated perceptions the two sides have over what these issues mean to them. Such Track Two projects often attempt to bring together subject-matter experts from each side for discussions, which if not negotiations over specific questions are very much intended to explore positions with a view to developing concrete proposals for new negotiating positions. There is often a belief that developing a joint proposal to manage a specific problem, such as water scarcity or the municipal governance of a shared Jerusalem, will forge ties between the participants. The outcome of such projects is thus not "just" a proposal for the issue in question, but a group bond between the participants which will lead them to work together to promote the project. Projects undertaken in this paradigm are often focused, or hard, Track Two.

Conclusion

As this brief overview of the dominant paradigms of the study of international affairs and their relationship to Track Two shows, many theories of international affairs and conflict resolution form the basis of such efforts and how they are perceived by both policymakers and scholars. No single paradigm fits exactly, nor are they even discussed exactly the same way by various practitioners. For example, though Çuhadar and Dayton are using terms like "constructivist" and "realist" in their typology, they do not mean exactly the same thing as when used by IR theorists. Similarly, Crocker, Hampson, and Aall speak of structuralism and social psychology as the primary paradigms to explain mediation, but mean, in IR terms, something close to realism and constructivism.

This set of discrepancies is maddening to social scientists trying to develop firm descriptions of, and explanations for, Track Two. As Rouhana notes,

> Interactive Conflict Resolution faces a host of core theoretical and methodological questions. As an emerging field . . . questions are raised about theories of conflict resolution that guide practice, methodologies used in research, and evaluation of interventions' impact on the macro-dynamics of conflict. To increase confidence in this approach to practice, establish its relevance for policy makers, and enhance its legitimacy as an academic field of study and research, interactive conflict resolution should be held to the same standards of scrutiny as other established fields.[76]

While Rouhana's concerns are valid, they miss the broader point that Track Two is action oriented. It is fundamentally concerned with what works in practice. This does not mean, of course, that those who undertake these activities should not be guided by a well-thought-out, conceptual sense of what they are trying to do and how they are trying to do it—that is, a theory of change. Absent this, Track Two becomes activity without higher purpose. What it does mean is that how this higher purpose is defined and pursued will not always conform to generally understood principles of IR theory, and should not be assessed against it. But Rouhana is right in the sense that Track Two can and should be assessed and held accountable. What a given Track Two project can be assessed against, in addition of course to its success in bringing together those in conflict in any given case, is how it handles a set of issues that have arisen in the field. Towards this end, those active in the field have developed theoretical propositions against which such interventions can be constructed and assessed. It is to some of these that we turn our attention in the next chapter.

3   Where Theory Meets Practice

WHILE MUCH OF TRACK TWO THEORY AND PRACTICE is not fully explained by mainstream theories of international affairs, this does not mean that it is without theoretical foundation. As noted in the previous chapter, several practitioners and students of the field have developed theoretical frameworks for their activities. Other practitioners have developed or borrowed concepts from other theoretical constructs and apply them in an eclectic fashion to what they do. In keeping with the action-oriented approach of Track Two, much of this activity is related to helping practitioners answer critical questions about how to make their efforts more effective and how to evaluate their work. Four particularly important aspects of this are the question of the "theories of change" that practitioners take into their cases; the way they conceive the conflict and what is necessary to address it; the question of when it is best to launch a Track Two process; and the ethical and cultural issues which arise when undertaking a Track Two project. These subjects will be explored in this chapter.

Theories of Change

The phrase "theories of change" relates to attempts by many in the field of conflict resolution to develop and test the implications of different theories of how people in conflict situations change; how their perceptions of themselves, of the conflict, and of the other side undergo a transformation. This is vital to the endeavor; in the absence of a theory of why such change happens and how it may be brought about, one lacks a set of markers against which to design a process or measure impact as the process unfolds. Moreover, one is unable to learn from previous practice or provide testable hypotheses for those who would come after. Cross-fertilization or even collaboration between projects becomes more difficult if they are working from different theories of change, or if those theories are more implicit than explicit and cannot be elaborated and compared.[1]

The literature on theories of change draws from the field of program evaluation. Such studies identify a theory of change as that set of explicit and, more often, implicit approaches to issues such as what kind of change is being sought, how much, how it happens, and how it is measured.[2] One of the earliest theories of change which took hold in the field of conflict resolution is known as "intergroup contact theory," which was first applied to attempts to reduce prejudice in domestic situations and later applied to international conflict resolution. This idea holds that bringing together those in conflict for discussions, which can be mediated or not but are aimed at breaking down stereotypes and deeply held suspicions, is in itself a useful exercise. It is not necessarily sufficient for resolving conflicts, but it has been seen as an important step on the road to changing people's views about the conflict.[3]

As we saw in Chapter 2, since the development of this theory of change, the field has grown in sophistication and complexity. However, Shapiro finds that most of those running Track Two processes continue to act on largely internalized theories of change rather than ones which are explicitly stated. These implicit theories are usually based on philosophically driven views of how and why conflicts come about rather than on objective research; they rely on "gut" feelings of how to resolve conflicts. Similarly, Çuhadar and Dayton, in their study on social psychology and conflict resolution, state, "We observed that an important number of practitioners have been undertaking their activities without formulating a theory of change."[4]

Theories of change are multilevel frameworks which Track Two practitioners take into their work, specifically around how their actions will bring about change at three levels: the individual level, the intergroup level (those participating in the process), and the broader societies involved in the conflict—or at all three levels. This recognition that change happens on multiple levels is an important though often unstated element, and it allows practitioners to organize their activities around particular levels of the complex and multifaceted situation they are working on. Some will try to effect change primarily on the individual level; others will seek change on the group level (often targeting particular groups of elites); and so forth. Some will try to effect change on all levels, or posit that a profound change on one level will affect the others. Further research indicates the existence of common underpinnings for most conflict resolution practitioners. For example, a sense of optimism pervades the field. Practitioners tend to believe that all conflicts, no matter how intense, contain opportunities for useful intervention in that those in conflict are capable of learning and growth; this is often expressed as the view that "people can change." The view is based on a fundamental belief that theories of inherent violence or Hobbesian views of the world are not correct, or at least are not complete. Instead, external influences are key to how people have developed, and such influences can be ameliorated through interventions.[5] In short, while theories of change do represent social science, they are also based on an element of faith.

When speaking of theories of change, mediators and more specifically practitioners of Track Two are trying to tease out the underlying conceptual and even emotional assumptions that they take into an intervention. They are doing so in the recognition that most of these theories are implicit, as opposed to explicit, and rest on deep-seated beliefs as to how and why people come into and resolve conflict. They also do so in the belief that these theories need to be stated and subjected to analysis in terms of the demonstrated effects of intervention strategies that are based on these theories. Marc Howard Ross suggests that there are six major "theories of practice" in the field of conflict resolution, particularly as it applies to ethnically based conflicts.[6] These are the theories of

- Community relations, the belief that ongoing polarization and distrust between groups exacerbate the conflict
- Principled negotiation, the belief that incompatible, zero-sum approaches to negotiations are the key reason that resolution is not possible
- Human needs, the belief that unmet or frustrated basic needs lie behind the conflict
- Identity, the belief by parties to the conflict that their basic identity is threatened by the other
- Intercultural miscommunication, the belief that incompatibilities between different cultural communication styles is primarily responsible for the conflict
- Conflict transformation, the belief that the key to the conflict lies in inequality and injustice, and that the basic situation which has produced these must be transformed

Ross notes that these six theories of practice are not exclusive of one another; conflicts often exhibit more than one of them. It is the job of those who would intervene to first deduce which of these theories are operative in the particular

TABLE 3.1 Major theories of practice of conflict resolution

	Causes and/or nature of ethnic conflict	Goals	Effects on participants in interventions	Mechanism for achieving effects	Transfer: impact on the wider conflict
Community Relations	Ongoing polarization, distrust, and hostility between groups exacerbate existing conflict	Improving communication and understanding; promoting tolerance acceptance of diversity; encouraging structures which safeguard rights of all	Build community self esteem through successful local institutions and projects making decisions on issues important in daily life	Self-esteem, efficacy and reinforcement from prior successes through local institution building	Increased community capability and self-esteem facilities cooperative problem solving on matters of mutual interest
Principled negotiation	Incompatible positions and zero sum view of conflict	Positive sum agreements between the parties — i.e. ones which provide for mutual gain	Build analytic ability to identify mutual interests and devise solutions which offer mutual gain	Separate people from the problems; focus on interests not positions; generate possibilities for mutual gain; use objective standards to judge outcomes	Spread of skills to others; increased sense that agreements are possible; benefits to communities from prior agreements
Human needs	Unmet or frustrated basic needs	Shared recognition of core needs and exploration of ways to meet them through joint action	Discovery of shared goals and objectives; recognition of common needs; greater sense of choices and options	Problem-solving workshops led by skilled third parties who encourage analytic dialogue	Transfer of new perspectives from influentials and near influences changes the idea of what is possible for the wider community
Identity	Threatened identity rooted in unresolved past loss and suffering	Changed relations through mutual recognition; development of a sense that agreement is possible; lowering fears to permit exploring options	Overcomes barriers to dialogue by focusing on deep identity issues involved in past losses so the parties learn what possible agreements can offer	Mourning past losses and suffering; track 2 and other channels which focus on identity threats and fears; symbolic and ritual action to affirm group identity	New understanding of the conflict through changes in discourse and symbolic actions which feed new understandings into the policy process
Intercultural miscommunication	Incompatibilities between different cultural communication styles	Effective intergroup communication; weakening negative stereotypes	Builds awareness of other cultures; develops new metaphors; information exchange to overcome cultural barriers to effective communication	Increased awareness of communication barriers; use of third-party 'translators'; deconstruction of historical accounts	Improved communication makes it easier to reach agreements and increased public support for cooperation
Conflict transformation	Real problems of inequality and injustice expressed through socially and culturally constructed meanings	Changing relationships and moral growth which produces justice, forgiveness and reconciliation	Transforms relationships to produce self-reliant persons; empowerment and recognition	Elicitive training which develops culturally relevant models of conflict resolution; mediation aimed at empowerment and recognition	Empowerment leads to transformation of relationships in the larger society built on culturally appropriate models

Source: Ross, M.H., "Creating the Conditions for Peacemaking: Theories of Practice in Ethnic Conflict Resolution," *Ethnic and Racial Studies* 23(6), 2000, pp. 1022–23.

situation and then to devise strategies to address them. Ross represents examples of such strategies in tabular form (Table 3.1).

Another example of a set of theories of change comes from Anderson, Chigas, and Woodrow, who posit fourteen generally accepted theories of change in the conflict resolution field. These are still quite general; nevertheless, they represent an attempt to comprehensively outline the theories of change which exist and to suggest the kinds of concrete activities that can go on around each. These are presented in Table 3.2.[7]

TABLE 3.2 Common Theories of Change

Theory of change	Methods (examples only)
Individual change: If we transform the consciousness, attitudes, behaviors, and skills of many individuals, we will create a critical mass of people who will advocate peace effectively.	Individual change through training, personal transformation, or consciousness-raising workshops or processes; dialogues and encounter groups; trauma healing
Healthy relationships and connections: Strong relationships are a necessary ingredient for peacebuilding. If we can break down isolation, polarization, division, prejudice, and stereotypes between/among groups, we will enable progress on key issues.	Processes of intergroup dialogue; networking; relationship-building processes; joint efforts and practical programs on substantive problems
Withdrawal of the resources for war: Wars require vast amounts of material (weapons, supplies, transport, etc.) and human capital. If we can interrupt the supply of people and goods to the war-making system, it will collapse, and peace will become possible.	Campaigns aimed at cutting off funds/national budgets for war; conscientious objection and/or resistance to military service; international arms control; arms (and other) embargoes and boycotts
Reduction of violence: If we reduce the levels of violence perpetrated by combatants and/or their representatives, we increase the chances of bringing security and peace.	Cease-fires; creation of zones of peace; withdrawal/retreat from direct engagement; introduction of peacekeeping forces/interposition; observation missions; accompaniment efforts; promotion of nonviolent methods for achieving political/social/economic ends; reform of security sector institutions (military, police, justice system/courts, prisons)
Social justice: If we address the underlying issues of injustice, oppression/exploitation, threats to identity and security, and people's sense of injury/victimization, it will reduce the drivers of conflict and open up space for peace.	Long-term campaigns for social and structural change; truth and reconciliation processes; changes in social institutions, laws, regulations, and economic systems
Good governance: Peace is secured by establishing stable/reliable social institutions that guarantee democracy, equity, justice, and fair allocation of resources.	New constitutional and governance arrangements/entities; power-sharing structures; development of human rights, rule of law, anticorruption; establishment of democratic/equitable economic structures; economic development; democratization; elections and election monitoring; increased participation and access to decision making
Political elites: If we change the political calculus and perception of interests of key political (and other) leaders, they will take the necessary steps to bring peace.	Raise the costs and reduce the benefits for political elites of continuing war, and increase the incentives for peace; engage active and influential constituencies in favor of peace; withdraw international support/funding for warring parties

TABLE 3.2 Common Theories of Change *(continued)*

Theory of change	*Methods (examples only)*
Grassroots mobilization: "When the people lead, the leaders will follow." If we mobilize enough opposition to war, political leaders will be forced to bring peace.	Mobilize grassroots groups to either oppose war or advocate positive action; use of the media; nonviolent direct action campaigns; education/ mobilization effort; organizing advocacy groups; dramatic/public events to raise consciousness
Peace agreements/accords: Some form of political settlement is a prerequisite to peace—we must support a negotiation process among key parties to the conflict and violence.	Official negotiations among representatives of key parties; "Track IV2" [track IV2 is not explained in the text] and "Track 2" dialogues among influential persons; civil society dialogues in support of negotiations
Economic action: People make personal decisions, and decision makers make policy decisions based on a system of rewards/incentives and punishment/ sanctions that are essentially economic in nature. If we can change the economies associated with war-making, we can bring peace.	Use of government or financial institutions to change supply-and-demand dynamics; control incentive and reward systems; boycotts and embargoes
Public attitudes: War and violence are partly motivated by prejudice, misperceptions, and intolerance of difference. We can promote peace by using the media (television and radio) to change public attitudes and build greater tolerance in society.	TV and radio programs that promote tolerance; modeling tolerant behavior; symbolic acts of solidarity/unity; dialogue among groups in conflict, with subsequent publicity
Transitional justice: Societies that have experienced deep trauma and social dislocation need a process for handling grievances, identifying what happened, and holding perpetrators accountable. Addressing these issues will enable people to move on to reconstruct a peaceful and prosperous society.	Truth and reconciliation commissions; criminal prosecutions and war crimes tribunals; reparations; community reconciliation processes; traditional rites and ceremonies; institutional reforms
Community reintegration: If we enable displaced people (internally displaced persons, refugees) to return to their homes and live in relative harmony with their neighbors, we will contribute to security and economic recovery.	Negotiation and problem-solving to enable returns; intergroup dialogue; excombatant–community engagement; processes for handling land claims; trauma healing
Culture of peace: If we transform cultural and societal norms, values, and behaviors to reject violence, support dialogue and negotiation, and address the fundamental causes of the conflict, we can develop the long-term conditions for peace.	Peace education; poverty eradication; reduction of social inequalities; promotion of human rights; ensuring gender equality; fostering democratic participation; advancing tolerance; enhancing the free flow of information/knowledge; reducing the production of and traffic in arms

Source: OECD (2008), "Encouraging Effective Evaluation of Conflict Prevention and Peace-building Activities: Towards DAC Guidance," *OECD Journal on Development*, Vol. 8/3. http:// dx.doi.org/10.1787/journal_dev-v8-art37-en

Shapiro, meanwhile, puts forth three broad theories, each with various sublevels.[8] At the level of **changing individuals**, practitioners seek strategies which will affect the perceptions and behaviors of those around the table and alter their feelings and motivations towards the other side. These strategies can include efforts to tackle prejudices and deep-rooted images of the other side. Change can take place at cognitive or behavioral levels, and can involve either (or both) intellectual or emotional changes in response to new ideas or to confronting long-held beliefs. At the level of **changing relationships,** Track Two efforts can seek to establish new networks between people involved in difficult conflicts. This is done in order to change the relationships of the individuals involved but also (if group members agree) to develop such networks into powerful forces for change in their respective societies. Finally, **structural, institutional, and systemic changes** are directly aimed at the institutions of societies in conflict through, for example, electoral or judicial reform or the creation of new mechanisms to address underlying problems like inequality or underdevelopment.

My experience is that as a practical matter a Track Two process is best aimed at the first of Shapiro's levels. It is then up to the participants, with the help of a third party, if requested, to use their influence to push change on the other levels through a mechanism known in the field as "transfer." Particularly in the initial stages, the people at the table are only in control of themselves; they cannot commit to changing others, much less to changing the institutional or structural issues of the conflict. As trust is built, relationships forged, and new ideas created, they may be willing to go further. But one cannot set out with a firm expectation; a willingness to transfer new ideas developed by the group has to grow out of the discussions.

Yet another example of a set of theories of change comes from Lederach, Neufeldt, and Culbertson, who posit four "strategies of change."[9] The first is **personal change**: changes in the attitudes, emotions, and behaviors of the individuals taking part in the effort. The second is **relationship change**: changes in the patterns of communication and intergroup dynamics of the participants, both within the group and in how they then interact with their home communities around the issues of the conflict. The third is **structural change**: attempts to address structural issues affecting the conflict, such as racist or discriminatory policies or underdevelopment.

Finally, **cultural change**: changes in the ways the "other" and indeed the conflict itself are understood. This set of theories bears some resemblance and relationship to those proposed by Shapiro.

Management, Resolution, or Transformation?

Another way to deepen our understanding of Track Two activities is by characterizing their objectives in relation to the desired impact on the conflict. Is the activity intended to manage a conflict, resolve it, or transform it?[10] This approach adds a new layer of complexity and granularity to the development of a theory of change: it posits that, as one is developing theories of change with respect to effects on individuals in the conflict, one should also lay out the intended impact of the intervention *on the conflict itself.*

Conflict **management** tends to see conflicts as the inevitable result of differences over such things as culture, values, and resources. Most conflicts cannot be fully resolved in that these differences cannot be eradicated, but conflicts over them can be managed and contained so as to reduce violence and improve the lives of people who are affected by them. Ultimately, if a conflict is properly managed over a long period, perceptions of the conflict, and therefore its reality, can change to the point that a historic compromise can come about. But those who develop Track Two projects aimed at conflict management believe that activities, especially at the outset of an intervention when the fighting is still going on or is fresh in memory, are best aimed at simply managing the situation in order to create stability and the long-term cessation of fighting. Attempts to fully end the conflict and change the reality on the ground may come later. As Bloomfield and Reilly put it,

> Conflict management is the positive and constructive handling of difference and divergence. Rather than advocating methods for removing conflict, [it] addresses the more realistic question of managing conflict: how to deal with it in a constructive way, how to bring opposing sides together in a cooperative process, how to design a practical, achievable, cooperative system for the constructive management of difference.[11]

Those who attempt conflict **resolution** are less swayed by this somewhat realist view of conflict and argue that people engaged in deep-rooted conflicts over identity issues will not agree to "manage" these problems, especially if that requires identity-threatening compromise over the issues on an ongoing basis. It is therefore necessary to find ways to help participants reframe their points of reference and reconceptualize the basis of the conflict so as to find common ground—to shift, that is, from so-called zero-sum positions to sum-sum positions. This is a different order of magnitude, and it requires an approach which goes beyond identifying workable compromises over the nuts and bolts of the conflict; it requires that the third party help the participants undertake a process, individually and jointly, of reconceptualizing the meanings of the conflict, why those meanings have become attached to the conflict over time, and whether new meanings—that are more amenable to possible solutions—can be developed and "sold" to their respective populations. Burton, among others, has been quite active in developing ideas along these lines, particularly as they relate to Track Two.[12]

Finally, those active in conflict **transformation** believe that the field must go far beyond the somewhat transactional approach of conflict management and even the conceptual approach of conflict resolution; it must do nothing less than help participants recognize that their conflict is deeply embedded in the very structure of their societies and polities, and then help them to develop the tools to change those structures.[13] Conflict transformation is therefore "a process of engaging with and transforming the relationships, interests, discourses, and, if necessary, the very constitution of society that supports the continuation of violent conflict."[14] Leaders in the conceptualization and development of this field include Lederach,[15] Galtung,[16] and Curle.[17] They might argue that the real pioneers were activists such as Gandhi and Martin Luther King Jr. Central to the methods of this field, particularly according to Lederach, is grassroots involvement at a level some have come to call "Track Three," as characterized by Chigas. This idea of Track Three is not to be confused with Track Three as identified by Diamond and McDonald in their work on multi-track diplomacy. As Reimann notes,

> Viewed this way, protracted violent conflicts turn out to be primarily the result of unequal and suppressive social and political structures. Dealing effectively with them, therefore, will call for the empowerment and recognition of marginalized groups in the form of non-violent struggle. Only in this way will it be possible to deal with issues of immediate concern at the local

level, or to put the appropriate pressure on Track One (and Track Two actors), to end the violence and enter into good-faith negotiations.[18]

Conflict transformation thus deliberately sets out to bridge the space between the dialogue-oriented processes that characterize much of traditional conflict resolution, and a hands-on form of advocacy-oriented activism which is carried out in the cause of social and political justice. The kind of third-party impartiality which most in the field strive for and believe to be essential in a conflict situation is not so important here. This blurring of the line between conflict intervention and advocacy/activism is difficult territory and not to be approached lightly.[19] An illustration of its inherent dangers comes from Sheehan, whose research shows that the US military has become adept at appropriating the language and concepts of conflict transformation to its needs, as part of its post–9/11 approach to counterinsurgency operations.

> In a search for ways to frame, legitimize and connect counterinsurgency, stability and "peace" operations, military strategists began invoking and using the term conflict transformation. . . . While a case can be made that counterinsurgency, because of its population-centric orientation, has distinct military benefits over conventional warfare and over counterterrorism . . . , it is a muddying of the waters to view conflict transformation as an integral or even complementary endeavor for two reasons. First conflict transformation is always nonviolent whereas counterinsurgency, even if it embraces population-centric operations, is a form of warfare that may employ violence . . . to achieve some of its objectives. Second, conflict transformation is an *elicitive* approach, designed to elicit structural issues and problems that give rise to conflict in the first place and bring about long-term structural change, whereas counterinsurgency and stability operations are *prescriptive* tactics and strategies designed to bring about particular forms of military stabilization and political order.[20]

Conflict management, conflict resolution, and conflict transformation are obviously different from each other in many ways. One way of illustrating this has to do with the interaction between each approach and the local elites. Conflict **management** does not attempt to change the underlying structure of the situation, but rather to find compromise within that structure. It is therefore aimed at persuading the elites to recognize the need to find ways to manage the conflict. Indeed, one of the best "selling cards" of those in this field is the argument that elites should listen to them because the conflict, if left unmanaged, may grow to the point that it affects their (the elites') ability to remain in control. Of course, this is not to say that those in the field of conflict management want to support or prop up the elites, but only that they do not *necessarily* see the way forward as being to challenge the prevailing political or social structure. Those active in the field of conflict **resolution** often take the view that elites, and the system they represent, are a major part of the problem. The elites therefore have to change their view of the conflict or get out of the way so that the system which sustains the conflict can be changed and the conflict resolved. So it is not necessary that the elites depart the scene or that the prevailing system be brought down; if the elites can accept the need for change, they can carry on—although carrying on depends on the nature of the system they represent and how much it needs to change to make resolution of the conflict possible. Finally, those in the field of conflict **transformation** see the existing political system as the problem and therefore believe that it must be tackled and changed. Their objective is to develop grassroots actions capable of doing so.

The kinds of activities that will be undertaken by Track Two actors are very different, depending on their objectives. Broadly speaking, as illustrated in Figure 3.1, conflict **management** approaches are favored by Track One, and by Track Two efforts—such as Track 1.5 and "hard" Track Two—which seek to support and assist Track One. Simply put, these approaches do not set out to fundamentally challenge the existing order but to assist that order in managing its disputes on an ongoing basis. Conflict **resolution** approaches are somewhat more removed from official diplomacy, as they recognize that significant change in the prevailing order may be necessary. Such approaches engage in a "first principles" review of the underlying basis of the conflict in order to develop new ways of seeing it and then to encourage the prevailing order change its policies and approaches. This may involve varying degrees of change to the existing order, depending on the nature of the solutions developed by the participants in such a process. Finally, conflict **transformation** actors see the existing order *as the problem* and seek to develop mechanisms whereby the grass roots of the societies in conflict can press for the necessary changes to create the basis for real and lasting peace.

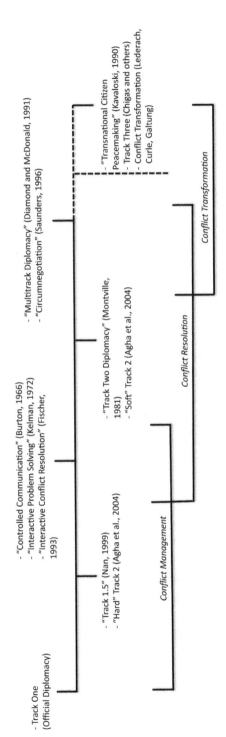

- Track One
(Official Diplomacy)

- "Controlled Communication" (Burton, 1966)
- "Interactive Problem Solving" (Kelman, 1972)
- "Interactive Conflict Resolution" (Fischer, 1993)

- "Multitrack Diplomacy" (Diamond and McDonald, 1991)
- "Circumnegotiation" (Saunders, 1996)

- "Track 1.5" (Nan, 1999)
- "Hard" Track 2 (Agha et al., 2004)

- "Track Two Diplomacy" (Montville, 1981)
- "Soft" Track 2 (Agha et al., 2004)

- "Transnational Citizen
Peacemaking" (Kavaloski, 1990)
- Track Three (Chigas and others)
- Conflict Transformation (Lederach, Curle, Galtung)

Conflict Management

Conflict Resolution

Conflict Transformation

FIGURE 3.1 Major Categories of Track Two and Conflict Resolution

The Ripeness/Readiness Debate

Another area in which much effort has been undertaken to develop both theoretical and practical underpinnings for the field concerns the question of when to launch a Track Two process. Indeed, when and how to launch a mediation process in general has been a subject of much discussion.[21] The various theoretical paradigms offer insights as to how conflict plays out over time. The best known approach to the question of when to launch a mediation effort is the concept of "ripeness," as elaborated by Zartman, Haas, Stedman, and others (though the term has been used by officials and observers of conflicts for many years).[22] Ripeness holds that intractable conflicts cannot be resolved until at least some of the disputants have reached a point where they begin to perceive that the costs of continuing to fight likely outweigh any benefits to be obtained—what Zartman calls the "mutually hurting stalemate." They must also perceive that there is a possible "way out" of the dispute which may be acceptable, and that at least some leaders on the other side are beginning to have similar feelings. Ripeness often occurs just after, during, or before a crisis; it is believed that staring catastrophe in the face, or having just survived one by the skin of one's teeth, has a galvanizing impact on thinking. As Greig puts it,

> mediation is most successful at two distinct points in time. Mediation can be successful early in a conflict, before the disputants have built up high levels of hostility that make compromise difficult. Yet, mediation can also become successful late in a conflict, after disputants have expended significant resources in conflict with one another and become more willing to improve their relationship.[23]

Greig further breaks down the concept of ripeness into short-term ripeness and extended-term ripeness. Short-term ripeness is more likely to lead to an agreement, but an agreement that will manage the issues rather than really resolve them and is therefore less likely to stick. Short-term ripeness generally concerns disputes over transactional matters, which are more likely to be susceptible to agreement than identity-based disputes. Fundamental change in the domestic politics of the rivals is often not required. On the other hand, extended-term ripeness generally applies to much deeper, identity-based conflicts. In this situation, the context under which mediation occurs is often more important than the mediation itself, at least at the beginning of the process. Situations of extended-term ripeness are less likely to lead to an agreement, but if an agreement is reached it is more likely to stick. Often a fundamental change in the domestic politics of the rivals (for example, towards greater democracy) is necessary.[24]

In situations of ripeness, the parties begin to consider whether alternatives to the present course of the conflict are possible, but they are still unsure how to begin and also unsure whether the other side genuinely feels the same way. Moreover, it is rare that everyone on each side holds the view that exploring compromise is a good idea. Rather, there are those on each side who think it might be beneficial but also powerful interests on both sides who do not think so; these moments are therefore dangerous, fragile, and uncertain. Ripeness is thus largely perceptual, not an objective or "real" thing in itself. There is no predetermined level of pain in a given circumstance that produces ripeness; a situation is ripe when at least some people on both sides begin to feel that it is ripe. Indeed, there are those who criticize the concept as being largely tautological, and maintain that ripe situations are only evident in retrospect.[25]

Moreover, ripeness is not a self-implementing condition, as Zartman himself notes. It requires someone (often a mediator or a third party) to make the connections between those on each side who feel the time has come to explore whether alternatives to conflict are possible. Considerable effort is thus expended in the literature on mediation which is informed by ripeness to identify markers of ripeness and to consider "entry points" that mediators may use to gain access to a conflict. One former US official with extensive experience mediating in Africa has elaborated on the various ways a mediator can induce ripeness and gain access, including coaching, legitimizing certain actors (and delegitimizing others), promising rewards, threatening punishments, and so forth.[26] These activities are largely the domain of official mediators, and moreover, "mediators with muscle," in Touval's words.[27] Ripeness on this level is thus largely a concept associated with official diplomacy and a realist approach to mediation (or a structuralist approach as Crocker, Hampson, and Aall would put it).[28] Power is important, and it gives the mediator the ability, if skillfully and judiciously used, to encourage ripeness within and between parties.

But what about situations in which the parties are not likely to be motivated or swayed by what realist-inspired mediators can offer, as enumerated by Crocker? What of Azar's protracted conflicts over identity issues which are nonnegotiable? What of situations where no group of people on either side are of the view that the situation may be "ripe"? What of situations where there may be ripeness but no potential mediators are interested in coming forward because the conflict does not affect their wider interests, or even where potential mediators may have an interest in seeing the conflict go on? Under these circumstances, is the fighting to continue indefinitely? Azar posed such questions when developing his theory of protracted social conflicts, and they were the reasons he felt that the traditional conflict resolution ideas of the time were inadequate.[29]

In these situations, Pruitt's concept of "readiness" can be useful. A conscious development of ripeness theory,

> Readiness is the extent to which an individual disputant is interested in negotiation. Ripeness is still a core concept in readiness theory, being treated as a function of the level of readiness on both sides. Negotiation will only start if there is some degree of readiness on both sides and, hence, some degree of ripeness. The greater the readiness and ripeness, the more likely is negotiation to occur. Readiness theory—in parallel to core ripeness theory—holds that two psychological variables encourage a party to be ready for negotiation: motivation to end conflict and optimism about the success of negotiation, or simply "optimism."[30]

In short, some individuals on either side may be "ready" to at least explore possibilities for compromise before the situation between their sides is considered "ripe." Readiness recasts conventional ripeness theory in more psychological terms that focus on individual actors rather than the search for a set of objective understandings on key elements of the situation, such as the mutually hurting stalemate, that are shared by groups of actors on both sides. Readiness theory thus allows for analysis on an individual basis of the processes that may contribute to ripeness, and also for exploration of whether there might be small groups of such individuals who are prepared to informally discuss the possibility of a new way forward.[31] Others have considered conflict resolution from the perspective of "grief theory" and concluded that a discussion of alternate futures is not possible until protagonists have gone through the stages of grieving for a future they cannot achieve and are ready to search for alternate futures. In such circumstances, informal discussions based on the concept of readiness can assist individuals in getting to this stage.[32]

Readiness is of interest to Track Two because it lowers the bar to entry for a third party; this may range from tangible things used to induce ripeness (that is, "sticks and carrots," which are generally the domain of states acting as mediators) to a search for individuals on both sides who are ready to consider change and to participate in informal and exploratory discussions. It is from such discussions that views may change and new ideas arise, contributing to what Pruitt believes is a central requirement of ripeness, "a broad central coalition of people across the political spectrum who are ready for negotiation."[33] As Bartoli reports on the efforts of a Catholic lay organization which mediated peace in Mozambique,

> But was the negotiation successful simply because after so many years peace was due? Was the conflict ripe for solution? The very concept of "ripeness" can be used in a tautological way. The only way to say for sure that a conflict is ripe for resolution is when it happens. . . . But what do we say about cases in which opportunities for such positive conclusions were missed? Are we to conclude that in those cases the situation was not ripe for resolution after all? In the debate over timeliness we tend to underestimate the power of the mediation itself—the transforming power of the experience of adversaries talking with one another and with others in a setting that is conducive to constructive dialogue. Therefore, it is probably more useful to say that violent conflicts are always ripe to end. At least we should always perceive them as such, thereby helping those involved and who have the power to stop the killing share this perspective.[34]

Different theoretical paradigms inform the concepts of ripeness and readiness. Ripeness is oriented more towards a realist analysis of structural factors which bring parties in conflict to the table, and towards what a third party can do to get them there. This in turn begins to define who such a third party is likely to be—very often in tough conflict situations this will mean a mediator acting on behalf of a state and with the ability to offer inducements and exact punishments. Readiness, by contrast, draws more on the social-psychological and constructivist traditions of creating informal contacts between small groups of individuals who are psychologically ready to consider alternate futures. The purpose of such encounters is a mutual exploration of the underlying causes of the conflict, leading, if successful, to an attempt to develop possible alternatives. Such conversations often happen before an official decision to negotiate has been made by either side and must, by definition, be informal and unofficial—that is, Track Two. The third party in such cases need not have power in a conventional sense, but rather must be able to inspire trust that the discussion will be fair and that necessary practical requirements, such as confidentiality, will be present.

We should not, however, see these concepts as mutually exclusive (Figure 3.2). Indeed, the true utility of readiness may lie in its ability to help bring about a situation of ripeness, particularly to help at least some on

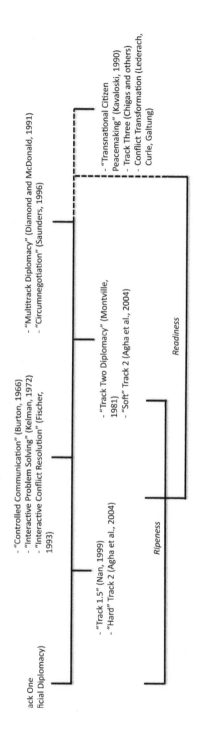

FIGURE 3.2 Major Categories of Track Two and Ripeness/Readiness

both sides identify a "way out"—one condition for ripeness. This raises the notion of sequencing different kinds of peacemaking efforts. In his "contingency model" of conflict resolution, Fisher discusses the relevance of different approaches and methodologies to different points in any "cycle" of conflict. He thus develops a model which encourages practitioners to recognize when different approaches are more appropriate. Key to successful peacemaking in such an approach is a recognition that the different levels of peacemaking (Track 1, Track 1.5, Track 2, and so on) bring different strengths to the table at different points in a conflict. Fisher encourages the field to broaden its understanding of the complementary nature of the different levels of peacemaking and to develop ways forward which are appropriate to each specific situation.[35]

Culture and Ethics

Finally, in the real world of Track Two, theory often meets practice in the areas of culture and ethics.

Culture

At least two dimensions of culture deeply affect those active in the field of Track Two. The first concerns the impact of working across different cultures as a Track Two practitioner. Much ink has been spilled over many years on the importance of culture in negotiations in general, and mediation in particular.[36] But as one might expect with so complex a subject, the field remains one of intense debate. Even the definition of "culture" itself is not entirely agreed on. As a Track Two practitioner, I have always found that a simple approach is best. I have tended to define culture as a set of shared norms, understandings, and values which a specific group of people have largely internalized and accepted as the basis of their communication and thought processes. The way members of a group approach their culture may be unconscious or conscious; most often it is a bit of both. And importantly, cultures are not monolithic; there may be cultures within cultures, or simultaneous cultures in play within groups, or even within individuals.

Docherty believes that there are three main levels of looking at the issue of culture as it influences negotiations. The first of these she calls the "tip of the iceberg." This essentially teaches negotiators to regard culture as a useful set of dos and don'ts of behavior in negotiations: never offer an Arab food with your left hand; learn the proper etiquette of exchanging business cards with

Japanese; and so on. This is a superficial level of analysis though popular in how-to books for negotiators.

Going more deeply into the matter of culture, Docherty's next level is what she calls the "patterns of culture" that various societies exhibit. For example, some societies are what is known as "low context" and others are "high context" when it comes to communication patterns.[37] High-context cultures are those which place a higher premium on unspoken signals and cues, such as body language and social pecking orders and other such codes, than they do on the actual spoken word; the context within which the words are delivered matters as much, or more than the words themselves. Low-context cultures, on the other hand, place much more emphasis on what is said. They value "plain speaking" and direct communication—the old saying that you should "say what you mean, and mean what you say." It is a vast generalization, but Hall's work shows that Japanese, Chinese, Arabic, and other Mediterranean languages are most often high context, while Swiss, German, English, and other Northern European languages are most often low context.[38]

This has obvious implications when people from these societies are trying to talk to each other. Westerners can be maddened by the apparent unwillingness of others to "say what they mean," and suspect many nefarious plots as a consequence. Those from other regions can be intensely suspicious of blunt messages which are devoid of the background and context that help these people determine the "true" meanings lurking behind the words. For example, scholars who study the impact of cross-cultural misunderstandings on international diplomacy point to the US-Iraq talks on the eve of the Gulf War (over the Iraqi occupation of Kuwait) as a case study in which cultural misunderstandings limited the ability of the two sides to communicate with each other, particularly when the United States attempted to inform the Iraqi leadership of the consequences of its actions. None of this is to say that war would have been avoided had the two sides been able to communicate clearly, but it raises the possibility that mistakes were made by one or both sides due to a lack of clear understanding of the other's "red lines."[39] In short, these concepts can have very real implications, as I have found many times when facilitating encounters between people from vastly different cultures, such as the United States and Iran.[40]

Docherty's final level is what she calls "symmetrical anthropology," which holds that people belong to multiple cultures simultaneously.[41] Every interaction is thus multicultural to some degree. Within any given process (or problem-solving workshop), multiple and overlapping cultural interactions are going on at any given moment. A third party can learn and make use of these. For example, in an India-Pakistan Track Two process on maritime issues that I have helped facilitate for some years, it is apparent to me that several cultures are in play simultaneously, and the "Indian" and "Pakistani" cultures are often the least significant of these. A first cultural subgrouping is based on where participants are from: Indians and Pakistanis from the divided Punjab region often have much more in common with each other than they do with their countrymen from other parts of India and Pakistan. They are thus a cultural subgroup around the table. A second subgrouping is based on the age of the participants and their training experiences. Those who joined the Indian and Pakistani navies before a certain date did much of their officer training in the United Kingdom. They thus have a bond around shared experiences (which expresses itself in shared and humorous stories of cold weather, harsh discipline, and bad food) which creates another subgroup around the table, distinct from those who joined in later years after the two navies had stopped sending their trainee officers to the United Kingdom. A third subgrouping concerns specialization in different fields of naval warfare. For example, submariners from the two navies have more in common with each other than they do with the surface warfare specialists of their own navies, and vice-versa. Maritime aviators of the two naval services are a different subgroup again.

The importance of these different bonds for the third party is that they can be called on to drive the process forward. When a difficult moment is reached, the third party can ask a smaller group composed of people from one of the different subcultures around the table to work on the problem and report back. It is no guarantee of success, but I have noticed that such smaller groups from the same subcultures have often been more able to reach a conclusion on a difficult matter than the broader group, which is composed of multiple, overlapping subcultures. It seems that the shared sub-culture provides a basis for communication and trust which may not exist among the larger group.

Docherty argues that it is important for negotiators, and mediators, to go much more deeply into the impact of culture on their activities. One should, for example, never assume that a concept such as rationality means the same thing to different people—indeed, the term can be misapplied when used to express a view that participants are not "rational" when, in reality, their culture leads them to see the balance of pros and cons around an issue differently.

One must therefore invest the time required to learn what those different ways of approaching the issue are and how they may manifest themselves at the table. Docherty advises skilled negotiators, and for our purposes, third parties, to be sensitive to "worldviews," metaphors, and social scripts and their impact on negotiations. The concept of "linguistic dissonance" is an important example here. Words and concepts may sound the same, especially when translated into a common working language in a problem-solving workshop, but can obscure very different ideas. It takes a skilled third party to recognize when this is happening and to persuade the participants to drill down in the search for deeper meanings as a way of exposing and coming to grips with different understandings of the issues in play. An illustration of linguistic dissonance is provided by Davidheiser's work, which examines how the differences between "Black" culture and "White" culture in America profoundly influence these groups' approaches to conflict and to conflict resolution.[42]

The second major way in which the issue of culture affects Track Two has caused heated debate within the field. Burton and his colleagues, writing in the early years of the field's growth, made some assumptions about the "generalizability" of the methods they were developing. They took the view that the techniques of facilitating their "controlled communication" workshops were essentially transferable across cultural settings, requiring only minor modifications. They went so far as to regard a "generic theory" of such interactions as necessary for the creation of a set of tools which could be used in different settings around the world.[43] In this view, they were at the time joined by others, such as Zartman and Berman, who wrote in 1982 that "negotiation is a universal process . . . and that cultural differences are simply differences in style and language."[44]

The generalizability assumption released a spirited discussion. Those who opposed Burton and others took the view that the specific cultural questions of each conflict are so critical and diverse that a universal, generic theory of conflict resolution is not possible—except at such a level of abstraction as to be useless, or even dangerous. Instead, they argued that it is essential that each intervention be solidly grounded in deep expertise of the specific cultural issues in play and that generalized concepts and methods of conflict resolution should be avoided.[45] The key issue in the debate was the extent to which such generalizations were actually possible. To Zartman and Berman's earlier notion that "negotiation is a universal process" others responded that "birth, life and death are also universal experiences, yet this has not prevented humankind, in its great cultural diversity, from evolving profoundly discrepant understandings of their significance."[46]

Today most who are active in the field would accept that the culture versus generic theory debate has been answered in favor of those who argue that the cultural uniqueness of each situation must be understood and respected by those who would intervene. But the issue raised by Burton and others remains valid. At the outermost levels of abstraction, the argument that every situation is unique would mean that there could be no cross-cutting discipline of conflict resolution, let alone of Track Two diplomacy. If every conflict was so utterly unique that no generalization was possible, then learning could not take place across cases. This is simply not true.

Common sense and sensitivity are called for. One cannot of course equate a conflict between indigenous peoples of the Amazon region with a conflict involving Afghan tribes. One should certainly never assume that techniques which work in one locale will automatically work in another. However, one equally should not assume that no learning can take place between one case and another, or that third parties cannot acquire enough sense of the local cultural and historical realities to become effective without necessarily being experts on the region. Maturity, experience, humility, and an understanding of the need to listen to experts regarding local conditions and issues are required in approaching these situations. It has been my experience that a third party cannot easily move between conflicts in different parts of the world, equipped with some "toolbox" of basic conflict resolution techniques as Burton and Sandole suggested might be possible. Most third parties tend to specialize in different regions and build up a deep knowledge of the conditions and cultures in play which informs their work. In my own case, I have worked for many years in the Middle East and South Asia, with some work also in Southeast Asia, and would not dream that I could simply hop on a plane and start doing effective work in Latin America or Africa. But I do believe that most who are skilled in the techniques, and possess the requisite interpersonal skills, can acquire the regional and cultural understanding and work effectively with local partners.

In practical terms, this debate often plays itself out in a discussion not so much over culture as over how much expertise the third party should have with respect to the specifics of the conflict. Most who are active in the field take the view that some knowledge is required, but not a deep expertise. Perhaps counterintuitively, too deep an expertise into the nuts and bolts of the dispute can blind the third party to possibilities for new ways of looking at things—possibilities to which the participants in the conflict may be blind precisely *because* they are so steeped in the minutiae of the dispute. It is the job of the third party to help participants gently move the conversation away from the detailed specifics of what has happened and towards the identification and consideration of new analyses and possibilities. What is needed then is sufficient expertise in the conflict to understand the debates and the history, but not to be captured by them; to recognize when the discussion is going down a blind alley where old positions are simply being repeated, and to help them move out of that alley (rather than contributing one's own perspective to the sterile discussion of the specifics, as an expert in the conflict might unconsciously do). As Mitchell and Banks put it, "The aim might be characterized as the cultivation of an 'innocent' eye that enables one to ask searching, fundamental questions,"[47] rather than becoming caught up in detailed debates over the conflict's history.

Ethics

Turning to the issue of ethics, it has long been recognized that an ethical framework is critical for those who would do this work. Absent a rigorous set of principles, the field can give way to unrestrained experimentation which can have devastating consequences. The lessons of Leonard Doob's early interventions in Ireland and elsewhere serve as cautionary notes to the field.[48] As Rouhana put it,

> The price of . . . mistakes [by the third party] can vary depending upon the situation: damage to participants' credibility, short- or long-term psychological harm, diminishing participants' belief in the possibility of arriving at a settlement with the adversary, or even threats to some participants' lives. Given the price participants might pay for third party's mistakes, this dilemma should be addressed by having practitioners design a broad set of guidelines within which experimentation can take place. While practitioners cannot prevent mistakes, they can reduce the likelihood of errors by designing an initial set of guidelines for practice, including training of third parties, ethical considerations, and boundaries of acceptable practice.[49]

All of this leads to the question of ethical frameworks for practice. Attempts have been made to develop such frameworks, of course.[50] Much of this work has drawn on codes of conduct for mediators as developed in domestic settings, such as labor mediation and marriage counseling.[51] Many of these early efforts centered on defining the role of the intervener (mediator, advocate, researcher, and so on) and developing appropriate norms of conduct for each. As time has gone by, those in Track Two have further ruminated on the question of ethics, often supplementing these codes of conduct with other ethical frameworks derived from fields such as international aid practices.

One question, for example, is that of the "neutrality" or "impartiality" of the third party. These two concepts are similar, but not identical. Various organizations have grappled with what they mean in practice. The International Committee of the Red Cross (ICRC) has defined *impartiality* in terms of nondiscrimination in responding to humanitarian needs—aid is provided to all who need it, regardless of race, religion, or political affiliation. At the same time, the ICRC defines *neutrality* as a conscious political stance with respect to the conflict, which takes no sides and makes no attempt to engage in the political issues motivating the conflict.[52] Other groups active in the field, and particularly in the growing number of civil wars that characterize modern conflict (as opposed to the state-to-state conflicts which predominated when the ICRC was established), have found it more difficult to adhere to these strict guidelines, and do take sides when they see atrocities being committed.[53]

The issue of whether the third party should be neutral or not has generated considerable discussion in the field. Much of this has been written in the context of more traditional mediation, such as in labor disputes,[54] and therefore may not be entirely applicable to Track Two. Essentially, the debate is divided between those who feel that impartiality is required, and an emerging group who believe that biased mediators can be more effective. For those who feel that an impartial approach is required, Kleiboer describes the chain of events which make the case: "mediator impartiality is crucial for disputants' confidence in the mediator, which, in turn, is a necessary condition for his gaining acceptability, which in turn, is essential for mediation success to come about."[55] Going further, Gent and Shannon studied the techniques used by mediators, and the qualities of the mediators which influenced their choice of those techniques. They found that "unbiased" mediators were more likely to use techniques that produced agreements, while "biased" mediators selected techniques more likely to favor a particular outcome. They thus argue that impartiality on the part of mediators influences their ability to choose techniques, which in turn affects their likely success in mediating the conflict.[56]

On the other hand, a body of scholars and practitioners advocates that biased third parties can be more effective in resolving disputes. This group holds that biased mediators are more likely to be personally invested in the outcome and therefore more likely to devote themselves to this work over the long term; they are more likely to develop a relationship of trust, and therefore an intimate relationship, with at least one side in the conflict because of their affiliation; and they may have access to privileged information as a consequence of their close relationship with one of the parties. Of course, counterarguments can be made that a privileged relationship with one side negates the mediator's ability to have such a relationship with the other. The advocates of biased interventions do not believe this to be the case, providing the intervener has a professional reputation for running fair processes.[57] In a study of mediator bias in the outcome of 124 peace agreements between 1989 and 2004, Svensson found that "biased mediators positively affect the likelihood of institutional arrangements in peace agreements . . . [while] neutral mediators tend to lead to outcomes without provisions for political and territorial power sharing, third-party security guarantees, government-sided amnesties and repatriation of civilians."[58]

In other words, while Gent and Shannon's research argues that unbiased mediators have more success in terms of the number of conflicts "resolved," Svensson argues that their track record is generally of resolutions which are not likely to be long lasting as they do not really address deep-seated problems. Biased mediators, on the other hand, will try to address these problems, as they have a personal commitment to at least one of the parties. This debate exemplifies the conflict management versus conflict resolution or even conflict transformation arguments we saw earlier. In effect, those who argue for third party bias are saying that it helps in staying the course, which is required to transform a situation of conflict; while those who argue against it are saying that it impedes a mediator's ability to help those in conflict to manage the situation. Of course, much will depend on the specifics of each case and generalizations must be approached with care.

Transposing these controversies to the field is a difficult and, ultimately, intensely personal business. Those who are active in the field must have their own moral compass. My own commitment is to conduct a Track Two process in as scrupulously impartial a manner as I can—no favors for one side or the other in how the process is organized and run. But that does not mean I can always claim to be neutral about the dispute or about the tactics that have been employed by one or both sides. In cases where a bias does exist, I will make it known to all sides before going forward. The process cannot work any other way. One case where I can make no claim to neutrality, for example, is where one of the parties has resorted to tactics which have targeted civilians. But conflicts are hugely complex and rarely is one side entirely right or wrong. Over the course of an intervention, I may come to some personal conclusions, and they may continue to change as my involvement deepens, but I will strive to ensure that these will not affect my impartiality in running the process.

This discussion raises the vexing ethical question of whether one should work with those who have committed atrocities. It is highly likely in the course of this work that one will come into contact with such people, or their agents. We are, after all, dealing with violent conflicts and the people who have fought them. It is also likely that at least some of the people around the table will have certain objectives from any process they agree to take part in—an amnesty being one example, and even a place in a transitional government. As a practical matter, it is of course entirely beyond the scope of Track Two, and that of a third party to grant any sort of amnesty or future official role. These can only be given by nations, peoples, or international organizations. But one must be conscious that one is putting in place a process ultimately intended by at least some of the participants to lead to those outcomes should the process come up with solutions that transition to Track One. What are the ethical considerations of doing so? Most often those engaged in this work take the view that stopping the fighting is more immediately important than addressing questions of international law; that the safety of those who are yet to be harmed or killed by the conflict is more important than the question of justice for those already affected, although they would not deny the importance of justice as well.

This is a morally defensible position, but it opens up a host of questions regarding how justice will ultimately be done for those who have already been killed or harmed.[59] Indeed, it is a point of considerable contention between the conflict resolution community and the community committed to the creation of international legal standards and processes devoted to the punishment of war crimes—often expressed as "the well-known tensions between stability and justice."[60] As Pauline Baker has put it, "Should peace be sought at any price to end the bloodshed, even if power-sharing arrangements fail to uphold basic human rights and democratic principles? Or should the objective be a democratic peace that respects human rights, a goal that might prolong the fighting and risk more atrocities in the time it takes to reach a negotiated solution?"[61] Babbitt also frames the issues nicely by pointing out that the concept of *impartiality* means different things to those who work in the field of conflict resolution and those who work for human rights and international justice.

> Both human rights and CR [conflict resolution] invoke principles of impartiality. However, the concept had completely different meanings for practitioners in each field. To a CR practitioner, impartiality requires an even-handed treatment of all parties, regardless of their status or resources. For a human rights advocate, impartiality refers to the application of human rights norms, most of which are constructed to protect the weak individual from the abuses of the state or other potentially exploitative authorities. Thus, the human rights result does not appear impartial, but instead looks like (and often is) advocacy for one party over another. This presents a conundrum for the CR practitioner who recognizes that social justice requires creating a more level playing field, but who needs to maintain even-handedness to be credible.[62]

While framing the essential dilemma, this line of thinking does not take one very far beyond a tit-for-tat exchange between the conflict resolution specialists and the international justice advocates who reside on the two sides of these issues. Perhaps the way forward for a Track Two practitioner is to conceive of what one is doing as being a small part of a much larger whole, as Saunders asserts is necessary.[63] Track Two's small part of the puzzle—to help those in conflict begin a tentative and semiofficial discussion that will likely last a long time and transition through many phases—may not be capable of adequately addressing the issue of justice for those affected by the dispute. But if Track Two does contribute to the creation of a larger peace process, the questions of justice and reconciliation will at least be confronted, if not addressed as part of the final settlement.[64] In short, if practitioners take an either/or approach to stability/justice issues, they run the risk of never being able to get anything going. Of course, those in the field who are seeking conflict transformation and with it the sweeping away of the existing order might argue that an emphasis on justice must be part of the solution, even if this means prolonging the conflict; they will be "biased," as Svensson argues they should be. They might say that leaving in place those who committed atrocities is morally wrong and does not lay the conditions for ending the situation which brought about the conflict in the first place.

Once again, it is ultimately a question of one's objectives in the field and of one's own moral compass. To do this sort of work, practitioners must determine whether they are able to work with people who have done terrible things. Much inner reflection is required; one must grapple with the deeper ethical question of whether the field of conflict resolution is adequately equipped to deal with the ethical dilemmas it generates. There are some who question whether the field of Track Two has not become a variety of things its founders never intended: a make-work project for do-gooders; a means whereby countries can shirk their responsibility to intervene in conflicts by supporting Track Two discussions as a low-cost alternative; a mechanism for some combatants to demonstrate an apparent willingness to discuss "peace" when they have little intention of actually compromising; and a means for certain types of scholar-practitioners to indulge their theories and their desire to be "part of the action" without having to confront what they are actually dealing with. As Fabienne Hara puts it in her stinging indictment of Track Two efforts (which she calls "parallel diplomacy") during the African Great Lakes crisis,

> For the sake of attracting the attention of financial backers, and thus ensuring institutional survival, several organizations desperately want to be seen at the forefront of the conflict resolution and prevention "industry." . . . Agents of parallel diplomacy are, for the most part, the inventors and players of a new kind of intervention by Northern countries in Southern countries. It is still a case of agents from Western civil society crossing over borders, no longer to save people, but this time to teach them to make peace and reach a Western-style consensus. . . . The field of conflict resolution until now has been dominated by Anglo-Saxon influence and marked by the rationale of democratic systems. Its operating concepts and lexicon are mostly inspired by theories developed by Americans. All these methods aimed at conflict resolution by means of dialogue are based on the precept that it is legitimate to include the authors of a violence perceived as obscene and primal in a rational process leading to a consensus.[65]

In response to these uncomfortable ethical points, much effort has been expended on such ideas as the "accountability" and "authenticity" of interveners and the processes they establish. These concepts hold that the third party must be accountable to those in the conflict above all others (such as those who might be funding the process) and that the process should be authentic in that it is the result of extensive consultation with those in conflict and reflects their needs and wants.[66] Both of these are fine principles, but they may require some modification in practice. For example, though an authentic process should result from consultation and agreement between the third party and those in conflict, sometimes getting the conflicting parties to agree on a process is more than the traffic will bear; they need to rely on the third party's impartiality, at least in the beginning, to design the process. As they become more comfortable with the process, and each other, the participants may begin to modify it. Indeed, when parties in conflict begin to jointly tinker with the dynamics of the process, it can signal that they are claiming control over the process and beginning to trust and work with each other.

An ultimate reliance on the practitioner's personal moral compass creates an unsatisfactory situation for many, in that differing standards can lead to a field which is marked by widely varying levels of professionalization, which in turn can be taken advantage of by those in conflict. That being said, it is still necessary for each practitioner to have his or her own personal ethical code. After many years of trial and error, my own code is as follows[67]:

- "First, do no harm." You are entering a complex situation where the consequences of mistakes are generally higher for the participants than for you; sensitivity, caution, and humility are called for.

- Be in it for the long haul. It is unfair to persuade those in situations of conflict to come to the table if you do not intend to be there for as long as it takes.

- You are not there to export your solution but to help participants find their own. You may have strong views as to how the problem should be solved, but what matters is whether the participants can jointly develop their own solution. Your role is to help them do so, not to foist your ideas onto them.

- You are not alone. Avoid the tendency to think that your activity is, by itself, going to "make peace." Real peace is the product of a multilevel, multiyear process of which your activity is likely but a small part.

- Honesty, integrity, and right intention: you must be scrupulously honest with the participants about your background, your intentions, and what you can deliver, and you must enter the situation motivated by a desire to assist them rather than for personal gain or glory.

Conclusion

The ideas and questions discussed in this chapter point to some of the theoretical and practical questions which inform the field of conflict resolution generally, and Track Two more specifically. There are multiple ways to conceive of the purposes of such interventions, to describe their objectives, and to assess when it is propitious to launch an effort. Further, a raft of ethical and cultural issues must be considered. How individual practitioners answer these various questions will have a significant impact on the kind of Track Two process they attempt to run, whom they recruit to participate, what they believe their objectives are, and when they try to begin.

Moreover, the different theories and points made in this chapter must be seen not only as individual issues but also in their relationships to each other. For example, is the Track Two in question motivated by a *theory of change* at the **individual, or personal** level, within a *conflict management* framework which holds that interventions are not likely to succeed unless the moment is approaching a level of *ripeness,* as defined by Zartman? If so, it is likely to engage in certain kinds of activities; for example, discussions of how existing policies and approaches could be tweaked to make them more acceptable to official diplomacy. It is likely to recruit certain kinds of people, such as retired senior officials who maintain close and trusted connections to their governments. And it is likely to take the view that such efforts have the best chance of success if they begin at a certain "ripe" moment; for example, at a point when the governments might be receptive to new ideas because of a perceived mutually hurting stalemate.

Alternatively, the intervention may be motivated by a desire to affect action in concert with a *theory of change* at the **relationship** level, within an approach which is agnostic as to an outcome of conflict *management versus resolution,* and which holds that *readiness* is the key—that at least some credible individuals are prepared to enter into serious conversations with each other, regardless of whether their governments might be looking for a way out at that particular moment. In this case, the Track Two project may be more likely to focus on actions which seek not to tweak or refine existing policy options but rather to examine the basis of the conflict in a more structural way so as to open up the possibility of quite new approaches—which may or may not include the survival of the existing order, depending on what is necessary to resolve what the participants define as the underlying issues of the conflict.

Finally, if an intervention is motivated by *theories of change* at the **structural, institutional, or systemic** levels and which seek to *transform* the conflict, it will be very different from the above two examples. Questions of *ripeness* or *readiness* will be irrelevant. The objective will be to launch a process for organizing and empowering civil society at the grassroots level and on a large scale in order to challenge the existing order and demand change capable of sweeping away the structures and individuals who maintain the conditions in which the conflict breeds and continues. Indeed, this is probably no longer Track Two as most in the field would define it and is more likely a form of advocacy.

These three examples are not the only possibilities. All of the variables discussed in this chapter can be combined in various ways which lead to different types of Track Two projects. When one adds **cultural** and **ethical** dimensions to these possibilities, the issues take on a whole new level of complexity. The key for practitioners is to use theoretical tools such as these to develop a firm and well-grounded idea of what they are trying to do and how they can best do it.

Such theoretical considerations, of course, are not perfect. We are, in the final analysis, dealing with a process which is about human beings—their needs, fears, and wants. Moreover, it is about human beings in situations of pain and suffering. No theory or set of theories can adequately explain how they will interact under such circumstances, useful as those may be to planning and evaluating Track Two projects. It comes down then to how Track Two takes place in reality. Who conducts these projects and what issues arise when they are doing them? We turn our attention to these questions in the next section of the book.

SECTION II
IN PRACTICE

4 On People: The Characteristics and Role of the Third Party

CENTRAL TO MOST TRACK TWO IS THE SO-CALLED third party. This is the name given in the literature to the individual, or the group of individuals, who convene and facilitate a Track Two dialogue. The term relates to the idea that most Track Two features two parties who are in conflict plus a third party who is present to arrange and facilitate the interaction. Not all Track Two requires an outside third party. But the majority of Track Two processes, and the great majority of conflict resolution–oriented Track Two processes, feature a third party.

Why have a third party? Who are these people and what do they do? Where do they come from and how are they prepared for the role? This chapter will explore these questions. There is no single, all-encompassing definition, nor are there agreed-on standards whereby people are prepared for this role. Instead, the idea of the third party has evolved through trial and error, and most who undertake this challenging role are prepared through study and through a long process of assisting others—a form of apprenticeship. Moreover, there are differing perceptions of what the third party does and how, often based on different conceptions of the primary purpose of Track Two and the underlying conceptual approach taken by those engaged in any particular effort. Some embrace an eclectic approach which stresses personal skills and indefinable qualities, while others believe that the field is in dire need of standards and professionalization. Finally, what "power" does the third party have and how does he or she use it?

Why Have a Third Party?

Why does most writing on Track Two take the view that a third party is necessary? Why can't people from societies in conflict quietly get together themselves to brainstorm about possible ways forward? This is a fundamental question and cuts to the heart of what Track Two is about. As noted in Chapter 1, a key objective of Track Two as it has been developed since Burton's original work on "controlled communication" is to create a setting within which participants can step back from their current positions and engage in a process of jointly analyzing the underlying causes of their dispute. From this discussion, if successful, a process can emerge whereby the two sides come up with ideas and proposals to change the situation.

But brainstorming by the parties themselves may not be enough. Indeed, under the wrong circumstances it may do more harm than good. As Chataway notes, "Unassisted, parties in conflict do not tend to engage in brainstorming, or even in effectively communicating perspectives. Rather, they tend to jump quickly to analyzing or dictating options, with the effect of polarizing the dispute even further."[1] Thus, the role of a third party is to gently steer the conversation down more productive paths; in effect, the idea behind Track Two is not just that the parties engage in brainstorming but that they engage in a particular kind of *facilitated* discussion. Absent this role, the conversation can degenerate into a frustrating bargaining session which holds little promise, especially in a highly charged, emotional situation where the conflict is deemed to be intractable; in such circumstances, what is there to bargain over?

Beyond facilitated brainstorming, experiments have shown that a workshop approach, which is usually featured in Track Two, is better at improving underlying relationships at the outset of a process than a strictly negotiation-based approach. A workshop approach improves the ultimate chances that the parties will be prepared to consider new ways forward on difficult issues; as people get to know each other, they are more willing to listen and explore alternative ideas.[2] Furthermore, if workshops are better at helping people overcome deep-seated distrust and begin to work together on new ideas, research also shows that *facilitated* workshops are superior to ones that are not facilitated.[3] There is empirical evidence then to support the specific kind of facilitated problem-solving workshop characteristic of much Track Two.

In my own experience I have seen this dynamic play out both positively and negatively. For example, for much of the US-Iran Track Two effort over the nuclear issue between 2005 and 2010, many on the US side tended to believe that a third party was not necessary.[4] If only the "right" people could be gathered into a room, then messages could be exchanged and solutions developed. There was a political and even a cultural belief that direct, unimpeded dialogue with the Iranians would solve the issue, or at least be necessary to see if it could be solved. People were brought into rooms, but the beneficial results did not happen. Instead, I repeatedly saw participants dive right into the latest issues in the relationship. Ideas on how to "resolve" the nuclear standoff were put on the table for discussion with little or no preamble. The results, not surprisingly, were disappointing. For example, there was simply no basis for detailed and productive discussion of the number of centrifuges Iran should be "permitted" to have and what sanctions should be removed first. The lack of trust was too fundamental, and the discussions quickly turned to frustration and a sense in many that the problem could not be solved, largely because the other side was not interested in solutions.

Perhaps these discussions would not have succeeded anyway; perhaps the two governments were not ready for changes in policy during this time. But I noted in most of the dialogues that I took part in between 2005 and 2011 that there was usually no third party in the sense accepted in the Track Two literature. Often a neutral government or NGO provided the space for the discussion, but they then stepped back or became a participant in the discussions themselves. These were thus essentially bilateral policy dialogues, sometimes with a few other people in the room to provide expertise or even to provide "cover" against charges that strictly bilateral talks were going on. Moreover, many on the American side in particular did not seem to feel that a third party was necessary. This is curious in that some who eschewed the idea of a third party in the Iran-US case were quite prepared to see the value of a third party in other disputes, where the United States was not directly involved. Indeed, they could see the merit of American individuals playing the third party role in other conflicts of this kind, but they did not seem to feel it was necessary or even desirable to have such a third party in dialogues where US interests were involved.

In taking this attitude, these people were mirroring the findings of interviews that Chataway carried out with US diplomats in the 1990s regarding their views on Track Two. She found that most of these diplomats were quite resistant to the idea that anyone should attempt to "mediate" any conflict involving US interests, while simultaneously believing that the United States had a responsibility, even an obligation to do so in many conflicts around the world. This was either because US interests were implicated in these disputes, thus requiring US involvement in the framing of the solution to make sure it was consistent with US interests, or more generally, an indication of US "leadership" in international affairs.[5] There may be truth in these points, but the apparent inconsistency in taking the view that the United States, or American individuals, can and should involve itself as a third party in other people's conflicts but has no need of such meddlesome services in its own disputes with others, is striking. It seems to speak to a notion that US interests are "too important" to permit others to be involved in these discussions. There may also be at work an unconscious idea that US power can be brought to bear on an opponent in a situation of direct dialogue. We shall consider the question of power asymmetry in the next chapter, but research shows that it rarely translates into success in such situations. Instead, the weaker party tends to resent the situation and digs in its heels.

Who Are These People?

If research (and much experience) shows that workshops facilitated by a third party are the most effective forum for coming to grips with intractable problems, who are the third parties in such situations? Are they born or made? What characteristics and training must they have? How do people become third parties in the first place? Lawyers take an exam and are called to the "bar" as proof of their mastery of a complex discipline and of their ability to carry out the functions of their calling. Medical doctors must go through a lengthy and rigorous education and practical training culminating in exams and the taking of an ancient oath, which leads to the granting of a license to practice medicine. Are Track Two third parties subject to any similar form of training and certification? One would think they should be; after all, they are intervening in situations of deadly conflict and the ramifications of poor practice can set back the hopes of reconciliation with serious real-world consequences. Such ramifications can include situations where stereotypes are reinforced rather than broken down and messages are misunderstood due to poor management of the dialogue process. In extreme cases, Track Two can constitute a danger to the participants. For example, though they contributed greatly to the development of the field, Doob's early and experimental interventions in Cyprus and Northern Ireland were also seen by many at the time, including Doob himself, as having made those situations worse.[6] As Burton wrote in 1987, "the intervention of a third party into relationships between others is a delicate task and can easily do more harm than good."[7]

It often comes as a surprise to those who are new to Track Two that there are no common training procedures, certification processes, or standards of conduct for the field. How could there be? Who would set and enforce them? Lawyers and doctors go through training and certification because they would not legally be able to practice within their chosen geographical or political jurisdiction if they did not. Professional associations, recognized and authorized for this purpose by the state, exist to enforce standards and discipline in these fields. Moreover, these fields have had centuries to develop their professions and the standards of practice that go with them. Track Two is a relatively recent international activity and there is no transnational authority that can lay down standards for the field. This has potentially dangerous consequences. As Chester Crocker, a retired US diplomat with much mediation experience, writes,

> in the absence of any recognized "gatekeepers" and with dramatically lowered barriers to entry, the conflict management space has become undisciplined and something of a free-for-all. This raises problems of institutional rivalry, uncertain tradecraft, and third party incoherence. The potential for effective, multidisciplinary and layered interventions is exciting and promising. At the same time, the risk of exporting third party confusion and fostering forum shopping and conflict party fragmentation is also very real.[8]

Also the danger of burnout (the same people being involved in multiple Track Twos, saying the same things over and over to the same people) is real, and participants in Track Two have written on this.[9] "Forum shopping," cited here by Crocker, is also a danger. This is the tendency of some conflicting parties to use the fact that many Track Two practitioners want them to participate in "their" (the practitioners') process as a means of demanding that the process favor the party's needs. It feeds a sense in some parties that they can get their way if only they can find the right process, rather than accepting that they must engage in a painful process of examining and changing their goals. It can also lead parties away from the official table in the hope that they can get what they want at a Track Two table, if only they can find the "right" one for their purposes.

In 1995, Rouhana wrote on the dangers of people establishing themselves as third parties without proper training or with improper motivations.

Conflict resolution in the form of unofficial intervention is a profession that as of now is best characterized as a free-for-all. Practitioners come from all kinds of disciplinary backgrounds and are more often drawn by sympathy to one side or the other in the conflict. Former diplomats, academics, psychologists, psychiatrists, and many others practice conflict resolution. Often, it is not their qualifications or training but their good will that motivates and sustains their efforts. In many cases, practitioners do not have formal training in conflict dynamics. . . . While such an approach may provide practitioners with the flexibility they need to adapt to changing conditions and the chance to try new methods and improve existing ones, it also allows for errors and mistakes for which participants and their communities need to pay.[10]

How then to correct for these dangers? There are many ways to "train" those who will participate in Track Two, familiarizing them in the abstract with the issues they will face. Conflict resolution has become a significant area of study and teaching at many universities[11]; a large body of literature exists in the field.[12] Some practitioners have published how-to handbooks, which demonstrate how such interventions are run and provide useful insights and checklists for those who would undertake them.[13] Graduate courses have been designed specifically to educate would-be conflict interveners.[14] Significant resources exist on the internet in the form of sites dedicated to conflict resolution, which provide readings and advice on key issues.[15]

All of these are useful but far from sufficient. Being a third party in Track Two is not something one can learn purely from reading, nor would the authors of these various resources claim that it is. Rouhana's preferred solution to these serious problems, for the purposes of properly preparing third parties and by way of strengthening the Track Two field's overall academic rigor, is to develop methods which will allow social scientists to empirically test hypotheses about how Track Two processes work by means of controlled experiments and field studies.[16] He therefore proposes that those running Track Two projects should, with the permission of participants, allow graduate students and independent social scientists to sit in in order to evaluate how the dialogue is meeting certain predetermined objectives. Such efforts would be compared with control groups comprising graduate students engaged in role-playing. Such controls could be subjected to different styles and methodologies of third party conduct in order to evaluate the effectiveness of different techniques. In addition, participants in Track Two projects could be asked to fill in detailed questionnaires over time to gather data on how various techniques are working.

Rouhana proposes these studies as part of an overall effort to increase the credibility of the field as an academic discipline, and not just as a way to train future interveners—though one of the primary benefits of such research will be to develop rigorous teaching and training materials for future third parties. He recognizes that these methods are not perfect, and that a variety of limitations and ethical issues would need to be overcome for such research to be possible and effective. Nevertheless, he believes that

> The refinement of intervention tools and the establishment of a repertoire of activities to be used in the problem-solving workshop require empirical examination of the elements in the problem-solving workshop and the methods of third party facilitation that lead to the intended outcomes. By using experimental research methods, it will be possible to examine hypotheses connecting some elements of the workshop package of activities with intended outcomes, to compare various methods of intervention, and to test and compare the effectiveness of various third party intervention techniques.[17]

Having been myself involved in Track Two for over two decades, I wonder how effective such research would be. Though the permission of participants would be obtained before field studies went forward, would having social scientists in the room, whose purpose was to evaluate the discussion rather than be part of it, alter the character of the discussion and thereby invalidate the results? These interactions can be extraordinarily intimate and highly emotional affairs. Would participants hold back if they felt their actions and words were being scrutinized for an alternate purpose, even if that purpose was a benign one to which they had agreed? Would the results of questionnaires given out during intimate dialogues over deep-seated conflicts really capture the beliefs of the participants? Similarly, one wonders whether control groups of students, no matter how well prepared, would be able to capture the decades-long (sometimes generational) feelings of hurt, anger, and mistrust which the actual participants in a real conflict bring to the table and which are a significant part of the situation a third party faces. Finally, effective Track Two unfolds with repeated meetings over time (sometimes several years) and participants return home, where they are subjected to the realities of the conflict between the meetings. Could these circumstances be replicated with control groups of graduate students?

In commenting on Rouhana's ideas, Saunders notes that the field is, in practice,

> an art, not a science. The art—and like creative politics or diplomacy, it is an art—is revealed in the capacity to draw out human ability to talk about what is on their minds in a way that induces mutual comprehension and opens the door to talking, thinking, and working together differently to solve problems out of mutual need and interest. . . . In reaching judgments about how such work contributes to peace making and peace building, we must probably reach beyond the methods of present social science. We must accept the fact that in complex political situations exact cause and effect or the precise contribution of ideas may be unknowable in any measurable terms. How ideas emerge from the shadows to center stage and the role they play in changing the course of events may belong more to the history of ideas than to social science research methods.[18]

In identifying the role of the third party as an art, Saunders opens the door to a discussion over whether such people can be trained. Can an artist be trained? Undoubtedly, those with artistic talent can be taught various techniques to make them more proficient artists; but can the basic talent be taught if it is not there to begin with? My own view is that it cannot. So it is with people who seek to play the role of the third party. The basic qualities of interpersonal relations—empathetic listening and interaction, patience, calmness under fire, firmness and flexibility (and knowing when each is called for)—and an innate ability to gain and retain trust are not things that can be taught to someone who does not have them. They can, however, be refined and sharpened through study and, more importantly, observation and practice.

What essential qualities must people have then to undertake this role? In reflecting on his own extensive experience and that of many others in the field, Saunders, a former diplomat who stresses the interpersonal aspect of this type of work, believes it is critical that the third party genuinely possess and be able to convey nine essential qualities:

- Sensitivity to the human dimension of problems, and the ability to relate to participants on that level rather than treating them as trainees to be instructed
- Commitment to the overall process of reconciliation between groups that have real grievances against each other

- Sensitivity to the cultural uniqueness of the groups involved
- The ability to convey genuine caring and commitment on a person-to-person level and gain respect from participants as a caring person and as a professional
- Realistic expectations of the pace at which people change
- Some depth of experience with related conflicts and the ability to conceptualize that experience so as to draw on it in a particular group
- The ability to help people see common elements in their experiences and views
- A sense of political process—the ability to see the whole picture, keep a destination in sight, and not take sides
- The ability to help participants organize their thoughts[19]

The picture that emerges is one of a politically and diplomatically sophisticated and experienced person who is also an empathetic listener and able to convey a genuine sense of compassion and caring. Elsewhere in the same article, Saunders writes of "wise citizens, well prepared." This definition stresses two characteristics of the third party: first, political sophistication, both of a general nature and relative to the conflict at hand, though not necessarily expertise on the specific conflict being discussed; and second, the ability to create an environment in which the people in conflict will gradually feel safe enough to open themselves up to the third party, and to each other. Specific training in the conflict resolution field is not required, though it could be helpful.

Academics such as Kelman and Fisher, who have come to this work through the study of such fields as social psychology, would not disagree with Saunders but would also stress certain types of formal professional training and preparation as key. While complementing the list of qualities that Saunders puts forward, especially in terms of interpersonal skills, Fisher also emphasizes specific training in the psychological and consultative aspects of this work, and more generally in conflict resolution. Fisher writes,

The characteristics of the third-party team or panel in workshops are fundamental to the . . . effective implementation of . . . interventions. Usually a few to several members are engaged in order to cover the knowledge areas and skill sets required. . . . The set of conceptual and behavioral skills required to implement the third-party role is daunting. . . . Team members require general knowledge of conflict etiology and dynamics and all need a working knowledge to varying degrees of the history and expression of the conflict in question. Members should also have a good knowledge of international relations, which provides the context for ethnopolitical conflicts, and a good understanding of intergroup relations from the various social science disciplines. . . . Personal qualities, such as self-awareness and tolerance for ambiguity, need to be blended with interpersonal skills, such as empathetic listening, with group skills, especially facilitative leadership and group problem solving, and with the capacity to manage interactions at the group interface. Overall, the third-party role is one of professional consultation, with all of the diagnostic, facilitative and evaluative skills and ethical competencies which that role entails.[20]

A particular expectation for the composition of third parties stressed by scholar-practitioners such as Fisher, Kelman, and Mitchell, who come from academic backgrounds, is that the third party be composed of a panel of some three to five people. A panel is seen as crucial in that a variety of expertise is required and no one individual can possess all of it. Moreover, some of the panelists should be dedicated on a rotating basis to observing the process rather than chairing it, in order to make sure that nonverbal and other indicators are picked up and fed into the ongoing evaluation of the discussions. Further, at least some panelists should be concerned with the business of evaluating the process in terms of lessons learned for the field overall.[21]

There is a disagreement between those, like Saunders, who believe an individual (or a very small panel) can play the role of the third party and those, like Kelman, Fisher, Mitchell, and Banks, who see the role as necessarily being played by a larger, multidisciplinary panel. Interestingly, Saunders comes to the field having been a former diplomat, while the others come to it from academic backgrounds. Perhaps this in part accounts for the difference of view: diplomatic mediators are used to acting, if not on their own, then at least as the head of a team. In my own experience, I have been involved with both panel situations and solitary ones. In those cases where I have been part of a panel, I have observed that much time is spent, even on panels where the rapport is very good, debating various approaches and trying to achieve agreement on the way forward. Such discussion is good for the development of practice but can slow the actual process. In projects that I have undertaken as the primary actor, I tend to be a single third party. However, such third parties do not act alone; other participants in the problem-solving workshop are selected on the basis of their ability to make contributions that help the process along, and there is an experienced support team as well.

John Paul Lederach, a practitioner and scholar of the field who is a leader in "transformation"-oriented conflict resolution, provides yet another set of characteristic abilities which he holds as crucial to the ability to play the third party role. Writing of a concept he calls "the moral imagination," an ability to comprehend and work within the reality of a violent present while inspiring those engaged in such disputes to gradually identify and work towards an imagined future, Lederach posits four key qualities. He believes that third parties must possess these qualities and have the personal and moral skills to help those in conflict find and nurture them too if they are to transcend their situation. They are

- *The centrality of relationships*: "the capacity of individuals and communities to imagine themselves in a web of relationship(s) even with their enemies"
- *The practice of paradoxical curiosity*: "a discipline that, in settings of deep-rooted violence filled with social polarization, views complexity as a friend and refuses to fall into the historic traps of dualistic divisions, which drive the cycle of violence . . . a permanent inquisitiveness that vigilantly explores the world of possibilities beyond the immediate arguments and narrow definitions of reality, whose shores are only attainable by taking the arguments seriously while refusing to be bound by their visions"
- *Providing space for the creative act*: "Providing space requires a predisposition, a kind of attitude and perspective that opens up, even invokes, the spirit and belief that creativity is humanly possible . . . even in settings where violence dominates. . . . People who display a deep quality of moral imagination in these settings of violence demonstrate a capacity to live in a personal and social space that gives birth to the unexpected. . . . They embrace the possibility that there exist untold possibilities capable at any moment to move beyond the narrow parameters of what is commonly accepted and perceived as the narrow and rigidly defined range of choices."
- *The willingness to risk*: "To risk is to step into the unknown without any guarantee of success or even safety. . . . People living in settings

of deep-rooted conflict are faced with an extraordinary irony. Violence is known; peace is the mystery. By its very nature, therefore, peacebuilding requires a journey guided by the imagination of risk."[22]

One of the striking things which emerges from the various definitions of the third party discussed in this chapter is that they both overlap and differ as to the personal qualities required of third parties and how they are to be prepared for the task. All the definitions stress the need for strongly developed interpersonal qualities. Saunders and Lederach, both of whom explicitly identify the role as being an "art," stress these qualities above all else—everything else can be learned. Fisher and those like him, who approach these situations as professional consultations informed by fields like social psychology, agree with the need for deep interpersonal skills but also stress the need for mastering a body of professional, academic training. Indeed, in their view, this is a key responsibility of third parties.

What Do These People Do?

If the set of personal qualities and the training which defines who a third party is contains a variety of meanings and definitions, so too does the accepted literature on what the third party does. Two of the more accomplished scholars and practitioners of Track Two, Fisher and Kelman, have generally defined the role of the third party. Fisher writes:

> The role of the third party is primarily facilitative and diagnostic, rather than directive or prescriptive; it can perhaps best be seen as a form of professional consultation. The demands of this role require that the team or panel of scholar-practitioners have moderate to considerable knowledge about the conflict and the parties in question, knowledge and expertise in conflict analysis, and human relations skills in interpersonal and cross-cultural communication and small-group processes. All this is necessary so that the participants can be assisted to engage in an in-depth (and in some ways threatening) analysis of their conflict and in productive confrontation on the issues and the interests, values and needs which underlie them.[23]

In the first chapter we saw Kelman's definition of the field, which included a short description of what the third party actually does:

The third party typically consists of a panel of social scientists who, between them, possess expertise in group processes and international conflict, and at least some familiarity with the conflict region. The role of the third party . . . differs from that of the traditional mediator. Unlike many mediators, we do not propose (and certainly, unlike arbitrators, we do not impose) solutions. Rather, we try to facilitate a process whereby solutions will emerge out of the interaction between the parties themselves. The task of the third party is to provide the setting, create the atmosphere, establish the norms, and offer the occasional interventions that make it possible for such a process to evolve.[24]

Common to these two definitions are the ideas that the third party role is undertaken by social scientist scholar-practitioners; that having some knowledge of the specifics of the conflict is desirable but a firm grasp of group dynamics is essential[25]; and that the fundamental role of the third party is to facilitate a process whereby the protagonists are encouraged to explore the deeper aspects of their understanding of the dispute and then together begin to come up with potential solutions. This is fully consistent with Burton's idea of "controlled communication," which launched the field many years before.

But *how* exactly is this done? Again, Kelman:

The third party provides the context in which representatives of parties engaged in intense conflict come together. It selects, briefs and convenes the participants. It serves as a repository of trust for both parties, enabling them to proceed with the assurance that their confidentiality will be respected and their interests protected even though—by definition—they cannot trust each other. It establishes and enforces the norms and ground rules that facilitate analytic discussion and a problem-solving orientation. It proposes a broad agenda that encourages the parties to move from exploration of each other's concerns and constraints to the generation of ideas for win/win solutions and for implementing such solutions. It tries to keep the discussion moving in constructive directions. And, finally, it makes occasional substantive interventions in the form of content observations, which suggest interpretations and implications of what is being said . . . to blind spots, to possible signals, and to issues for clarification.[26]

This is a significant list. Recruitment of the participants and establishing and enforcing the norms and ground rules will be discussed in the next chapter on the problem-solving workshop, as they are central to the organization and success of such workshops. We will also deal with the role of the third party in assisting the transfer of the results of Track Two processes to the official track in Chapter 6. Next we shall consider two of the roles identified by Kelman: the "repository of trust," and "interventions."

The Repository of Trust

Trust is central to all human relationships at some level. The subject of trust has received considerable attention in the social science and conflict resolution literature from a variety of standpoints.[27] Research has revealed a number of different elements of trust. These include the differences and similarities between professional (including institutional) and personal trust[28]; differences between various *kinds* of trust; and the fact that trust and distrust are "fundamentally different from each other, rather than more or less of the same thing."[29] These kinds of trust and distrust are arranged in a "ladder," from the lowest levels of trust to the highest:

- Calculus-based trust: a strong sense within the individuals or organizations in the relationship that all will do what they promise to do because they fear the consequences of not doing so, or anticipate rewards for adherence[30]
- Calculus-based distrust: a confident sense that the other side in the relationship will not adhere to promises because they will calculate that the benefits of not doing so outweigh the rewards for adherence
- Knowledge-based trust: a sense of trust based on repeated observation of the other in various situations, which allows one to develop a strong knowledge and understanding of the other's likely behavior in circumstances where trust is called for
- Knowledge-based distrust: a sense that the other cannot be trusted, which is based on experience and observation of their likely behavior over time
- Identification-based trust: a more developed form of trust than either of the two above, this form of trust stems from an ability to identify with, understand, and appreciate each other's desires and wants to such an extent that parties can begin to share some of the same needs and choices with respect to the issue at hand[31]

- Identification-based distrust: a perception within one or both parties that the goals and choices of the other are not compatible with one's own

Once broken, trust is not easily regained. In the case of mediation or conflict resolution, the environment within which the third party begins working is, by definition, particularly lacking in trust. In his survey of thirty mediators who had each been involved in fifty or more cases of mediation, Goldberg found that 75 percent of them identified the ability to gain and retain the trust of the parties in the dispute as the single most important factor in their eventual success, something which Goldberg's interviewees referred to as "their ability to develop rapport with the disputing parties—a relationship of understanding, empathy and trust."[32] In their study on mediation of managerial disputes, Ross and Wieland probed why this ability to gain and retain the trust of the disputing parties is so fundamental to a mediator. They found that trust

> serve[s] a doubly useful purpose: not only do[es it] give the mediators the credibility to offer suggestions designed to resolve the dispute, [it] may also create a climate where the parties trust the mediator, allowing the mediator to attempt relationship building between the parties.[33]

Trust is therefore of fundamental importance to conventional mediators operating in situations such as industrial disputes. It not only allows the mediator the access required to understand the two sides' deeper concerns; it is the coin of the realm in creating the space whereby the mediator is allowed to build a relationship between himself and the parties, and ultimately between the parties themselves, which is sufficiently strong for the mediator to propose solutions and to have them be taken seriously.

This need for trust is perhaps even greater for those who would play the role of the third party in a Track Two process. In cases of Track Two efforts where the parties at the table represent larger groups that are actively fighting each other, or have been recently, one is dealing with people who have been killing each other, often for an extended period. Moreover, as noted by Kelman that third parties in Track Two are not mediators and do not seek to propose solutions (but rather to create circumstances in which solutions will emerge from the analytic discussions among the parties themselves), the third party is not seeking a level of trust sufficient to permit him or her to propose ideas—either to both parties simultaneously or separately in the form of "shuttle mediation." Rather, the third party in a Track Two context hopes to build a relationship of trust *between the parties in the conflict* to a level that is sufficient for them to be drawn into a conversation in which they will gradually reconsider the meaning of the conflict and simultaneously reveal their innermost perceptions of the conflict to each other. This is a different order of magnitude.

The role of the third party also points to the need for a different *type* of trust, in that it is fundamental to Track Two that a situation ultimately be created whereby the parties in conflict deal directly with each other rather than go through a mediator. It is in this context that Kelman's concept of the "repository of trust" is important. If two parties who profoundly mistrust each other are to begin a face-to-face interaction and sustain it over time, they must be able to trust at least someone in the room; they must be able to designate someone present as the *repository* of their trust until they can come to feel at least some trust for the other side. This is the role of the third party. It is also the third party's role to gradually relinquish the function of "repository of trust" as parties in conflict develop the necessary rapport with *each other* (as opposed to the mediator, which Goldberg's interviewees identify as critical in conventional cases of mediation) and begin to interact over their deep-seated views of the conflict. As N. Ó Dochartaigh puts it in his study of "back-channel" negotiations over many years in Northern Ireland, "the development of a sense of mutual solidarity between negotiators from opposing sides and their cooperation in moving forward the positions of their respective parties . . . is facilitated by the presence of an intermediary with whom both parties can legitimately build a relationship of solidarity, thus generating a sense of solidarity that stretches across the divide."[34]

How is such a level of trust obtained? In their study on running Track Two processes, Burgess and Burgess have considered how the third party can develop the trust of the participants, and increase the participants' ability to trust each other over time. They consider seven qualities and strategies to be key:

- Treat all participants equally and with respect and dignity at all times, and encourage all participants to do the same
- Create an environment that makes participants feel comfortable and safe
- Let each party know that the trainer, mediator, or facilitator is listening to them, understands their problems and how they feel about them, cares about their problems, and can serve as a resource to help

them address those problems

- Show that the trainer, mediator, or facilitator has no stake in the outcome of the conflict that would prevent participants from pursuing their own interests and goals ("stake" can include high pay, as highly paid interveners may be suspected of wanting a settlement for their own financial benefit)
- Never assign blame, criticize, or judge a participant or party, or tell the participants what they must do (although one can enforce mutually accepted ground rules in a respectful way[35])
- Ask nonthreatening, open-ended questions
- Listen empathetically, reframe unclear or unnecessarily hostile language sympathetically, and encourage others to do the same[36]

From my own experience I would agree with these points. I also believe that one of the most important keys to success, building on the points made above, is scrupulous honesty on the part of the third party. If the participants from the conflict zone are to trust the third party, they must believe that she is being honest with them in all respects. This has to do in part with honesty about the mechanics of the process—where the funding is coming from, what the third party's affiliations really are, and so on. This is a very practical but important set of considerations. If participants enter into a dialogue only to find out that the third party is not who he says he is, or that financial support for their discussions is coming from a concealed source which may have ulterior motives, confidence will be lost immediately, never to be regained.

Scrupulous honesty also has to do with the third party's motivations and objectives. This point is complex. Those who seek to play the role of the third party do so out of a mixture of motivations and objectives. They may be motivated by moral or religious ideas, for example. They may have a deep belief about how the conflict in question should be resolved, based on many years of observation or interaction with it. They may be motivated by compassion for the suffering of those caught up in the conflict. They may be individuals who desire to excel in the field of conflict resolution, either out of a professional desire to be active in the field or an academic interest in developing theories about how conflicts should be resolved. Often there is a mixture of such motivations in play. Whatever the third party's motivations are, it is vital to reflect on them and be honest about them up front. If a third party brings conflicting parties to the table under the impression that her interest is one thing, only to have it subsequently revealed that she is motivated by other factors, credibility will suffer seriously and trust will be lost.

The third party does not have to be absolutely neutral in its attitudes towards the conflict. This point takes us into the vexing question of whether a third may bring its own deep-seated beliefs about a conflict to the table. As we discussed in Chapter 3, for many years it was widely felt that the third party must strive for a position of neutrality. Thus there has been a belief that this sort of work is best undertaken by people—Scandinavians or Swiss, for example—who come from far-away, smaller countries that have no local interests. Others have taken the view that it does not matter where the third party comes from but that it must be totally neutral and not have ties to any government, even as a retired official of one.[37] Obviously, many retired government officials who play the third party role would disagree with this.

More recent scholarship, however, makes the point that neutrality may not always be necessary.[38] So-called insider-partial third parties, those who have well-developed and well-known views on the conflict, may be just as effective. What seems to be necessary is that the third party be able to convey that it will run the process in a fair and impartial way and will not, due to its own views, disadvantage anyone at the table. As noted earlier, Burgess and Burgess say that it is not necessary for the facilitator to have *no* stake in the conflict, but it is essential that the third party not have a stake "that will prevent the participants from pursuing their own interests and goals."[39] In reality, one can never be completely neutral anyway. In my own work, I tell the participants whether I have any biases. I may have sympathy for a side's basic objectives, for example, but deplore the methods they have used to pursue them, especially if these have involved the indiscriminate killing of innocents. And one must confront the fact that there is rarely an entirely virtuous or entirely evil side in any complex and long-standing conflict; as a retired senior diplomat once said to me in the context of an India-Pakistan Track Two I was running, "There are no saints here, only sinners."

The need for the third party to be absolutely honest can have interesting consequences. Especially at the beginning of the dialogue process it is to be expected that the participants will be hedging their bets and not be completely open with each other, or even with the third party. How could it be otherwise with a group of people who have lived in the middle of a conflict for many years? Often their survival has depended on concealing things, and on keeping options open. And so, at the beginning of a dialogue, the third party is sometimes the only person in the room who is being completely honest about his motivations and objectives. This can create a situation of emotional "nakedness" for the third party, which requires considerable self-confidence and moral authority to deal with. But it is essential for the third party to project this confidence and authority to the parties in conflict. Anything less and one cannot establish oneself as the repository of trust.

Substantive Interventions

Having achieved this trust, how does the third party use it? Sparingly, is the answer. In keeping with the point that the third party is there to encourage the participants to have their own dialogues, its interventions and comments should be kept to a minimum. Indeed, biting one's tongue and *not* speaking is sometimes the most challenging task, especially when one sees that participants are going down alleys of conversation that are time consuming and not likely to be terribly productive. One wants to intervene, but it is often much more effective for the participants to discover together that a particular idea will not work than to have that pointed out by someone else. In addition to the fact that ideas discovered by the participants themselves are more lasting and authentic than lessons imparted by someone else, one must always remember that the dialogue is *theirs* and they must genuinely feel they are deciding where it goes and how it gets there. This is part of their process of developing the kind of deeper relationship that will ultimately be necessary, and it sometimes requires "excursionary" discussions, however frustrating these may be.

Consequently, one of the most important qualities of the third party is patience. This is not simply the patience to sit through what one knows is likely to be an unproductive discussion, but a kind of patience linked closely to a sense of where the dialogue needs to go which is aligned with an innate ability, developed with experience, to gently steer the dialogue there over time. The third party must also understand that even the inevitable detours along the way have their purpose, rather than setting a firm agenda and pushing people as rapidly as possible. One must avoid conveying to the participants a sense that there is a preordained timeline they have to adhere to, or a set of subjects they must discuss; fundamental changes in antagonistic and deep-seated perceptions of the other side do not happen according to a timetable or an agenda, especially not one introduced by an outsider, even a well-intentioned and trusted one.

There are times, of course, when it is useful for the third party to inject itself into the dialogue. In their description of the dynamics of the so-called problem-solving workshop, Kelman and Cohen identified three types of interventions the third party might make to stimulate reflective analysis among the participants or to gently encourage them down productive paths of conversation.[40] In each case, timing is everything: the third party should make these interventions when they are relevant to the course of the discussion rather than to demonstrate their own mastery of the issues. Above all, such interventions should be made sparingly.

First, there are "theoretical inputs." These are comments which introduce "concepts, models, and empirical findings from conflict theory and research."[41] Sometimes used at the beginning of a process to provide a starting point in conversations about the objectives of the process, and sometimes used as the process is underway to introduce ideas which may help it along, these interventions can assist participants to stand back from the details of their own conflict and develop a broader view of what they hope to accomplish. Burton wrote about such interventions or inputs in the context of his "controlled communication," and his writing on the subject was among the first.[42]

A second kind of third party intervention, as identified by Kelman and Cohen, are "content observations." Such observations take the form of "interpretations of the content of what is being said by the parties."[43] The third party can use such observations to invite the participants to probe the meaning of what they are saying, particularly when they are using what they regard as obvious phrases or buzzwords to convey meanings which may not be properly understood by the other side due to linguistic or cultural barriers. I have found this to be an effective method of helping participants overcome such barriers as the high-context/low-context communication problem discussed in Chapter 3. For example, in a US-Iran Track Two that I was facilitating some years ago, the Iranians kept insisting that the United States did not show Iran the proper respect it is due as an ancient and great civilization. The Americans would brush this off, saying that they respected Iran's history well enough but wanted to talk about present-day issues dividing the two countries, such as the nuclear question or Iran's attitude towards Israel. After a few hours of this back-and-forth, I noted that the Iranians were using the word "respect" without defining what they meant by it, and I asked them to do so. The next two hours revealed to the Americans the extent to which the Iranians base many of their policies on historical myths regarding the negative way in which Persia, and Persian culture, have traditionally been treated by outsiders.

It cannot be said that these insights helped resolve any of the issues on the table, but I was subsequently told by some of the Americans in the room that the discussion had opened their eyes to Iran's very different way of seeing things. To that point, they had viewed Iran's use of what one of the Americans called the "respect card" as a rhetorical device to evade discussions over difficult issues and to deflect blame onto the Americans for any misunderstandings. Many Americans still took the view that at least some of the Iranians present were, at least to some extent, doing this (and they probably were), but the Americans also conceded that future solutions will have to take into account the respect question if they are to be saleable in Iran. Meanwhile, some of the Iranians told me that having to actually define what they meant by "respect," and to do so under relentless and somewhat skeptical American probing, had forced them to jettison some of the more rhetorical flourishes they often relied on in their use of the term in internal discussions and come to terms with the policy implications of what they had always presented as a rather abstract and open-ended complaint. The discussion had an impact on how each side listened to the other as the dialogue went forward.[44]

The final kind of third party observation identified by Kelman and Cohen are "process observations." These observations are meant to call attention to the manner, or process, in which the dialogue is unfolding and what that means in the larger conflict. For example, if either side in the room is ascribing to the other characteristics which are reflective of broader attitudes its society has towards the other's, these can be pointed out by a third party as a way of inviting analysis of whether these characteristics are true or are stereotypes.

Some years ago, while facilitating an Israeli-Iranian dialogue, I noticed that each side took the view that its own members were acting as individuals, giving their own interpretations of events, while those on the other side were reciting official policy because their society would never allow them to come to such a meeting without a firm "policy line." In effect there was a tendency on the part of individuals on both sides to consider statements made by individuals on the other not as personal analyses or expressions of opinions but as statements of policy, while their own statements were being made in an individual capacity. I suggested that this might be reflective of each side's tendency to view their own political process as multilayered, chaotic, and ill disciplined, while seeing the other side's as highly disciplined, controlled, and always "on message." I suggested that this had to be impossible for *both* sides at the table, and was perhaps a projection each was making onto the other. The participants agreed that they had been subconsciously thinking this way and we began probing the implications. It was a fascinating discussion. One implication, which we discussed at length, was that each side believed the other side would have to make the first move with respect to concessions in order to get a process of rapprochement going, because the leadership on their own side was not authorized to act or enforce the discipline to make far-reaching changes, while it innately suspected the other side was capable of doing so. Obviously, this was a recipe for a dead end, and each side would have to come to a more sophisticated understanding of what would be required if official talks were ever to begin.

Power and the Third Party

These qualities and roles are important to understanding who the third party is and what it does, but there is another element that needs to be understood: power. As Aall notes, "Talking about power and mediation in the same breath may strike many as odd."[45] Power is generally associated with the deployment of punishments or rewards in order to achieve objectives. Where power and mediation do intersect, it is generally held to be the realm of statecraft, especially that of great powers, who use rewards, incentives, and even punishments to bring conflicting parties to the table to get them (force them, if necessary) to agree. As discussed in Chapter 2, Touval has coined the phrase "mediation with muscle" to describe such situations.[46]

But there are many kinds of power in a mediation situation, some of which are highly relevant to those who would play the role of the third party in a Track Two setting. Rubin has identified six kinds of power in mediation situations. Each can be used in different ways by different kinds of mediators to gain access to the conflict and to achieve legitimacy in the eyes of the combatants. They are

- *Informational power*: access to specialized information, either about the other side, or about how to structure and run dialogues, that the parties may want and which can be used as the basis for a facilitator or go-between role

- *Expert power*: a belief by parties to a conflict that the third party has useful expert knowledge, perhaps in the field of conflict resolution or some other highly sought area, that they can benefit from
- *Referent power*: the value that parties place on their relationship with the mediator, possibly because of his broader standing, which allows the mediator to command their respect for and attention to his ideas and suggestions
- *Legitimate power*: the perception of parties that the mediator has a right to be playing the role, perhaps because she represents an institution they cannot ignore
- *Reward power*: the ability to deploy incentives to get parties to change their behavior
- *Coercive power*: the ability to punish, or threaten punishment, in order to bring about changes in behavior[47]

Some of these kinds of power are beyond the grasp of a third party in a Track Two setting. To paraphrase Stalin: like the Pope, third parties have no divisions. Thus, reward and coercive power are almost always beyond the scope of this kind of work; they belong to states, and likely the bigger states at that. Legitimate power, on the other hand, may derive from the mediator's having been appointed by an institution that the parties in conflict accept as a legitimate actor. Even if that institution, and hence the mediator, have no reward or coercive power, those in the conflict do not feel they can simply dismiss the mediator without suffering negative consequences of some kind; they may or may not like the fact that the mediator has been appointed, but they cannot easily ignore him. Examples of such mediators would be the various Special Representatives appointed by the United Nations Secretary General to many conflicts, or by various regional bodies such as the Organization for Security and Co-operation in Europe (the OSCE) or the African Union.

If coercive, reward, and legitimate power are the province of states or official international institutions, then referent, expert, and informational power can be exercised by nongovernmental actors (though they may be used by officials as well). Referent power derives from the perception of the parties that it is in their interest to cooperate with the mediator (or at least appear to), even if she is not directly representing a powerful state or institution. An example of referent power would be the conflict resolution activities of former US president Jimmy Carter. The parties to the conflict may believe that he carries in some sense the weight of the United States into these situations or, at the least, that he has the ability to influence the perceptions of the United States towards themselves and the situation. This may or may not be true, but if it is *perceived* to be so by the conflicting parties then the mediator has a certain referent power. The parties thus place a value on cooperating, or at least appearing to cooperate with him. This does not necessarily mean they have any intention of changing their approach to the conflict; it could mean they don't want to be seen (by various audiences) as unwilling to talk. This type of power can thus be exercised by a nonofficial, but a rather special kind of nonofficial.

Informational and expert power, on the other hand, are most often the kinds of power exercised by third parties in a Track Two setting. Indeed, "power" may the wrong word in the context of third parties, and may more properly be thought of as forms of "influence." In these cases, the third party gains and maintains access to the conflict and establishes legitimacy in the eyes of the parties by virtue of the personal and professional qualities we identified and discussed previously. The greater the value the conflicting parties place on the dialogue, and the more they believe that the third party is key to running it, the greater the influence (power) of the third party to shape the discussions. But it's a tightrope; the third party in a Track Two setting has no actual *power* to compel the parties to take particular courses of action, or even to force them to stay at the table. If either or both of the conflicting parties come to the view that the dialogue is no longer worth the effort, or that the third party is not being impartial or otherwise doing a good job, they can walk away; the third party has no power to force them to stay or to bring them back.

As noted before, this delicate situation reinforces the idea that this sort of work is an "art." It also supports the notion that the role of the third party in a Track Two setting is not to dominate the proceedings or impose a certain solution on the conflicting parties, but rather to *facilitate* a dialogue out of which the parties will themselves develop ideas and possible solutions. In this sense, the "power" enjoyed by a third party in a Track Two setting is exactly right for their task: any greater power to coerce or reward, assuming it could be accrued by a third party, might lead to the temptation to drive the parties to certain kinds of solutions or outcomes. But a third party cannot do this, or even attempt it, because the parties would simply walk away—there is nothing the third party could do to keep them. In a real sense, the relative powerlessness (in a realist sense) of third parties is precisely what makes a Track Two possible; it creates an environment in which it is up to the parties to reach solutions because there is no one else to do it for them. There is only a trusted person to help facilitate their discussions towards the achievement of this task: the third party.

Conclusion

This chapter began by asking who these people are and what it is they do. It also asked where they come from and how they are prepared. Finally, it explored what power is available to the third party and how it uses it. There are no universally accepted answers to these questions, just as there is no universally accepted definition of Track Two. Experience demonstrates that certain interpersonal skills are very helpful, as are certain kinds of training and experience. Some who have written on these questions stress the necessity for training based on empirical research, both to prepare third parties and to enhance the standing of the field in the social sciences. Others believe that such research can be useful in developing the field but can never truly capture the reality on the ground.

In my own view, the development of someone into an effective third party is about already existing inner qualities sharpened by experience over time, preferably working with someone (or better still with a variety of people) already well versed in the field. The study of technique from academic sources, though a necessary element of preparation, does not and cannot "make" a third party. In a sense, the development of a third party is a form of apprenticeship. During this period, the "apprentice" will gradually experience greater levels of responsibility and will be evaluated at each step by those with whom he is working. But there are no standardized courses or texts, and there is no certification at the end of it. He either develops the ability to do this work or he does not. This may be profoundly unsatisfying to some who seek to make the field into a science, but it is the reality.

This does not mean that the field should be a free-for-all as some have described it. While it is probably unlikely there will ever be a transnational body to formally certify third parties, there is a group of people who have demonstrated repeatedly that they have the aptitude and ethical qualities for this role. These practitioners could (and should) establish a self-selecting network of those who meet the standards and epitomize the best of the field.

Reputation and word-of-mouth do matter. Perhaps in the end the people who should decide whether a certain individual has the required qualities should be the consumers of the product—those who are in situations of conflict. To be invited by them to undertake an intervention is perhaps the true sign of one's mastery of the art.

Having been invited to undertake such a project, how does one do it? What kinds of meetings should one hold and how should they be structured and run? We turn our attention to these questions in the next chapter.

5   On Method: The Problem-Solving Workshop

NOW THAT WE HAVE A SENSE OF WHAT TRACK TWO IS, or rather a sense of the multiplicity of things it is, and also a sense of who does it, the question arises as to how. What are the key techniques and settings of Track Two efforts? Perhaps the most critical is the "problem-solving workshop" (the PSW), and it is the subject of this chapter.

The PSW is a rather specific type of interaction. It has evolved through trial and error over five decades, and is arguably the key tool of Track Two, especially Track Two aimed at promoting the kind of deep, mutual examination of intractable conflicts which many practitioners from Burton onwards have held to be at the heart of the field. The PSW is not a chance occurrence, nor is it best implemented as a onetime event. It is, rather, a series of workshops over an extended period. It is also a carefully planned encounter, which the third party and the participants must approach with great care. Through a series of such meetings over time the goal is to achieve new and practical ideas regarding the dispute but also more profound psychological outcomes among participants. In effect, the meetings become a kind of shared, cathartic learning experience, within which parties to the conflict can step back from it, develop joint understandings of its deep-rooted aspects, and come to more fully understand themselves and each other, both as individuals and as the larger groups they are "representing" within the PSW process.

The Theory of Problem-Solving in the Social Sciences

The idea of the so-called problem-solving approach emerged in the mid-1960s from social science theory and practice. Its application to international conflict resolution is generally attributed to Burton and his colleagues. Mitchell identifies four trends of thinking in the social sciences in the late 1950s and early 1960s which influenced Burton[1]: social case work, which at this time was developing a set of theories on the role of the case-worker as being to help the client identify and implement solutions, not to impose solutions[2]; work being done in the Human Relations Department at the Tavistock Institute in London on how small groups of people in conflict could be formed into working groups focused on tasks related to, but much larger than, the specifics of their problem, the objective being to develop alternate ideas for moving forward[3]; work being done on industrial problem-solving in corporations like Gulf Oil to develop discussion groups across levels of management and labor, which were focused on cooperatively identifying, anticipating, and developing solutions to problems within the organization[4]; and work being done on problem-solving in the field of mathematics, which brought together small self-managing groups around specific mathematical problems that required crosscutting innovation and creativity in order to be solved.[5]

Combining these inputs, and his own evolving ideas on alternate ways to solve international disputes, Burton developed what became known as the problem-solving technique as applied to conflicts. As discussed in Chapter 1, the key to this approach is small groups of people from the conflict being brought together by the third party facilitator for an intensive and repeated process of discussion. These discussions are not meant to be forums where positions are repeated but rather where joint analysis can lead to agreed-on understandings of the underlying causes of the dispute, followed by joint development of ideas and options that would not be apparent from traditional zero-sum bargaining.

There is a tendency among those who do not know the background to equate this process with concepts such as brainstorming. But as noted in Chapter 4, brainstorming by itself may do more harm than good. As Chataway commented, "Unassisted, parties in conflict do not tend to engage in brainstorming, or even in effectively communicating perspectives. Rather, they tend to jump quickly to analyzing or dictating options, with the effect of polarizing the dispute even further."[6] The role of a third party in a PSW setting is to gently steer the conversation down more creative and productive paths. Beyond the question of facilitated brainstorming, experiments have shown that a *workshop* approach is better than a negotiation approach at improving underlying relationships at the outset of a process.[7] Furthermore, if workshops are better at helping people overcome deep-seated distrust and begin to explore and develop new ideas together, *facilitated* workshops are superior to ones that are not facilitated, as also demonstrated in research studies.[8]

A large number of studies drawing on the "social contact" theory from social psychology have accumulated a substantial body of evidence that unstructured and unfacilitated contacts between people from groups in conflict do not change the hostile attitudes between them; indeed, such attitudes can even deepen. Conversely, such encounters are more likely to succeed where four basic conditions exist:

> (i) where members of each group have equal status (professional, educational, etc.); (ii) where each group is working towards a common goal; (iii) where each group is cooperatively interdependent; and (iv) where group contact is supported by laws, customs, or institutions.[9]

These are the conditions one strives for in a PSW: equality of status among the participants, regardless of asymmetries within the conflict; a sense of common purpose; cooperative interdependence; and a set of rules and structures which a facilitator employs to guide the conversation towards cooperative and reflective analysis rather than an exchange of positions.

The PSW in Theory

What exactly happens in these workshops? As noted by those who have written representative overviews of hypothetical PSWs, no two are alike.[10] Moreover, these authors subscribe to particular methodologies which may not be shared by others. It is thus a curious situation that the field of Track Two has no agreed-on methodology for how its (arguably) primary tool should be planned, conducted, analyzed, or assessed. Rouhana has attempted to deconstruct the PSW in order to more fully represent in theoretical terms its activities, objectives, and goals and how these relate to each and can be measured (Figure 5.1).[11]

Possible activities (the column on the left) are relatively self-evident and do not require further discussion. Which of these or other activities are selected will be a function of what the specific Track Two project is intended

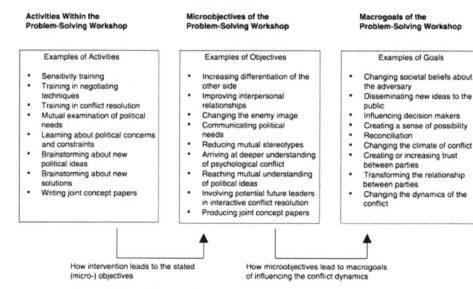

FIGURE 5.1 The Problem-Solving Workshop
Source: From, Rouhana, N.N., "Interactive Conflict Resolution: Issues in Theory, Methodology, and Evaluation," in *International Conflict Resolution after the Cold War*, Druckman, D., and P.C. Stern, (eds.) (Washington, D.C.: National Academy Press, 2000), 297. Reprinted with permission from the National Academies Press.

to achieve. The objectives (the middle column), which Rouhana calls the "micro-objectives," require further elaboration.[12] For example, *differentiation* is drawn from research showing that individuals from societies in deep and long-standing conflict often develop an image of the other side as a monolithic "they." "They" are all unreasonable; "they" are all religious fanatics; "they" are all governed by an irrational hatred of everything "we" stand for.[13] Such images provide a comforting and all-encompassing source of support of our own narrative of the conflict and nurture strong explanations for those elements of our conduct which would otherwise be unacceptable. ("Of course, we would rather not have to do x, but 'they' are so brutal as to require it as our only possible response.") When such monolithic images exist on both sides, the sense of intractability is enhanced, particularly where individuals from the two sides do not meet frequently, if at all. Differentiation is thus a process whereby individuals from each side come to understand that the other side is not monolithic; it is a *differentiated* political and social entity characterized by a wide variety of viewpoints and ongoing debates over policies and which courses of action to take. In this sense, "they" begin to look a lot like "us." The fact that this set of revelations is being achieved mutually through direct contact can be a very powerful outcome of the PSW process.

Similarly, the ideas of *changing the enemy image* and *reducing mutual stereotypes* can be powerful when they result in a humanization of the enemy. Each side may know intellectually that the other has also suffered in the conflict, but to hear and experience firsthand their stories of grief and suffering is to learn that the real enemy is the conflict itself. Alone, these objectives will not change long-standing positions, nor should they be expected to. But they can increase the complexity of each side's understanding of the conflict in both cognitive and emotional terms.

The "macro-goals" of the PSW process (the column on the right) set out by Rouhana require little elaboration. Once again, which of these is selected for a particular PSW process will have much to do with the objectives of that exercise and the needs of the moment.

Rouhana also warns us that the PSW's effects can be overestimated. He identifies four potential dangers:

- Deemphasizing the reality of the conflict on the ground: The reality of the PSW becomes confused with the reality of the conflict itself—especially for the third party, which does not experience the day-to-day reality of the conflict—leading to discussion of ways to improve and maintain the PSW that have less and less to do with the need to affect the conflict itself.

- Treating the PSW as the conflict reality: Once again, the third party begins to imagine that what he is seeing in the PSW mirrors the way people interact in the conflict on the ground.

- Overemphasizing the dynamics in the PSW: Efforts to develop ways to address the conflict in the PSW are held to be so important that the reality on the ground is given secondary attention as the process goes on; people begin to search for theoretical solutions to what is increasingly seen as a theoretical conflict.

- Overestimating the participants' influence: believing that participants from one or both sides have the ability to influence the political reality at home, when they do not.[14]

Beyond deconstructing and analyzing the specific issues of the PSW itself, Rouhana challenges its proponents to justify claims they may make as to its effectiveness. As noted in Chapter 3 in the discussion of theories of change, most who are engaged in Track Two do not take the time to explicitly outline their theory of change—their concept of how their activities will actually produce change in the participants—or to develop tangible yardsticks whereby it can be measured and evaluated.[15] Rouhana notes that much is claimed of the PSW, and many proponents are quick to relate changes in the broader conflict dynamic, when they happen, to PSW efforts. But there is little measurable proof that a given PSW has had the claimed effect. Often the claims are so general ("We got people together and showed them that new ways of thinking are possible") that one cannot deny them but one can question whether they actually have had any impact on the reality of the conflict.

Rouhana's analysis remains the most thorough attempt to date to deconstruct the PSW and ask fundamental questions about how it works. Yet while he has identified the questions, crosscutting answers remain elusive, except at the level of generalities. His preferred method of doing research into these issues—simulating PSWs with students and assessing the impact of various techniques—is unsatisfactory. However carefully selected and trained to play the role of conflict participants, graduate students cannot adequately represent the pain, fear, and anger felt by participants in a real intractable conflict, or the complexity of the issues they face. As two authors who have run one of the more respected such studies admit, "one limitation of the current study involves the use of college students. . . . They had neither the knowledge base nor the vested interests of real international negotiators. Thus, it may be inappropriate to use these results to describe or predict the behavior of real-life international negotiators."[16] Moreover, an actual PSW process plays out over several encounters, sometimes over a number of years. It is the repeated exposure to the PSW experience over time, interacting with the reality of the conflict on the ground between sessions, which must be replicated if "gaming" is to adequately capture the PSW for study This is not possible in a research setting. Rouhana's analysis of the issues and concepts behind the PSW is highly useful in setting forth a number of propositions, but we are left with case studies and experience to guide us in further developing our understanding of the PSW.

The PSW in Practice

A number of issues confront the organizer and participants in a PSW process. These include the question of the "rules" that will govern the discussions; the recruitment of participants; the location of a PSW; the question of funding; and a phenomenon known as the "transcultural island effect." The question of how to transfer results of the PSW process to the intended audience will be discussed in the next chapter.

The Rules

For many Track Two practitioners, the "rules" are central to the success of any PSW process, especially at the beginning before participants have built a personal relationship. The rules exist to prevent the workshop from degenerating into an exchange of recriminations and accusations. Much evidence exists from the social sciences that unstructured and unfacilitated contact between people from groups in conflict can perpetuate and even deepen hostile attitudes between them. Conversely, such encounters are more likely to succeed if, to quote Çuhadar and Dayton, "group contact is supported by laws, customs, or institutions."[17] Obviously, the rules established at the outset of a PSW process are not laws in the conventional sense, and there is no enforcement mechanism. They are more to be thought of as a mutually accepted set of customs or norms that participants agree to follow in their interactions within the PSW context. One practitioner, Saunders, has elaborated on the rules as follows:

- Participants will interact civilly, listen actively to each other with attention and respect, not interrupt, and allow each to present her or his views fully.
- Speakers will observe time limits to allow genuine and balanced dialogue.
- Participants will speak from their hearts as well as their minds. Because they need to speak about feelings and relationships behind specific problems, feelings will be expressed and heard with mutual respect.
- Participants will respond as directly and as fully as possible to points made and questions asked. Each will make a real effort to put himself in others' shoes and learn to speak with sensitivity for their views and feelings.
- Participants will try to learn from these expressions of others' views and feelings to increase the complexity of their thinking about the other side and the relationship.[18]

All of this seems to be common sense, but it is important. Interactions in PSWs take place within situations of immense suffering and mistrust, often over many years if not generations. Left to themselves, conflicting parties would be in danger of degenerating into an unproductive recitation of grievances and allegations. Some means must exist whereby the third party can steer the conversation around to a mutual examination of the underlying perceptions and core beliefs which lie at the heart of the conflict. As we noted in the previous chapter, the "power" enjoyed by the third party is limited; it is effectively the power that participants have given her by their acceptance of the rules and of the third party as the voice at the table which will oversee their observance.

In my experience, I have noted that the rules play subtly changing roles in the discussion as a PSW process goes along over time. At first they are quite important. When the parties are meeting for the first time, or the first few times, there will be considerable apprehension and mistrust. Adherence to the rules is a means of convincing all that the discussion will be a fair one, and that all participants will have the chance to make their views known without anyone being allowed to dominate the process. At a first meeting it is often necessary to invest time in allowing the two sides to air their narratives; they must put some things on the table before they are willing to go forward. This can be a difficult time. It is hard for people to sit and listen to the other side recite its narrative without interrupting; the third party must gently but firmly maintain the integrity of the rules. Similarly, when the time comes to discuss these initial statements, the third party must use the participants' commitment to respect the rules to insist that questions and comments about the other side's narrative be reflective and analytical rather than accusatory. The session must not be allowed to lapse into bargaining over whose narrative of the conflict is most accurate. Since bargaining is the normal reflex reaction of many participants when asked to speak about their conflict, it is often not easy to prevent. The rules give the third party an agreed-on means to bring the conversation back on topic whenever it threatens to stray.

As the participants gain confidence in the process, in the third party, and in each other, strict adherence to the rules is no longer quite as necessary. If the discussions have been successful, the urge to score debating points will naturally decline in favor of a growing mutual desire to better understand each other, and ultimately a desire to jointly develop new understandings about the conflict. In these circumstances, the discussion can be more free-flowing with fewer interventions from the third party regarding the rules. But the development of this dynamic takes time, and it cannot be rushed.

While most who are active in the field would agree on the important role that the rules play for the reasons elaborated above, there is a strain of thought from some quarters that mechanisms such as the rules are evidence of cultural bias in this type of interaction. In his studies of conflict between Americans of different racial backgrounds, Kochman argues that white Americans are culturally disposed to favor the kind of logical, orderly problem-solving mode encouraged by such devices as rules.[19] Black Americans, according to Kochman, are more inclined to an interactive style characterized by rapid exchanges in which the orderly turn-taking styles emphasized by the rules is not as prized. Kochman also reports that black Americans in mediation settings are suspicious of outside authorities who establish themselves as arbiters of the conversation.[20] Though such cultural generalizations must be approached with care, these findings do suggest that third parties need to be careful in making assumptions about the applicability of the rules in cross-cultural settings. At the least, the rules must be discussed with the participants in each case and adapted by the consent of all.

One question which arises in PSWs, particularly at the beginning of a process, is whether emotional outbursts should be allowed. In reality, they usually cannot be stopped. Such outbursts are a double-edged sword. On the one hand, they reflect the reality of the conflict. While the rules exist for a purpose—to control and improve communication—they should not stifle interaction to such an extent that the discussion becomes divorced from the harsh reality of the conflict these people are living through. Trying to completely prevent reality from asserting itself at the table can result in a dialogue which seems somewhat unreal. On the other hand, such outbursts, when they are accusatory in tone, can seriously detract from the atmosphere necessary for constructing a process where the deeper issues of the conflict are jointly examined and eventually understood. There are no guidebooks on this question, as everything depends on the circumstances.

In my own experience, outbursts of emotion will happen and cannot be stopped. They can be useful in educating each side as to the depth of feelings that exist on the other—a profound reality check. What the third party can do is appeal to the rules when outbursts do happen, and insist that they do not become personal or accusatory. Accusations are simply not productive and lead to a bad atmosphere that cannot easily be recovered from.

Some practitioners advocate the venting of emotions as a necessary first step before the group can move on to problem-solving. Rothman's "ARIA" model (antagonism, resonance, invention, action) of conflict resolution specifically seeks, in its "antagonism" phase, to bring enmities to the surface as a necessary precondition for later phases.[21] I have never encouraged venting in my own work, but I do not stop it either. I do insist that it take place within the rules. Again, this is an instance where the "art" of Track Two comes to the fore—the ability to manage such difficult moments so as to make something productive come from them, while retaining the trust and respect of the participants.

Recruitment

What kinds of people does one seek to recruit to a PSW process? How does a third party recruit those who will participate? There are no set answers; each process goes forward in its own way.[22] Much depends on the kind of process one is running and the outcomes which are desired (Figure 5.2). As we saw in the first chapter, there are many kinds of Track Two. Projects at the Track 1.5 end of the spectrum, and that are focused on outcome rather than process, will usually seek participants who have close connections to their governments—retired senior officials or others who have intimate connections to those in power. Track Three, or grassroots projects, will be looking for leaders of civil society movements, who are often people who oppose governments. And there is an unlimited range of projects and desirable participants in between. It is important for the third party to think about recruitment carefully when designing a process. The participants recruited need to match the nature of the intended process and its "theory of change." Bringing together a group of people suitable for one kind of Track Two, and then engaging them in another, can lead to frustration.

Whatever the objective of the project, at a basic level one is looking for people who are open to the idea of change without being so starry-eyed as to be unrealistically optimistic. The credibility of the process requires participants who are deeply aware how difficult this will be even as they are willing to give discussions a try—as called for by the concept of "readiness," discussed in Chapter 3. The recruitment of those predisposed to go further for peace than their general populations would consider acceptable is known as the creation of an "easy coalition," and it renders such efforts less than credible in the eyes of their leaders and populations.[23] Moreover, one seeks a range of views in order to have a somewhat representative discussion. While extremes (those

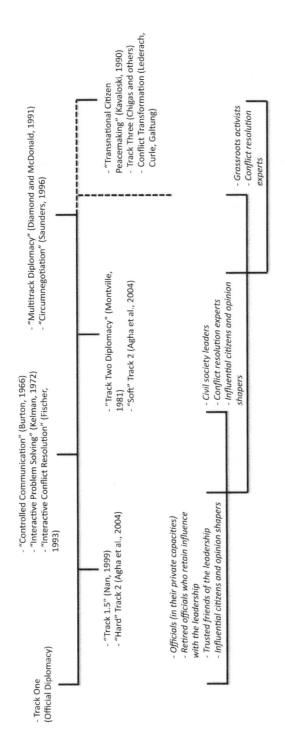

- Track One
(Official Diplomacy)

- "Track 1.5" (Nan, 1999)
- "Hard" Track 2 (Agha et al., 2004)

- Officials (in their private capacities)
- Retired officials who retain influence with the leadership
- Trusted friends of the leadership
- Influential citizens and opinion shapers

- "Controlled Communication" (Burton, 1966)
- "Interactive Problem Solving" (Kelman, 1972)
- "Interactive Conflict Resolution" (Fischer, 1993)

- "Track Two Diplomacy" (Montville, 1981)
- "Soft" Track 2 (Agha et al., 2004)

- Civil society leaders
- Conflict resolution experts
- Influential citizens and opinion shapers

- "Multitrack Diplomacy" (Diamond and McDonald, 1991)
- "Circumnegotiation" (Saunders, 1996)

- "Transnational Citizen Peacemaking" (Kavaloski, 1990)
- Track Three (Chigas and others)
- Conflict Transformation (Lederach, Curle, Galtung)

- Grassroots activists
- Conflict resolution experts

FIGURE 5.2 Major Categories of Track Two and Their Typical Participants

who are unrealistically optimistic about the prospects for change, and those who refuse to even consider it) are not useful at the table, one needs groups from both sides of the conflict who represent a range of views on the issues and different beliefs as to how likely it is that change can be achieved. This makes the conversation more difficult to manage but more authentic and useful in the long run.

Thus while one seeks a group of people who represent different views, it is important to recall the basic requirement that they be people who are intellectually and emotionally open to the idea that change is necessary—even if they represent a variety of perspectives on how possible change will ultimately be. Third parties should not fool themselves into thinking that such a group is necessarily representative of the population as a whole. The wider population can include significant constituencies who for ideological, religious, or other reasons simply do not accept the need for accommodation and change at any level. It is not useful to have these people around the table of a Track Two process, but it must be borne in mind that they exist, sometimes in significant numbers. Moreover, if one is putting together relatively small groups from each side, thereby permitting an intimate dialogue, it would be impractical in the extreme to imagine that six to ten people from each side could represent the totality of views in their societies, particularly if they are drawn from a specific segment of the population, such as elite former officials. One must be mindful of the limits to how representative these exercises can be.[24]

Beyond these considerations, one does need a range of disciplines, professions, backgrounds, and viewpoints. If the project is aimed at a specific technical issue, such as water-sharing, one obviously needs several people around the table who have expertise in that area. But the group should not solely comprise such experts. Often the technical issue in play, be it water-sharing or anything else, is a microcosm of the larger problems that bedevil the relationship. Having people at the table who are generalists in the broader issues of the relationship is important. This may result in a slower discussion, and some frustration for the experts who arrive ready to deal professionally with technical issues on the basis of shared expertise and training, but it will be crucial when the time comes to develop transfer strategies.

I often begin recruiting for a new process by dealing with selected individuals on the two sides—people with whom I have worked for many years and whom I trust deeply—to help identify potential participants. I will talk at length with one or two people on each side to develop an idea of the project and an outline of the kinds of people who might be suitable. I will then ask them to help me find such people, using their own contacts and local experience. Before the first meeting of the PSW I will (resources permitting) travel to meet with all of the individuals on both sides, talking at length with each of the potential participants. There is no set interview process, but one seeks a sense of whether the individuals are going to be suitable. Characteristics I look for include a realistic view of the problem and how difficult it will be to tackle it; a willingness to recognize that the process they are about to embark on will challenge them to revisit their perceptions of the causes of the conflict, even if they believe those perceptions to be right; a propensity to abide by the rules, which are discussed at length in these preliminary meetings; and being connected to their government, even as they also express readiness to look beyond official positions to develop alternate ideas. There is no ideal person who meets all of these criteria, but one looks for a range of people who collectively do.

As a rule of thumb, I have found that personality and general experience matter more than expertise, though both are needed within the group as a whole. It is critical to remember that one is dealing first and foremost with individuals. Though one may be seeking to develop a group from each side which is somehow representative of the middle ground in their societies, they are *people*, not units. They will thus have their own idiosyncrasies and personalities and cannot be selected solely on the basis of their ability to play a foreordained role in the process. Once these people are at the table, a unique dynamic will begin to unfold, one that cannot entirely be foreseen, which the third party will have to manage as best it can.

For all this effort, rarely will the initial group of participants in the PSW be ideal, or even remain intact, as the process goes forward over several years. Some people will move on or drop out of the process (in some cases, they go into government and take the ideas they have learned with them). Others prove not to be the participants one had hoped for and need to be replaced. Further, new perspectives need to be brought in as the process goes along. Sometimes a need for different expertise arises as the discussion shifts to new subjects. Recruitment therefore continues, and the third party should always be on the lookout for new participants. Often this is done in collaboration with those already in the process. One must also make sure that the group does not grow, as through accretion, beyond the small, intimate number required for a real discussion. One of the more difficult things can be letting someone go, yet this is sometimes essential for the health of the process and must not be shied away from when required. Above all, it is in this matter of recruitment that the third party's judgment is on the line. It is here that Saunders's notion of Track Two as an art, and his list of the personal qualities of those who would play this role, are important.

Location, Location, Location

Location is an element of structuring and running workshops that is often overlooked in the literature, but which has a significant real-world impact, in my experience. The selection of a location should not be an afterthought but rather a prime consideration in planning the PSW. As Agha and colleagues remind us, "Track-II talks are convened specifically to foster informal interaction among participants. The purpose of Track-II exercises is to provide participants with a setting that is conducive to achieving such objectives."[25]

There are several considerations. First is the convenience and safety of the participants. In cases where fighting is going on or has recently ended, it can be dangerous for people from the two sides to be seen as having met—dangerous to their reputation or even physically dangerous. The location must thus offer a degree of privacy. Yet participants are busy and do not have much time to devote to travel. The location thus has to be close enough to be accessed relatively quickly; there should be good air connections; visa restrictions and other bureaucratic aspects should be as light as possible. In my work in South Asia, I have tended to use cities like Bangkok and Dubai, for example.

Second, the setting should help remove disparities in the power balance between the participants. Places which appear to offer one side or the other greater "control," either physically or symbolically, must be avoided. This is particularly important for the weaker side in asymmetrical discussions. As Gibb noted, an atmosphere in which one side feels weaker leads to a form of interaction called "defensive communication,"[26] in which speakers spend "a good portion of their time defending themselves, thinking about how to win, dominate and impress the other, how to escape punishment and/or how to mitigate an anticipated attack." Meanwhile, "defensive listening" is characterized by "postural, facial and verbal cues that raise the defenses of the partner in communication."[27] Settings in which one side or the other feels it has power, or even more importantly, where one side *perceives* that the other has greater power, are not conducive to the goals of a PSW. In a study of dialogues between Jewish and Arab Israelis, Maoz noted that unequal power relationships between the two communities often produced great difficulties at the dialogue table, including defensive behavior in place of analytical discussion.[28]

Several years ago, when I was quite new to this business, I was asked to be on a third party panel facilitating an Israeli-Palestinian discussion. I was not involved in the administrative setup of the discussions, which was handled by another group. The group organizing the discussion booked us into a hotel in Jerusalem that both sides could access physically and which offered good meeting facilities at a reasonable price. But what they did not understand was that this particular hotel had been built by Jewish interests in a part of Jerusalem the Palestinians felt should be part of their future state, and it was primarily used to house right-wing religious Jewish tourists from the United States visiting "biblical" Israel, including tours of the settlements. When they learned of the location, the Palestinians simply refused to take part in the discussions. We were able to move the meetings quickly to another hotel regarded by both sides as neutral ground, and the discussions were able to go forward. I learned a valuable lesson the hard way: being asked to facilitate a process is about more than what happens at the table—where the table is situated and how you get there is also critical. Ever since, in all cases where I have been asked to facilitate a process being organized and run by another group, I have insisted on having a say in the logistical arrangements.

Third, while one should avoid overly lavish locations,[29] the comfort of participants is a consideration. This idea is sometimes difficult for those who fund these exercises to grasp, but it is important. Workshop participants are busy people; they are often leading figures within their societies. They are not financially remunerated for participation in the process, participation that can mean several meetings a year over several years, each over several days, including travel (which they usually already do too much of), and that can also involve taking personal and reputational risks. While they should of course participate because they believe in the process, they should not be asked to endure hardship. Good accommodations, business-class airfare, and decent facilities are a mark of respect for those who are giving their time freely and taking risks to participate. I have seen many important people not ask for a penny for their time but balk at spending that time in a setting they view as beneath their status.

Furthermore, a suitable location is a facilitator of relaxed dialogue. Locations which are experienced in offering conference services at a high standard allow the dialogue to proceed smoothly, both during the time at the table and during the informal times—coffee breaks and meals—which are crucial to breaking down barriers and building up the spirit of the group. It may sound trite, but "breaking bread" together is a powerful tool for creating a sense of community among participants in a process. So too are off-site group excursions to cultural or other places of interest. All of this contributes to what Rouhana calls "creating a sense of possibility" within the PSW.[30] This is a difficult task which requires a place within which the participants can step back from the day-to-day realities of their lives and imagine alternate futures. As Çuhadar and Dayton note:

> The designing of social time together during the initiatives is extremely important in facilitating the generation of affective ties. The social time should allow for self-disclosure and the discovery of "commonalities" across categories.[31]

In my own work, I have many times seen contentious points from the discussion table slowly worked through over the dinner table, or during a relaxed walk around a local site of cultural significance. To the funder who, after looking at the website of the hotel I had used for a meeting, grumbled about "Track Tourism" rather than Track Two, I replied, "We are spending all this money on airfares and other costs; a few extra thousand on a nice hotel where we know we will have excellent facilities and a comfortable environment is surely a worthwhile investment." This does not mean that Track Two requires five-star resorts. Smaller, out-of-the-way, intimate locations can be better, and sometimes physical comfort can be compromised for a site of great interest. Whatever the selection criteria used, the location should be a place worthy of the stature of the participants and their investment in time and reputation. Of course, it would be wrong to assume that being in a nice place will always have a positive impact on the discussions; however, being in an unpleasant place will almost always have a negative effect.

Funding

The question of setting naturally brings up the question of how all this is paid for. As a first point, Track Two projects are inexpensive in the overall scheme of things. A dozen airfares and three or four nights in a hotel, along with meals and other conference costs, is not that much when compared to other international gatherings. Even when the third party does not have an independent source of income (as in the case of an academic salary) and therefore requires support, the overall costs of these processes are not prohibitive. But they do have to be paid for. So who pays and why? Funding is invariably one of the first topics potential participants will ask about during recruitment. They are, rightly, concerned that an interest could be supporting the process out of a desire to exert influence, and they will be reluctant to associate themselves with any interest that may have motives contrary to those of their group. The third party must be totally honest in reply. Failure to fully disclose the sources of funds will destroy the credibility of the process, and of the third party, should hidden sources of funds be revealed later.

Several times I have been approached by various interests who wanted to help pay for a PSW but who insisted that their sponsorship be kept anonymous. Sometimes these were governments who may have wished to influence the process or whose motives were benign but who were concerned that their sponsorship would have been controversial if made public. Sometimes they were wealthy individuals from one side in the conflict who did not wish their sponsorship to be revealed lest it cause them problems at home or taint the process. In all cases, I have turned down any funds which could not be disclosed to the participants in the process. The risk is too great.

Full disclosure means that one must invest significant time in fund-raising. As Fisher has noted, a catch-22 exists around the issue of funding as it applies to Track Two:

> To do the work, you need funding. However, to demonstrate that you deserve the funding, you need to do some of the work, because this convinces funders you can meet their requirements and produce positive effects. Because you cannot do the work, because you do not have funding, you cannot demonstrate that you deserve funding. There is nowhere to go.[32]

There are two primary sources of potential funding: official funds, and foundation money. With respect to official funds, there is a debate in the field over whether to accept them. Some scholar-practitioners, such as Mitchell and Banks, believe that all government funding, from any government, should be rejected. They speak of "the dangers of being supported from government funds (which will give the impression that any proposal for a problem-solving exercise is merely another, if more subtle, attempt to further national interests.)"[33] Others, myself included, will take funding from governments but only if it comes from governments that are seen as acceptable to the participants; if it is provided in a "hands off" manner (the government does not manage the project); and if the source can be disclosed to the participants. Obviously, these points, except the last one, require some discussion and negotiation. The question of what makes a government acceptable is interesting. While certain countries, such as the Scandinavian states, are widely seen as acceptable because they are not usually perceived as having a direct interest in a dispute, money from the United States or from countries with historical interests in a given region, such as Britain or France, can be trickier, though it can still be acceptable. In fact, I have experienced occasions when participants actually *wanted* at least some US government support as a sign of engagement from Washington, but they also wanted it to be "hands off" in the sense that I would be running the project and US money would not be the sole, or even majority source of support. It is particularly important in these cases that the funder be disclosed up front to the participants and that their views be sought on whether this type of arrangement will work.

The question of hands-off money requires discussion between the third party and the potential funder. It is naïve to expect a government to simply hand over money with no expectation of a say in the process. The question is about what say is expected and how it will play out. I do not accept funds if the funder, be it a government or otherwise, believes it will get to dictate such matters as who comes to the meeting, what the agenda is, and so on. Since the third party will take the blame if the process goes wrong, so too it must have the ultimate freedom to act in these respects. Also, participants from the conflict must play the determining role in developing the process as it gets going. Still, it is only natural to listen to ideas or suggestions the funder may have. Obviously, much personal investment in time is required to get to know the funder and develop a close relationship of mutual respect.

An interesting wrinkle that can come with official funding is when a country's policies impose limits on how the money is spent. This is often a source of great frustration to officials in the country itself, yet laws must be respected when public funds are being used. For example, some years ago in pulling together a Middle East dialogue partly funded by the US government, I was told I could not use US funds to pay for Iranian participation due to US law. However, the US government funder also told me that it was particularly important to them that there be Iranian participation in the project, as official contacts were impossible and the chance to engage Iranians unofficially was a prime consideration in funding the project. In this case, I was able to get a non-US source of funds to pay for the Iranian participation, while US government money paid for the rest.

Foundations are another source of funding. The better-known ones, such as the United States Institute of Peace, Ford, Rockefeller, and Carnegie, in the United States, and others in Europe, generally have good reputations for hands-off policies, and their funding of these dialogues is seen as consistent with their broad missions. Other foundations have an agenda. As Burgess and Burgess note, "Their RFPs (Requests for Proposals) are very specific, and they essentially want to find someone who will carry out a process that they, the funders, have designed."[34] There is not necessarily anything wrong with this, but care must be taken that the project's objective as designated by the funder is consistent with the interests and needs of the participants. Regardless of which foundation one goes to and any conditions it may impose, one again has to be completely open with the participants as to where the money is coming from and what stipulations may apply. Foundation funding, particularly from the better-known foundations, is generally regarded as "cleaner" than government funding, but it is rarely granted for more than a year at a time, is subject to renewal, and can suffer from rapidly changing priorities within the foundation. Sudden change can happen with government funding as well, of course, but at least some official money can often be established on a multiyear funding track, subject to performance reviews along the way. I have found European governments, particularly the Scandinavians, to be good at this.

Beyond the question of who funds, there remain some key issues. The funder must be willing to have its name disclosed to the participants. At the same time, it must be willing to be relatively anonymous because the process may well go on quietly, so the funder should not expect public kudos. Indeed, the existence of the process may not be made public for years, if ever. The funder must also be prepared to invest in a rather tenuous and perhaps controversial process aimed at the deep-seated causes of the conflict but with relatively little chance that the process will lead directly to a breakthrough (more likely, it will contribute a small piece to a long-term reconciliation, which will be important but never made public). For these reasons, Jan Egeland, a Norwegian diplomat who has undertaken many mediating roles, both as an official and in unofficial capacities, refers to these investments as "venture capital for peace,"[35] in that the investments are relatively small and the chance of success per investment is also small, but the potential payoff is great. Egeland goes on to state that

> international diplomacy is surprisingly underprepared in terms of providing the personnel, the expertise and the material support necessary for effective multiparty peace facilitation. Sufficient discretionary funds . . . are needed to flexibly finance meetings, travel, expertise and logistics in an often prolonged negotiation process.[36]

Often the third party works with multiple funders, and the funding arrangements evolve over time as a project goes forward. An India-Pakistan Track Two that I have been running for some years, known as the "Ottawa Dialogue," began with funding from the Canadian government for a single meeting in Ottawa. When the regional participants decided they wanted to continue, the Canadian government decided not to extend its funding because of budget cuts and other considerations. The US government did agree to fund ongoing work. As the dialogue has developed into a group of discussions around different issues, additional funds have been obtained for the various dialogue tracks from combinations of the US government, the Danish government, the UK government, the US Institute of Peace, and the Carnegie Corporation of New York. Specific meetings and activities have been funded on a one-off basis by the Hoover Institution at Stanford University and by the Hewlett Foundation.[37]

This kind of juggling of multiple sources of funding is very much the norm for Track Two and it takes time and effort to set up and sustain. Complex and time consuming though it may be to manage such a situation, my experience with multiple funding arrangements is that they can enhance the credibility of a Track Two dialogue for two reasons: they demonstrate that several different authorities value the work enough to support it; and they allow participants to feel that no one funder has an undue degree of influence over the process. Finally, funders themselves generally like it when they are not alone in supporting a project. The fact that others are also willing to assume some of the costs is a form of reassurance and spreads the risks.

The Transcultural Island Effect

The final issue we must deal with in our exploration of the problem-solving workshop is sometimes known as the "transcultural island" or "bubble" effect. This occurs when the participants in an ongoing series of PSWs develop such a bond over time that they effectively become removed from the reality of the conflict—what Rouhana referred to as treating the PSW as the conflict reality, or overemphasizing the importance of the PSW. In the transcultural island effect, participants essentially come to see the continuation of the PSW process as being of greater importance than dealing frankly and honestly with the issues they were gathered to discuss in the first place. The workshops thus become for the participants an "island," removed from the conflict reality to such a degree that the discussions no longer represent anything useful or real.

It is of course an objective of the PSW that the participants should bond and come to trust each other. This is required if they are to open up to each other concerning their fears and aspirations. This idea that the people at the table come to value their relationship with each other highly and thus modify their stands to preserve it is not new to the analysis of negotiations. As Walton and McKersie report in their study of labor negotiations, in some instances, the participants gradually come to see the need to maintain their relationship with their opposite numbers as being as or even more important than defending the positions of their own side: "an awareness of a common experience or fate . . . [between the parties at the table] . . . produces positive feelings between participants. . . . The negotiator comes into conflict with his own organization because he cannot, or prefers not to, ignore the demands and expectations of his opponent."[38]

There seems to be an added dimension to this phenomenon when discussions are taking place in secret and there is a danger involved for the participants if they became public. In this case, a degree of joint enterprise is built into the process from the start, keeping the shared secret of the talks, which can build a strong bond of trust over time. Moreover, participants are a very small minority within their larger societies or organizations (most of which do not know that the discussions are underway) and are being exposed to new ways of seeing the conflict. This leads to the reinforcement of a shared sense of the dialogue as a special place which is separate from the reality of the conflict as experienced by most. As Dochartaigh reports in his study on the unofficial dialogues which went on for many years between British officials and representatives of the IRA:

> The higher levels of trust required in secret contact may well intensify the need for strong personal relationships if contact is to be sustained. Back channels gain an added intensity by binding individuals together through their shared secrets. Negotiators on both sides are very susceptible to criticism from those on the other side because of strong opposition to the very act of "talking

to the enemy." As a consequence, their professional and personal reputations are extremely dependent on the discretion of their opposite numbers.[39]

As noted, this sense of the special quality of the discussion space is necessary and can be beneficial. However, when it reaches the point where it is an impediment to frank exchanges of views, especially when participants are dealing with uncomfortable but necessary subjects, it begins to erode the usefulness of the process. In such circumstances, the third party must step in to "shake things up." This can be done by adding new people to the process, who have not been part of the development of the special relationship that the others have come to enjoy over time. This must be done extremely carefully, as confidentiality issues are involved and one does not want to destroy the process by bringing in people who are too disruptive to the character of the discussions. A third party can also use what power it has to steer the agenda towards difficult issues which the participants may be avoiding. Again this must be done with care, as the bulk of the effort to this point has been to create a space where participants feel that they control the process, not the third party who is there to facilitate.

The limited research on the matter shows that particularly effective Track Two projects are those which manage to create a transcultural island within which participants can work extremely closely, while also permitting individuals on each side to remain equally members of their own national groups. While being able to work within the transcultural island, they remain able to credibly take part in and lead discussions within their own group and not be seen as people who have sold out because of their close relationship with people from the other side. In an Israeli-Palestinian project on water, it was found that

> the group members maintained their separate salient group identities as Israelis and Palestinians and at the same time succeeded in forming a superordinate group identity based on their professional group memberships as "water professionals" who share the same views and values about water regardless of their national group memberships.[40]

Conclusion

As this examination of the problem-solving workshop has shown, there are no all-encompassing answers to any of these practical issues, but there are useful guidelines for planning and conducting such meetings that are supported by experience and, in varying degrees, by research. Research and theory have helped us understand PSWs in greater detail but cannot provide hard-and-fast answers, not least because there are such different theoretical perspectives on key questions. Moreover, theory has limitations because such encounters are profoundly human experiences which defy detailed categorization; no two PSWs will be the same. The third party and the participants must feel their way through the PSW process, informed by theory but guided ultimately by common sense and the intangible qualities that make one good at facilitating or participating in this sort of high-wire interaction.

There is one more thing we must examine: what happens to the ideas and proposals which, hopefully, are developed in the PSW process? How do these ideas and proposals go from the PSW into the hands of an intended audience? And what is the intended audience, anyway? Finally, how do we measure the results of Track Two? These issues are known as the questions of "transfer" and "evaluation," and we turn to them in the next chapter.

6 On Impact: Transfer and the Evaluation of Track Two

IT IS A DEFINING CHARACTERISTIC OF TRACK TWO THAT
the process is meant to influence events in some way. These discussions are not, for want of a better word, "academic"; they are meant to affect the real world. One of the key questions in the field of Track Two thus surrounds how to promote the "transfer" of the results of these processes to their intended audience. Absent a concerted effort to transfer the results from the problem-solving workshop to places where they can make a difference, the exercise has been for naught in terms of influencing the situation. Transfer is thus the business of moving the results of Track Two dialogues into the official process, or into a broader dialogue in each society, or to some other audience. Sometimes it can mean transfer to multiple audiences simultaneously.

In thinking about transfer, Track Two practitioners must always ask themselves, "Transfer of what to whom?" The answer to this question will influence one's strategy for transfer and the tactics selected to achieve it. If one is engaged in a Track Two process meant to influence decision-making elites, then a strategy for gaining the confidence of that elite as a prelude to exposing them to new ideas is called for. This carries with it a number of issues. Secrecy, for example, may well be necessary in order to give elites time to consider new proposals without the pressure of having to respond immediately in public—which usually brings about a "no" if a new and perhaps radical approach to a long-standing problem is being proposed. If however one's objective is to influence a broader mass of people in society, possibly as a prelude to inspiring *them* to force change at the elite level, then a media-savvy, grassroots approach is called for. In some cases, one will be trying to do both, though perhaps in a sequenced manner.

Transfer is thus a complex, risky, and subtle business. It is difficult to get right and easy to get wrong. Done improperly, or too soon, and the results of many years of quiet work may be wasted. Done too late, and a potentially transformative idea may be overtaken by events before it gets into the hands of those who could make a difference. Done too aggressively, and those who might have been the champions of a new idea will be put off; too softly, and the ideas being espoused may not make it through the noise of a complex and dangerous situation to reach their intended target. In my experience, practitioners and participants in Track Two dialogues often think about transfer only at the end of the process, almost as an afterthought, once they feel they have a "product to sell." This is a mistake; both the third party and the participants should be thinking about and planning for transfer throughout the process, and they should be updating their ideas about transfer as circumstances change.

Beyond transfer is the vexing question of measuring the impact of Track Two. How does one know if these discussions have produced any real result? What is meant by a "result" anyway? These are more than academic questions. If the field is to progress in its understanding of best practices, it is necessary to develop some ideas on how it achieves results against which specific dialogues can be measured and assessed. Moreover, those who fund and support such dialogues want some indication that their money was well spent, not simply in terms of value for money and proper accounting, though that is obviously important, but well spent in the sense that it was a worthwhile investment in affecting policy, as against other possible uses of the same money. As with everything else about Track Two, the answers to these questions are highly context-specific. In each case, those seeking to assess a Track Two effort will have to develop a firm understanding of what the project was intended to achieve and how it was structured: a Track 1.5 project involving retired senior officials and aimed at conflict management should not be assessed by the same metrics as a Track Three project aimed at training grassroots peace activists, for example. Yet even with this broad range of activities, there must be some basic tools and concepts with which the field can measure its activities.

Transfer: The Evolution of the Idea

In reviewing the scholarly work on transfer, one notes an evolution of think-ing that is associated with specific authors who often wrote about their per-sonal experiences.[1] In Burton's first effort in Southeast Asia in the 1960s, transfer was predicated on the assumption that the ideas generated would make their way through to the official process because he had included people who were from that process or had very close links to it. Burton assumed that these people would take the ideas home and lay them in front of the right audience; he thus spent little time planning for the transfer of the ideas or outcomes generated by his workshops to the official process. Burton's concept of transfer held that the ability to get new ideas directly to decision makers was central; if one could get ideas to the key decision makers, then conflicts could be resolved. In this approach, Burton may have been influenced by his growing belief that official diplomacy was not well suited to resolve intrac-table, or as he called them, "deep-rooted," disputes; this was one reason why he moved away from the realm of Track One diplomacy to develop alternate methods of dispute resolution. Thus, "once the outcomes of problem-solving had accrued," Burton, in his "controlled communication" workshops, "down-played the role of [Track 1] negotiations, seeing these simply as a discussion of administrative details."[2] As time went on, he became even more dismissive of Track One as a vehicle for resolving deep-seated disputes.[3]

In Burton's first case, transfer seemed to go well and without much obvious effort. In retrospect, and even at the time, questions were raised as to whether Burton's Southeast Asian experience was easily replicable. He believed strongly that it was, but others noted that the dispute he and his colleagues had tackled was not a particularly long-standing one, and the parties may well have been looking for a way out anyway. If true, this would indicate that the conflict was not so deep rooted as he imagined and that the parties were unusually receptive to the ideas the workshops were generating, in contrast to disputes which are long-standing and intractable. Obviously, this situation would have the effect of greatly facilitating transfer and making Burton's model of a "decision-maker-centric" approach more effective here than it might elsewhere be. Subsequent history proved this to be the case.[4] As Çuhadar notes,

> the early practitioners of Track Two diplomacy assumed that the innovative analysis of conflicts and positive changes in the attitudes in the Track Two

meetings [would] later on transfer to the official policymaking automatically. However, this idea was simplistic and inadequate to help understand the processes that take place.[5]

Kelman and others began to consider transfer as an issue requiring further thought in the early 1970s. A central goal of their interactive conflict resolution model was to influence Track One; they acknowledged that transfer is complex and difficult and that Track Two practitioners have to think seriously about it and plan for it. Two basic elements were identified: changes in individual perceptions and attitudes that participants in the PSW experience originally held; and how these changes went on to affect the larger policymaking process on both sides.[6] Kelman developed further ideas on how transfer takes place. He identified three key ways in which Track Two assists Track One and also transfers its results to Track One:

- Developing cadres of people who may take part in future official negotiations
- Providing specific substantive inputs into a negotiation process, or even discussions about the possibility of negotiations
- Developing a political environment in which negotiations may be possible[7]

One problem of transfer, known as "re-entry," is how those who have participated in PSWs, and whose attitudes have been altered by the experience, are affected when they "re-enter" their own societies.[8] The great majority of their compatriots will not have been through the PSW experience, and their attitudes about the other side will not have had the opportunity to be transformed. This is true for re-entry among one's professional peers and for re-entry among the general public, although the specific issues attending these forms of re-entry are different. The essential question is thus twofold: will PSW participants revert to their previous attitudes once they re-enter their familiar surroundings, or will they attempt to introduce into their domestic debates the notion that change is possible? How can Track Two processes be designed to promote the latter?

Writing in the early 1980s, Mitchell considered the issue of re-entry in detail.[9] Like Kelman before him, Mitchell distinguished between two separate but related levels of transfer. The first is the *internal* effectiveness of a PSW process—how the perspectives and views of the participants themselves are changed by the workshop process. The second level is the *external* effectiveness of the PSW—how the broader nature and course of the conflict are influenced by the ideas that come out of the PSW, and how participants in the PSW can contribute to this. Mitchell acknowledged that objective factors on the ground influence how much decision makers will be able to use the results of Track Two, even assuming they are disposed to do so. This leads to the recognition that real peace is made as a result of a complex and interlocking web of factors, and that Track Two, however important in getting a dialogue going, is but one of these.

Mitchell also pondered the question of how "close" participants in Track Two exercises should be to the leading figures in their respective power centers. Proximity is a double-edged sword, he noted. The closer the participants are to powerful people back home, the more likely they are to enjoy a relationship of trust with key decision makers and thereby engage personal networks to effect transfer. This is the most direct and arguably the most effective means of transfer, as Burton surmised. On the other hand, the closer participants are to power in their respective societies, the more likely they will conform to the perspectives and interests of those in power and thus resist the kinds of far-reaching ideas for change that may be necessary in a situation of long-standing and intractable conflict.[10] This idea has surfaced in the writings of several people who study Track Two.[11] In the context of Southeast Asian Track Two (even though this is a very different kind of Track Two conducted for different purposes), it was summed up by Kraft as the "autonomy dilemma." Kraft states:

> The linkage between tracks one and two provides track two diplomacy with access to privileged information and a position from which it could directly influence official policy. At the same time, it affects track two's potential for critical thinking, and, consequently, the quality of analysis and discussion. This problem is becoming more evident as the distinction between the tracks becomes increasingly blurred.[12]

In other words, if a critical element of a Track Two project's success is that participants be able to "think outside the box" and come up with novel ways to address intractable problems, then people close to those who wield power may not be the best participants—they may resist ideas that require significant changes in the prevailing order. On the other hand, those who are most disposed to reframe the conflict in new ways may not have the ear of those in power who can make change happen. If the intended audience is the grass roots, in an attempt to force change in the elite, that is a different matter. As noted in Chapter 3, this issue cuts to the heart of whether a Track Two process is about the management, resolution, or transformation of a conflict.

This is another indicator that one is looking for extremely rare people when one recruits participants for a Track Two. If one hopes to affect official policy but *also* to produce new ideas which challenge existing norms, then participants should be both well connected and able to think outside the box. Furthermore, they should have the courage to explore new ideas and then take them into the official process or into the public debate in their respective societies, even if the ideas are seen as being radical. In this sense, the qualities that Lederach discussed as defining "moral imagination" (explored in Chapter 4 in the context of the third party) also apply here, particularly in the ability and willingness to look beyond the present, and to take risks.[13]

In 1996, Keashly and Fisher stated that there was "no conceptual model of the transfer process itself, let alone a comprehensive model of political decision-making and interstate relations into which it could be integrated."[14] In the late 1990s, Fisher developed a schematic model of transfer.[15] This model depicts the likely lines of transfer between Fisher's interactive conflict resolution (ICR) model and key official constituencies (Figure 6.1). It locates ICR closer to "intersocietal relations" than to "international politics" (Track One) but shows the paths by which Track One actors can be affected by Track Two along the dotted lines of "transfer effects." The exact mode of transfer will of course depend on the specific circumstances, but Fisher's model represents an important attempt to lay out the key issues and actors.

Though Fisher's model appears to depict likely lines of transfer in cases where two relatively equal and largely similar parties are engaged in a dispute, he readily acknowledges that in reality such situations are rare. Most disputes are characterized by asymmetry of power and differences in the composition of the disputants—between states and substate actors, for example. The model also assumes that ICR will in most cases be located closer to civil society dialogue than it is to official diplomacy. If one "moves the dot" to make the ICR attempt more akin to Nan's Track 1.5 diplomacy,[16] or Agha and colleagues' hard Track Two,[17] some interesting things happen to the transfer lines. If the dot representing ICR is located close to the "official interactions" line, the transfer effects lines will run more immediately towards the diplomacy and leadership circles.

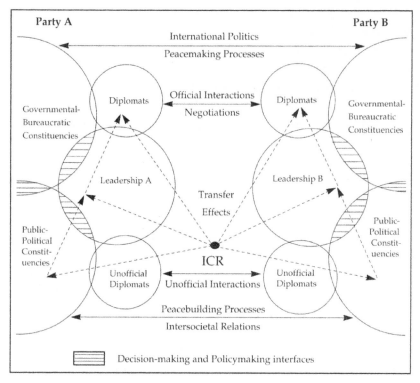

FIGURE 6.1 A Schematic Model of Potential Transfer Effects of Interactive Conflict Resolution (ICR). Source: Fisher, R.J., "Interactive Conflict Resolution" (Syracuse: Syracuse University Press, 1997), 202. Reprinted with permission.

Fisher's model is a useful tool with which to understand transfer dynamics. But its applicability in reality (as with any social science model) requires an intimate knowledge of the individual parties—their characteristics and asymmetries. It also requires a well-developed sense of the fluid dynamics of the discussions; of the way events flow and circumstances change over the life of a project. It could be that the dot will move several times over the life of a Track Two project. The "transfer effects" lines will adjust correspondingly. In his edited volume looking at different cases of transfer, Fisher identified critical factors influencing the extent to which transfer is likely to be possible. These include such matters as the kind of conflict (interest-based or needs-based); the power balance between protagonists; the stage of the conflict in the conflict cycle (see Chapter 3); and the "culture of conflict" which the groups in conflict assign to their struggle.[18]

Regarding the mechanisms of transfer, Fisher's findings showed that successful transfer takes place on a variety of levels and through a variety of means. These include personal contacts between Track Two participants and leading figures in Track One, often based on trust established over several years; private briefings and memos to leaders and also to members of the larger bureaucratic establishments on both sides; and speeches, interviews, op-eds, and other mechanisms intended to reach a more public audience, where that is deemed an appropriate and useful goal. Notably, however, Fisher pointed out that "on a more sombre note, the evaluation of transfer mechanisms and effects is in an anemic state. . . . The most common measure of success were positive comments by officials from the parties or third parties who maintained that the unofficial work had made a significant contribution to the peace process, whether or not it had culminated in a resolution at that time. . . . Overall the evaluative element of the work appears to be thin and in need of increased attention."[19]

Fisher introduces once again a key question which arises in assessing transfer and, more generally, Track Two: how do we evaluate its contributions? Much of what happens takes place privately, or has an incremental effect over time (if it has an impact at all). Rouhana's criticisms of the lack of methodological rigor with which most problem-solving workshops are structured and assessed carry over to the issue of transfer as well.

Another set of critical concepts for the evaluation of transfer comes from Fitzduff and Church.[20] In looking at how NGOs affect official policy, they have divided transfer strategies into two broad categories: *insider* and *outsider* strategies. Insider strategies seek to influence elite insiders, either the decision makers themselves or those close to them. Most Track Two at the elite level is explicitly aimed at insiders; the potential shortcomings of the approach are alluded to in debates over such concepts as the autonomy dilemma. Outsider strategies are aimed at influencing public opinion and civil society. Often the objective is to affect official policy from the bottom up, it being felt that elites will not change their ways unless confronted with significant pressure to do so. This kind of transfer has only more recently come in for serious scrutiny and study.[21] It is even more difficult to quantify in terms of results than elite-level transfer, but it is increasingly recognized as playing a key role in some circumstances.[22]

In their study of Israeli-Palestinian Track Two over time, Agha and colleagues have probed the internal processes whereby transfer takes place within governments that are receiving the results of Track Two dialogues.[23] In terms of "insider" Track Two, or what Agha and colleagues would call "hard" Track Two, the authors identify the role of an intermediary as one key to transfer. This is someone who acts between the Track Two process and the highest levels of leadership on the official track. Known as a "mentor," the role is defined as "a high level political leader who serves as a chaperon for the talks." Mentors take the risks associated with getting the Track Two going and sustaining it, and they sometimes do this without the leaders' formal knowledge in order to insulate them from negative fallout should things go badly. They also "[bring] the information and impressions gained in the talks, as well as understandings and agreements reached in their framework, to the leaders' attention."[24] Crucially, in identifying the key qualities of mentors, Agha and colleagues note that

> effective mentors may need to meet three requirements beyond access to the top leaders: a belief that Track-II talks may be a useful tool for conflict resolution; sufficient time and energy to initiate, navigate and orchestrate such talks, or at least to monitor these talks on a regular basis; and a readiness to "enlarge the envelope" by encouraging Track-II talks without necessarily obtaining their leaders' approval for the talks—or at least not initially, when the results of the talks are far from certain.[25]

At least in this case, then, transfer seemed to depend on the existence of a key individual or individuals who were within government and who were able to act semi-independently in order to provide the Track Two process with cover and support while simultaneously shielding political leaders from exposure. Many of the personal qualities identified by Lederach as constituting "the moral imagination" seemed to be at work here.

Çuhadar explored transfer in the context of specific Track Two projects between Israelis and Palestinians on the questions of water and Jerusalem.[26] Building on the work of those who had studied this problem before her, Çuhadar noted that transfer can happen in three directions: upwards (to policy elites); sideways (to others involved in conflict resolution or dialogue projects); and downwards (to grassroots, civil society actors). In a sense, Çuhadar's upward transfer is akin to "insider" strategies, while her downward transfer is similar to "outsider" strategies. Çuhadar's identification of sideways strategies is an interesting and previously neglected element of transfer and speaks to the fact that Track Two projects can influence each other, both simultaneously and sequentially. I have seen ample evidence of the sideways effect when working on long-standing issues which have been the subject of repeated Track Two efforts over time. Ideas explored some years ago in one Track Two process, which has since lapsed, can be reevaluated and updated in a subsequent Track Two effort to take account of new developments. Often participants from the earlier Track Two are still active and revive the idea in a new Track Two. Sideways transfer can also be simultaneous, when more than one Track Two is going on at a time and some participants are active across the different efforts—a kind of "cross-fertilization."

My own experience, particularly in South Asia and the Middle East, has been that Çuhadar's three target groups (upwards, sideways, and downwards), or Fitzduff and Church's "insider" and "outsider" strategies, are not necessarily exclusive of each other, though most Track Two processes aim primarily at one, or (in the case of Çuhadar) perhaps two, target audiences. If multiple target levels are being aimed at, there usually has to be a sequencing strategy. For example, if the primary intention is to influence Track One officials, it must be recognized that officials often resent hearing the results of a Track Two discussion at the same time they are released publicly; officials want time to absorb and reflect, and they require time to prepare the political and bureaucratic ground for policy changes before being forced to respond publicly to new ideas. Even those individuals within Track One who support what is happening—Agha and colleagues' champions and mentors—need time to prepare the ground. If results are released upwards and downwards simultaneously, the response at the official level may be a reflexive no. This happened to a Track Two I was facilitating between India and Pakistan, when an idea for a far-reaching "confidence-building measure" that had been developed in a PSW was placed on the internet prematurely by a participant in the process and then seized on by those in the two societies who were opposed to any compromise. This premature disclosure helped to create a public controversy before the champions of the idea within the Indian and Pakistani governments had time to prepare for a more nuanced internal debate.

The case of transfer intended upwards toward elites can be further subdivided, according to Çuhadar, into two categories: transfers intended to affect the official *process* of negotiations, and transfers intended to frame an *outcome* of an official process. The latter is the rarest and most difficult form of transfer and depends on timing as much as anything else.[27] This distinction between process and outcome adds a necessary layer of complexity to our understanding of how transfer affects Track One. All too often we seek evidence that a Track Two dialogue has directly affected the outcome of a negotiation, when it is more appropriate to look for evidence that the ideas generated by the dialogue somehow stimulated the official process to look more deeply at issues. Even if Track One adopts outcomes different from those which the Track Two process had suggested, Track Two may still have had an impact by virtue of opening doors to new thinking.

Of course, it is much more difficult to quantify and measure this kind of transfer. In her analysis of the cases of water and Jerusalem, Çuhadar found an impact had been achieved by various Track Two projects in educating officials from both sides (and the United States) on complex points they had been unaware of, or had initially given short shrift. This was particularly so for the Palestinian side, which lacked the negotiating and expert infrastructure to probe these issues deeply at the official level, and which benefited greatly from expert inputs from Track Two discussions. Again this is an example of Track Two discussions having had an impact, if difficult to measure, on the *process* of official negotiations, if not necessarily a direct impact on the outcome.

Broadly speaking, Çuhadar's findings indicate that Track Two is relatively poor at transferring specific policy proposals into official negotiations, particularly if they are expressed in terms of "draft agreements." My own experience, both from government and as a Track Two practitioner, is that officials prefer to come up with written agreements themselves and are skeptical of documents or draft agreements which are "negotiated" between nonofficials, even those who once were officials. They prefer to receive concepts or ideas, which they can then translate into documents over which they will feel some ownership. Of course, sometimes a Track Two will deliberately try to "negotiate" an agreement to make a point. The "Geneva Initiative" is an Israeli-Palestinian Track Two which has set out to develop a detailed version of a final Israeli-Palestinian peace agreement in order to demonstrate that it can be done—that acceptable solutions can be found. They have done this because they feel that some politicians and officials on the two sides are making too much of problems and using them as an excuse not to negotiate an agreement, which would require each side to take on powerful internal constituencies who do not want to compromise on certain issues.[28]

But this strategy of using Track Two to overtly jolt Track One forward is comparatively rare. More often, where Track Two can make a contribution, if the political environment is "ripe" and officials are prepared to receive its results, is in the development of new concepts and ideas which officials can then further develop into written agreements. Track Two often plays its greatest role then in assisting the *process* of developing new ideas and incorporating them into negotiations, rather than in necessarily providing specific *outcomes* to officials. More broadly, Track Two can help the two sides learn more about each other and develop more accurate understandings of the complexities each side must deal with. In this sense, Track Two is useful in breaking down previously monolithic interpretations each side may have held of the other, and allowing for learning and differentiation about the deeper realities and constraints that the other faces.

On the key question of *how* this transfer takes place, Çuhadar's research shows that

> there were mainly four transfer mechanisms used in both water and Jerusalem initiatives. These were: (1) exporting key influential participants from Track Two initiatives to negotiations and policymaking institutions, (2) contacts and consultations with decisionmakers and/or official mediators, (3) serving as advisors to policymakers of negotiation teams, and (4) creating, publicizing, and sending artifacts comprised of ideas, maps, and policy recommendations for decisionmakers' attention.[29]

In short, and this is also borne out by my own experience, transfer is largely done by people. The role of papers, either broad conceptual papers or draft agreements, can of course be useful in summarizing the ideas in play. But these papers will not be trusted by senior officials if they seem to come out of the blue. In cases where transfer was successful, participants in the Track Two process went on to become participants in the official process, or were able to call on extremely close connections—often built on many years of trust—to those running the official negotiations. These people were able to interpret the papers to their official colleagues, because they were intimately familiar with the papers and the colleagues. In this sense, an indirect and difficult to measure aspect of transfer is the transfer of skills, knowledge, and understandings which had not previously existed in the official track.

Writing about Track Two in the Southeast Asian context, Capie has also probed the question of how and when transfer takes place in that regional setting. As noted by Kraft and others, Track Two in this case is noted for its particularly close relationship to Track One. But Capie tells us that we should not just assume that the results of such dialogues always find their way into official action.[30] He shows that such dialogues have had high-water points of influence, usually during moments of rapid change when officials were searching for new ideas and constructs, but he also shows that such dialogues are not so successful in stimulating official changes in times of relative stability when officials do not perceive themselves to be in *need* of new ideas—if success is defined as promoting change that makes it into official channels. Above all, Capie tells us that certain factors must be present for unofficial dialogues to "succeed" in terms of directly bringing about change at the official level:

- Structural opportunity: a moment when the regional system is looking for new ideas and policy proposals
- Sound ideas: ideas which are viewed by regional governments as realistic and also capable of addressing the needs of a moment when there is great flux
- Influential proponents: people who are regarded by regional governments as trustworthy and whose ideas will be listened to by elites

Capie then notes that these conditions do not come together all that frequently. In a way, he is describing the qualities of a "ripe" moment as defined by Zartman and others (Chapter 3). Does the fact that such moments are rare invalidate an ongoing unofficial dialogue process in the region? Proponents, especially those who subscribe to the notion of "readiness" (Chapter 3), would say no; they would say that maintaining a dialogue creates a structure-in-being which is capable of generating ideas and proposals, and a trusted core of proponents for those ideas who can be effective at moments when Capie's conditions come together. In the meantime, the ongoing development of ideas and concepts has an incremental impact. Gradually, such ideas can suffuse themselves into the official process and into the broader societal discourse. But incremental change in the way people think about complex issues is hard to measure and track. If one is trying to develop hard-and-fast indicators for the "success" of Track Two, this can be a frustrating reality.

Taken beyond the Southeast Asian context, Capie's three conditions are useful in considering transfer more broadly. The implication is that the moments when his three conditions come together to bring about direct transfer are relatively rare. But one must ask whether Capie is referring (in

Çuhadar's terminology) to transfer related to process or outcomes? If the latter, then he is probably right: transfer which directly leads to a changed policy outcome is rare. But process-oriented transfer goes on all the time, often unseen, and in the eyes of its proponents it has had a significant impact on the Asian security environment at the level of ideas and concepts. Job, for example, specifically argues that Track Two's primary impact in Southeast Asia has been "ideational"; that it has stimulated new thinking about basic security concepts in the region and then helped move new ideas into the mainstream political discourse of the region.[31] Acharya similarly argues that a decades-long process of dialogue, much of which took place at the unofficial level, was a primary force in shifting the Southeast Asian region from one of mutual hostility to the emergence of a nascent regional security community.[32]

Some Practical Issues of Transfer

If these are the key issues which surround transfer in conceptual terms, we are left with some issues of transfer in practice. For example, relatively little has been written on what the third party can do to assist in transfer. A notable exception is Cynthia Chataway's work.[33] Looking in detail at the role played by Kelman in helping to transfer the results of his ongoing Israeli-Palestinian workshops, Chataway found that Kelman had used his trusted position to publish, with the dialogue participants' knowledge and permission, key findings from the discussions. This had the effect of putting ideas into play in the wider discourse, which the regional participants in the Track Two were not yet comfortable doing. In effect, Kelman took upon himself the risks associated with putting new ideas onto the agenda, thereby relieving the Israeli and Palestinian participants in his dialogue from having to do so. In this, Kelman was protecting his participants from at least some of the risks associated with the concept of re-entry. As his work became better known and respected by elites on both sides, Kelman was also able to engage leading figures, such as Peres and Arafat, during his trips to the region and transfer ideas to them directly. As a final point, Chataway notes that Kelman as the third party was able to move freely between the two sides in ways the Israeli and Palestinians participants could not.[34]

In reflecting on Kelman's work, Chataway noted that his status as a non-official, who had scrupulously avoided taking on any official role or even receiving any funding from the US government, helped in that he was "less easily associated with the kind of negative expectations that predominate for the politically active, and less easily discounted as having a hidden political agenda." Chataway found that "facilitator analyses may be delegitimized, at least within the societies in conflict if not in the international community, by association with external parties that are perceived to have engaged in coercive influence."[35] Her statement echoes Mitchell's view (Chapter 3) that accepting funds from governments can seriously affect the perceived impartiality of a Track Two process.

In my own experience facilitating Track Two in the Middle East and South Asia, I have accepted funding from the United States, Denmark, and other governments on the firm understanding that my relationship with them would be at arm's length; even so, in some cases those who disagreed with the results of the discussions charged that I was acting as a proxy for these governments. Fortunately, these claims were mostly dismissed, as they were clearly intended to devalue the quality of the work so as to discourage officials and the wider public from examining the ideas on their own merits.

Another issue is that of "asymmetric transfer." There are at least two aspects of asymmetry in the context of transfer. The first is elaborated by Mitchell as the problem of achieving transfer in a situation where a power asymmetry exists between the protagonists in the conflict, and the more powerful side (which Mitchell calls the "lion") lacks interest in the output of the process because it perceives it is "winning." In such cases, the problem is not merely having a good idea and respected proponents of it. The problem is how to induce the more powerful side to change its view on whether exploring compromise is in its interest. Mitchell holds that in such circumstances it is necessary for the Track Two process, as part of its analysis of the situation, to have developed strong arguments which will convince the lion to *cost out the future*. Even if the lion is likely to remain the more powerful actor, there may be arguments that a continuation of the conflict will impose a variety of costs which will mount over time and become painful; better, perhaps, to see if an alternate future is possible before these costs grow.[36]

The second aspect of asymmetry has to do with the efficacy of transfer in any given case: how does one know that transfer is taking place on the other side with the same efficacy as it is on one's own? How does one know if those across the table have the kind of access that is required to effect transfer? How does one know if there is a "mentor" on the other side who is shepherding the results of the talks to where they matter? Absent intelligence into the inner workings of the other side, or informal contacts with figures who can validate progress on an ongoing basis, one cannot know with certainty. Of course, if official discussions are going on at the same time as the Track Two discussions, then presumably the two delegations will note changes in official positions which reflect the learning that is taking place through Track Two. But what if there are no official discussions and knowledge of the other side's internal processes is incomplete?

This lack of certainty is a real problem for Track Two, especially Track Two aimed at influencing outcomes as opposed to longer-term, process-oriented Track Two. If one side erroneously believes that the other side enjoys greater access to its decision-making elite than it actually does, ideas may be sold to one's own leadership in the expectation of reciprocity at an equivalent level of seniority on the other side. When this reciprocity fails to materialize, the entire process can be discredited in the eyes of those who took the risks. In her analysis of the cases of water and Jerusalem, Çuhadar provides examples of unequal transfer, either because of competing channels on one or both sides or because of vastly different levels of access to decision makers.[37] All of this is yet another reason why it is necessary (particularly for those engaged in Track 1.5, hard Track Two, or outcome-oriented Track Two) to have some sense that the other side is approaching the talks at a similar level of seniority and commitment. This may not be apparent at the outset but will have to become so as the discussions go on, or they may fail. The situation is less a problem for those engaged in soft or process-oriented Track Two, as the purpose of such discussions is to develop ideas that will be of use in a broader or background sense. One is not expecting these ideas to show up quickly in official negotiating stances on either side.

Finally, one must consider that situations can sometimes evolve rapidly. A Track Two process which has quietly gone on for some years as a soft, process-oriented exercise can suddenly become a hard, outcome-oriented discussion. New parties may come to power on one or both of the conflicting sides and express greater interest in exploring a possible solution. Some of the participants in the Track Two discussions may go into official service, taking with them a desire to move things along quickly. Track Two practitioners should always have their ear to the ground and try to sense when these moments are happening. Strategies should be in place to deal quickly with rapidly changing circumstances.

The question of transfer is thus critical to Track Two. As experience has been gained in different settings and in work on different problems, the thinking about transfer has evolved considerably, especially since Burton's first efforts in the 1960s. We now regard transfer as a critical issue, one which operates on multiple levels, often simultaneously. As we have come to recognize different kinds and models of Track Two, we have come to see the need for different approaches to transfer (Figure 6.2).

Once again, the key question is "Transfer of what to whom? The objectives, mechanics, and dynamics of the transfer process in each case will be vastly affected by how this question is answered. If a Track Two aims at directly influencing the *outcome* of a Track One discussion—an agreement or a treaty—then transfer will require fairly close access to senior figures on the two sides. Under these circumstances, a Track Two process is trying to feed rather specific inputs into an ongoing and rapidly evolving negotiation, or into rapidly evolving considerations of the possibility of such negotiations at the Track One level. Transfer will likely have to be made directly to the leaders on both sides, perhaps through trusted "mentors," and be done with considerable discretion in order to allow leaders to reflect on the new ideas and proposals without having to fight public battles before they are ready to decide whether to accept them.

Track Two projects which are aimed more at broader background questions, also known as the questions of *process*, are somewhat different. Here a rapid acceptance of new ideas by officials is unlikely, for any of a variety of reasons; the objective is to have new thinking gradually seep into the discourse—to create over time new possibilities by slowly influencing how people at various levels think about the issue and by inculcating in them a sense that new approaches are possible. Under these circumstances, transfer will be less about trying to get leaders to buy in to specific ideas right away, and more about reframing the argument on both sides. This may be done by trying to get elites to accept new ways of thinking (upward transfer), or by trying to get society as a whole to debate new approaches to long-standing disputes (downward transfer). Both may be necessary, though discrete approaches may be required in each case.

By contrast, Track Two aimed at stimulating change on the grassroots level in societies in conflict will not direct transfer strategies at officials. In their efforts to *transform* the conflict, such projects will seek to empower and motivate ordinary people to rise up and demand fundamental change. This is an altogether different form of transfer.

Finally, what about cases where the objective of the Track Two is not so clear, or where it evolves quickly from one kind of exercise to another? How

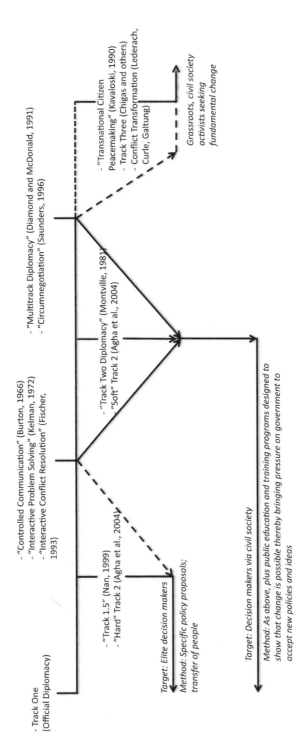

FIGURE 6.2 Major Categories of Track Two and Transfer Targets and Methods

- Track One
(Official Diplomacy)

- "Controlled Communication" (Burton, 1966)
- "Interactive Problem Solving" (Kelman, 1972)
- "Interactive Conflict Resolution" (Fischer, 1993)

- "Multitrack Diplomacy" (Diamond and McDonald, 1991)
- "Circumnegotiation" (Saunders, 1996)

- "Transnational Citizen Peacemaking" (Kavaloski, 1990)
- Track Three (Chigas and others)
- Conflict Transformation (Lederach, Curle, Galtung)

Grassroots, civil society activists seeking fundamental change

- "Track Two Diplomacy" (Montville, 1981)
- "Soft" Track 2 (Agha et al., 2004)

- "Track 1.5" (Nan, 1999)
- "Hard" Track 2 (Agha et al., 2004)

Target: Elite decision makers

Method: Specific policy proposals; transfer of people

Target: Decision makers via civil society

Method: As above, plus public education and training programs designed to show that change is possible thereby bringing pressure on government to accept new policies and ideas to develop transfer mechanisms which can succeed in such ambiguous cases or which are capable of evolving to meet changing needs? This is where things get very tricky. Transfer mechanisms designed to help broad, process-oriented ideas seep slowly into official and public discourse may suddenly be inappropriate if the situation shifts and one finds oneself running a Track Two which has made the jump from soft to hard. In such a case, it is vital that the third party and the participants in the dialogue recognize that the shift is happening and discuss how to modify and calibrate their transfer strategy to accommodate it. Once again, this speaks to the need for transfer to be more than an afterthought; it must be an ongoing issue to which careful attention is paid as the Track Two process begins and then unfolds.

Evaluation: Measuring the Impact of Track Two

Evaluating Track Two projects is difficult, but there are at least two reasons why it is necessary to think about this subject. First, if the field of Track Two is to learn about itself and improve its understanding of what works and what does not, it is necessary to evaluate activities and outcomes. Only by this means can useful comparisons of different techniques be attempted. Second, those who fund and support such activities are, understandably, interested in having mechanisms whereby the impact and efficacy of these investments can be measured and demonstrated.

Much research and discussion have taken place around evaluation.[38] Unfortunately, the means for undertaking evaluations are less than obvious. Each Track Two project is unique, and a wide variety of things go on under the rubric "Track Two." For example, evaluation in active conflict zones presents very different methodological and ethical challenges from those in relatively stable conflict situations, where fighting is less in evidence even though political and other differences remain.[39] A challenge is thus developing the means to evaluate particular projects so that valid comparisons are possible.

Moreover, different constituencies may have different goals for each project, and therefore for what they want from an evaluation. The funder may wish to determine whether good "value for money" was achieved. But how can we determine if the same money spent elsewhere, or in some other way within a Track Two process, would have produced better value? Some funders may wish to achieve a degree of publicity for their efforts—but what of processes which must remain quiet, or which are destined to play only a small role in an overall peace process? What credit can be claimed? Third parties, meanwhile, and conflict resolution experts more generally, may have other issues they wish to see evaluated. They may be interested to know if particular conflict resolution techniques or theories work better in some circumstances than others, for example. They may wish to evaluate whether a given project was conducted in accordance with ethical norms in the field. Participants in a Track Two project themselves may be motivated by still other concerns, for instance a desire to explore the other side's motivations and capabilities over a desire to "make peace" as such. Which of these shall be deemed the most important to be evaluated? Can we consider different things in the same evaluation process?

With a variety of interests and objectives at play, there is also the question of *who* shall do the evaluation. Should it be done by the third party itself? The third party is closest to the process and understands the intricacies and subtleties better than anyone else. Could evaluation be done by the participants in the process? Or should it be done by an external expert, possibly appointed by the funding agency? What issues and biases arise in each case and how can they be corrected to produce a useful evaluation?

There is also the question of timescale for evaluations. Track Two processes rarely lead directly to "peace." They might be thought of as small stepping-stones in a much larger process that unfolds over a long period. As Elliott, d'Estrée, and Kaufman put it, "Because intractable conflicts involve a series of interconnected disputes and complex social dynamics, they usually require a series of interventions. Cumulatively, these efforts may allow for significant change over time, yet each effort by itself is likely to produce only marginal de-escalation in an overall pattern of escalatory behavior."[40] In a comparatively rare kind of study, Malhotra and Liyanage tracked the views of participants a year after a Sri Lankan workshop that was based on the *intergroup contact* theory of change; they found that participants were more likely to have strong feelings of empathy towards civilians and victims on the other side than two similar groups of individuals who had not participated in such a workshop.[41] A similar study, done in the Israeli-Palestinian context, revealed similarly positive findings concerning the impact of encounters between Israeli and Palestinian youth on long-term feelings towards each other.[42] If feelings of empathy are a building block of the eventual acceptance of compromise, these studies suggest that individuals who have taken part in Track Two exercises would be more likely to respond positively to initiatives aimed at resolving the conflict than others who had not been part of such dialogues. However, maybe these individuals were more likely to favor peace in the first place. And is empathy enough? Should we not be evaluating whether the individuals who participated in this PSW actually *did* anything to promote peace? And , if they did not, perhaps they would have under different circumstances; maybe they would have acted had the political situation been ripe. The list of questions goes on and builds relentlessly.

How then do we evaluate the contribution of a specific Track Two process in relation to the ultimate resolution of a conflict if that resolution does not happen for many years after the Track Two process ended, or never happens at all? Perhaps the Track Two made a contribution to the ideas about the conflict, but that contribution lay dormant for many years until the situation had changed to the point that the ideas were able to be incorporated into policy. Maybe an individual or two in a Track Two process had their thinking changed significantly but were unable to do anything until they joined the government many years later. Or perhaps something else influenced their thinking, some other event which pushed them toward the real change that made peace possible. How should we evaluate the significance of a Track Two project in this case? We are dealing with a situation in which individual perceptions have changed, or new ideas have been created, but these have not had time to have an impact on the macroscale. Yet most of those who evaluate projects want to do so when they are underway, perhaps to determine whether to continue funding them; or just after they have concluded, as a means of "wrapping up" the project. For most Track Two, this is far too soon to measure the impact of the process.[43]

In her study on regional-security Track Two processes in the Middle East and South Asia, Kaye argues that the concept of success, and by implication evaluations of how success is achieved, must be approached with care. In particular, it is dangerous to conceive of success in terms of agreements signed or official positions changed according to some sort of schedule or agenda. Instead, we must think of success in terms of new thinking which has been spawned and new relationships which have formed.

> While such dialogues rarely lead to dramatic policy shifts and [the] resolution of long-standing regional conflicts, they have played a significant role in shaping the views, attitudes and knowledge bases of core groups of security elites, both civilian and military, and in some instances have begun to filter the ideas discussed into wider segments of society. . . . Thus track two

dialogues on regional security are not as much about producing high-profile diplomatic breakthroughs as they are about socializing an influential group of security elites to think in more cooperative ways. . . . Such processes are thus best viewed as social processes whereby problems and their responses can be defined by influential groups leading to the *potential* for greater regional cooperation and perhaps other related policy shifts over time.[44]

Yet another issue concerns the multiplicity of projects that are often under-way around deep-seated conflicts. In looking at high-profile conflicts, such as the Israeli-Palestinian or India-Pakistan conflicts, there are dozens if not more Track Two projects of varying types underway at any given time.[45] These projects may be proceeding on the basis of different theories of change; some of them may be oriented towards conflict management, while others are oriented towards the resolution or transformation of a conflict; some of them may involve small elite groups in Track 1.5 discussions, while others are devoted to training in peace and reconciliation techniques at the grassroots level. Sometimes participants will cross between these projects, participating in more than one at a time, or in several over a period of many years.[46] How then to measure any one of these projects to see what specific impact it may have had?

All of this raises the question of the purpose of the evaluation itself. Çuha-dar, Dayton, and Paffenholz have considered evaluation methodologies from the standpoint of the objectives of the exercise.[47] In reviewing the literature and practice, they have developed four broad categories for evaluation:

- "Lessons-learned" studies: these attempt to study several projects to deduce practical lessons that can be used by funding agencies and by practitioners to help them design and conduct future projects.
- "Research-oriented" case studies: a more theoretical form of evaluation, this method uses individual or multiple cases to consider whether and how the experiences of given conflict resolution projects validate, test, or build theory in the field.
- "Key questions/reflection" studies: these attempt to provide a set of questions to help practitioners and researchers better design and implement evaluations themselves, both as projects are ongoing and in retrospect.
- "Overall frameworks and methodologies" studies: these attempt to develop general frameworks of activity in the field against which

specific projects, and strategies within those projects, can be evaluated and improved.

In their study on the debate over "success" in conflict resolution efforts, d'Estrée, Fast, Weiss, and Jakobsen argue that there are three purposes to the evaluation of conflict resolution efforts. The first is to provide feedback based on progress made to date in the dialogue, which allows those running a Track Two process to better meet their goals or to alter them to make them more realistic; the authors apply the term "formative evaluation." The second is "to provide summary information on project or program outcomes and processes for making choices, decisions or policies (summative evaluation)." The third goal of evaluation is "to create knowledge based on accumulating information across projects and programs for use in theory-building and intervention design . . . to evaluate current processes in order to advance theory development and to further improve reflective and ethical practice."[48] In a subsequent article, d'Estrée along with two coauthors reduced this list of the purposes of evaluation to two:

> *Knowledge-oriented evaluation* seeks to accumulate lessons across cases and to build theory, contributing to our overall understanding of conflict. The products of knowledge-oriented evaluations are often aimed at understanding conflict dynamics and improving the general practice of dispute resolution, rather than attempting to improve a specific intervention. . . . [And second,] an approach that integrates evaluations into the conflict resolution intervention itself, to help promote "success" of the intervention, as determined by the disputants, conflict resolution interveners, and other stakeholders. The participants in the process become partners in the evaluation, generating goals for both the evaluation and their own efforts at resolution. Because this evaluation is situated within the intervention and actively involves participants in the process, it is known as *action evaluation*.[49]

But how to perform these evaluations? From the many approaches which have been developed, Deutsch and Goldman identify two which they believe are most promising in the evaluation of projects (which they refer to as "conflict resolution initiatives"): the "framework for comparative case analysis," and "action evaluation research."[50] The "framework" approach emerged from a study by d'Estrée and colleagues on how to consider and measure "success" in this type of work. The authors developed a framework with four categories.[51]

The first category, "changes in thinking," includes a set of criteria concerning new types of knowledge which participants may take away, and what use they may make of it in problem-solving and communicating new ideas. The second category, "changes in relations," contains a set of measurable indicators for whether and how the relationships between the parties have changed. The third category, "foundations for transfer," contains criteria for assessing how a dialogue process has established mechanisms for transfer. Finally, the "foundations for outcome or implementation" category establishes criteria for measuring the extent to which a process has influenced official policy over the short to medium term.

D'Estrée and coauthors caution that these criteria are dynamic and need to be thought about in relation to each other and over time; above all, they are not meant to be linear, as Track Two processes do not unfold in a linear fashion. The authors also caution that each Track Two project should be evaluated on its own terms; for example, a Track 1.5 process aimed at elites should not be evaluated the same way as a Track Three process aimed at grassroots activities. As to methodologies, the authors advocate a variety of unobtrusive means of gathering data for evaluations, including interviews, observations, discourse analysis, and surveys.

A second major evaluation approach identified by Deutsch and Goldman as being particularly relevant to Track Two is "action evaluation research."[52] As the name implies, this approach asks participants in the Track Two process to become involved in an ongoing process of identifying their key goals; discussing why they care particularly about these goals; and identifying strategies which will help them reach them. This process is built in to the project as it moves forward to foster continuous evaluation and discussion of goals, objectives, and strategies. The evaluation thus becomes an ongoing part of the Track Two process itself.

As the Track Two intervention unfolds over time, the evaluation process goes through three phases. The first is called "establishing a baseline." During this phase participants are encouraged to develop individual and group goals and to agree on ways they can be achieved. It is expected that this will be an ongoing and dynamic phase. As the process unfolds, new understandings about the goals will arise and these will be discussed by the participants. As a means of reshaping and tuning the project plan, the next phase, "formative monitoring," engages participants in an ongoing evaluation of the process. In particular, a structured review of the ideas and plans that were established in the baseline phase is built in to the dialogue process to encourage reflection and analysis comparing what the process set out to achieve against what is actually being accomplished. Finally, the "summative evaluation" phase is the period "in which defined criteria of success are used to see how well an intervention has met its own internally derived and consciously evolved goals. As a project reaches an intermediate point, or its conclusion, participants use their evolved goals to establish criteria for retrospective assessment. Stakeholders will, for example, examine whether they have reached specified goals, and ask themselves, 'why?' or 'why not?' They will ask themselves how and what they could have done differently or better."[53]

Three leading figures in the field (Kelman, Saunders, and Fisher) have developed models of evaluation which stress the need to break Track Two interventions into discrete phases and then develop evaluation criteria and methods appropriate to each phase. The idea is that even if an entire Track Two process cannot be evaluated as well as one might like, certain aspects or phases of it may be susceptible to more rigorous evaluations. Over time the accumulation of a body of such evaluations will assist in the development of theory and practice.

Though subtly different, each of these author's models proceeds from the assumption that transfer is a two-stage process: first, one seeks to identify and measure transfer *within* the PSW—that is, changes in the attitudes and ideas of discussion participants themselves; and second, to identify and measure transfer which takes place *beyond* the PSW—steps taken to advocate the ideas to a broader audience. Kelman writes of a "links in the chain" approach, which breaks each intervention into nine steps and provides "testable propositions" for the evaluation of each.[54] Saunders takes an approach which breaks down interventions, which he calls "sustained dialogues," into five phases and then evaluates each phase on whether and how participants were changed as a result of their interactions, and then whether they sought to and were able to change the views of others beyond the process.[55] Finally, Fisher also uses a phased approach which breaks the process down into eight phases and proposes steps to evaluate each.[56]

Of course, these evaluation methodologies are not the only ones available.[57] But they represent ideas as to how evaluation can take place. Interestingly, a number of commonalities emerge from these methodologies:

- They stress the need for the Track Two project *itself* to establish its own goals and then develop ways to measure them rather than be measured against goals established by outside agencies.

- They recognize that projects should be evaluated against their own objectives and methodologies rather than against different Track Two projects which may be active at the same time on the same issue. Each project is sufficiently unique that detailed comparisons between projects are not useful, although generalized comparisons may be possible for descriptive purposes.

- They recognize that evaluation must take place over time and that Track Two projects go through different phases, each of which will require a different approach within the overall evaluation process.

These observations are important. As a practitioner I have found it critical to evaluate each project *on its own terms*. This approach requires much intellectual honesty on the part of the organizers and participants in a process. The alternative—attempts by outside agencies and particularly funders to introduce cross-cutting criteria which allow different projects to be compared to each other—should be approached with great care. Comparisons run the risk of skewing projects towards goals that did not originate with the participants themselves. Some years ago, the Canadian government adopted an approach to project evaluation based on methodologies and criteria in use by its then existing international development agency. Foremost of these was a device known as the "results-based management framework," which had been adopted more widely across the government.[58] There were many reasons for this, including a spate of small but highly public scandals involving public spending. The objective was to put in place procedures to govern public spending which would make sure that public funds were disbursed according to strict and transparent rules, and for purposes that could be evaluated and measured against objective criteria.[59]

Those applying for Canadian government support for a Track Two project were thus required to complete a complex template, filling in a series of boxes that outlined in considerable detail what the project intended to do, how it planned to do it, and what outputs it expected to achieve.[60] This information was assessed to determine whether to fund the project and in its eventual evaluation. Unfortunately, anyone who has actually done a Track Two project will know that such information is practically impossible to provide in advance with precision. Track Two projects are dynamic; they follow their own logic and they evolve as the thinking and experiences of the participants evolves.

This does not mean of course that one cannot establish a general outline of activities and a budget as planning and management tools—one should have a sense of how many meetings there will be and how much they will cost. But what exactly will happen at each meeting, when and where they will be held, and precisely what outcomes will be achieved cannot be known at the outset. And yet those who administer the completion of the "performance measurement framework template" require just such information. The template thus leads to a complex and frustrating discussion. It also encourages the creation of performance indicators which can be "measured." These are largely artificial and may well hamper project development.

Some years ago, for example, I applied for support from the Canadian government for a Track Two project. After much discussion with the official assigned to oversee my application, one "indicator of success" established for the project was the level of seniority of participants in the discussions, both at the outset of the project and as it went along—the progressive recruitment of more senior participants would be seen as a sign of success. As this project brought together retired military officers from various Middle Eastern countries for dialogue about regional security, a built-in bias was introduced towards the recruitment of progressively more senior retired officers. But were these the right people? Were retired generals better than retired colonels in being able to think outside the box and consider new approaches to security? Why should this be so? As we saw earlier, might it be the case that the more senior the participants, the more likely they were to be bound by intellectual and policy orthodoxy rather than willing to think new thoughts? Surely the goal should have been to find the right participants in terms of their intellectual and personal qualities, regardless of their rank on retirement. This artificial criterion, in addition to creating scope for much humor within the project (was a retired Tunisian major general worth two retired Jordanian colonels?), made no sense within the needs of the project. But it was quantifiable, and that was the main requirement from the point of view of the funder.

The adoption of such tools as the results-based performance approach is understandable, but it has stultified the creativity and risk-taking which are the hallmarks of Track Two. Because those running such processes cannot know in advance where the work will take them, and cannot establish measurable criteria for success, this approach is frustrating and distorting. It also limits Canada's ability to play a role in the field.[61]

What is ultimately required of a useful evaluation is common sense. If Saunders is correct in his belief that this work is an art, it must be recalled that art cannot be measured scientifically. Of course there needs to be evaluation for those who fund projects; but projects must be evaluated on their own terms and against realistic criteria, both in the sense of what they seek to measure and in terms of recognizing that flexibility is often a key to Track Two processes as they evolve. Similarly, evaluation for the purpose of developing the field must also recognize that the development of cross-cutting best practices for the field is an important goal, but that no two projects are exactly comparable. Best practices are therefore going to be general in nature and will need to be developed, and then applied and assessed, on a case-by-case basis.

In my own work, I tend to hold the following as keys to the useful evaluation of a Track Two project:

- Focus at the outset of a project on working with participants to identify the theory (or theories) of change that will underlie the project, and then measure the evolution of the project against that, remaining alive to the idea that the operative theory of change may evolve as the project does and this should be factored into any evaluation process.

- Avoid tying the measurement of a project's impact to its influence on official diplomacy within a certain timeframe. It is laudable to achieve an impact on official diplomacy, but you cannot plan on it and you certainly cannot plan for it to happen according to a certain timeframe.

- Measure the changes which take place within the group and the willingness of group members to work for change beyond the group. You can only really observe the changes which take place among the participants in a project—whether they have achieved new understandings as a result of their discussions and are willing to advocate these ideas to audiences outside of the process.[62]

- Measure how transfer is done and track it to the extent you can.

- Above all, remain flexible. Continuously, and in partnership with participants, revisit all of the above steps in an iterative and ongoing evaluation of goals and methods which recognizes that circumstances can change quickly and need to be responded to.

These may sound somewhat flimsy as a set of criteria against which to evaluate a Track Two process, but they represent an honest recognition of the limits of the field. Approaching each of these tasks with care and integrity, one can achieve a reasonable assessment of what is happening, or has happened, which can be useful to funders and to other practitioners.

Conclusion

Transfer and the evaluation of Track Two are among the most difficult challenges confronting the field. They require Track Two practitioners, supporters, and participants to be honest about what they can achieve and how it can be measured. For a field which thrives on ambiguity and, for some, a certain hyperbole as to the importance and impact of their work, having to specify what has been accomplished—which is often far less than one set out to accomplish—and how much impact a process has really had can be disquieting. But this is necessary if the field is to realistically understand what it is capable of achieving, and if it is to be taken seriously by others.

Practitioners and participants in Track Two projects must think about the problems of transfer and evaluation early and often, not merely as afterthoughts. The fluid and dynamic nature of Track Two means that situations can shift quickly. One needs the ability to flexibly adjust the methods of transfer and the basis for evaluation.

Conclusion

TRACK TWO DIPLOMACY IS A MULTIFACETED PHENOM-
enon. It is frustratingly difficult to nail down in both theory and
practice; even more difficult is nailing down the relationship *between* theory
and practice. Many kinds of activities go on under the banner of Track Two,
from those which are closely aligned with official diplomacy and which seek
to manage conflicts, to those which seek to empower grassroots activists who
wish to fundamentally transform the existing order. Other kinds of Track Two
are concerned with training those who will serve as peacemakers within their
own societies; yet others, with stimulating dialogues over regional norms of
conduct and stability in different parts of the world. For those who do not
follow the field closely, it can all be quite confusing. This book has attempted
to provide the reader, whether a practitioner of official diplomacy who has to
interact with Track Two or a student interested in international affairs, with
tools to understand and assess the many versions of Track Two. It has also
sought to situate Track Two within contemporary international affairs, and
to point out and assess the key issues confronting the field. If there are no
hard-and-fast answers to these issues at the end of the book, however, that is
the nature of the beast.

And yet Track Two seems to be a fixture of the international scene that
shows no sign of going away. In all its various guises, it is increasingly called
on, for better or worse. There are more NGOs, individuals, and scholar-practitioners active in the conflict resolution field today than even a few years ago.[1]

They are part of a general process of change in the field of diplomacy which is seeing the increasing empowerment of nontraditional actors and networks in international relations.[2] While some decry the increasing number of "conflict resolution" practitioners who are involving themselves in disputes around the world as a "free-for-all," it is incontrovertible that they are. It thus behooves all who are interested in the field, and in international affairs more generally, to understand Track Two—its possibilities and its limitations. And it is essential that those who practice it should justify themselves by demonstrating a serious approach to their business.

Part of the title of this book, *In Theory and Practice*, is hardly original in the social sciences. In fact, it appears so often and in so many settings that one thinks twice before repeating it. However, I decided to do so because it captures perfectly the objectives I had in writing the book; namely, to bridge the gap between the two with respect to Track Two diplomacy. If these chapters have gone some distance in helping the reader to grasp and break down the barriers between the two, this book has achieved its aim.

For many years there has been a view in some quarters that theory and practice must somehow be opposed to each other—theory versus practice. In fact this was the title of a symposium which formed the basis for a series of papers published in a special issue of the journal *International Studies Review* in 2011.[3] These papers illustrated the basic debate. For those interested in developing theory, activities which cannot be subjected to rigorous, fact-based, empirically informed analysis are suspect. Moreover, activity which does not further the development of generalizable theoretical ideas is suspect in that it is regarded as being of little use to academe. Dismissal, or at least a degree of incomprehension, can greet those who argue that activities which cannot be categorized can still be the subject of good scholarship. On the other side, as Weiss and Kittikhoun state, "practitioners and activists . . . associate 'theory' with abstraction and irrelevance."[4] The requirement for parsimony and generalizability which marks the theorist's endeavor is seen as unrealistic, as no two real-world situations can ever be sufficiently exact to permit comparisons beyond a very abstract level.

The divide between theory and practice is not new, of course, nor is it as great as it is often portrayed. A rich literature exists on how the divide might be bridged.[5] Moreover, there is evidence that academic debates have an impact on policy. The special issue of *International Studies Review* noted evidence that scholarly work has penetrated and affected the policy community in such areas as the development of the "responsibility to protect"; policy on approaches to fragile states; the development of new kinds of sanctions; and international development, to name a few.

But the creation of new ideas and approaches is one thing; actual action by scholars and other nonofficials to bring people together to address their differences is, for some scholars, quite another. They have good reasons to believe that the academy should be wary of involvement in "real-world" issues. History is replete with examples of theories being misused for political ends, bringing much misery.

The upshot of this difference of view has been a wary stance between the two poles. One outcome of this standoff, as Babbitt and Hampson have noted, is that conflict resolution is seen by more mainstream scholars as soft theoretically and has had difficulty establishing itself as a serious field within academic circles.[6] In a special issue of *Negotiation Journal* devoted to the problems encountered by conflict resolution practitioners who seek to advance their careers within traditional academe, many issues were pointed out. These included the fact that developing and managing Track Two projects are not seen as traditional academic endeavors which should be credited in tenure, promotion, or in time away from teaching and committee work; that Track Two projects often require confidentiality, which is resented and scoffed at by those doing more traditional academic work as evidence that something "unserious" is going on; and that the results of Track Two projects are sometimes not susceptible to being "written up" in traditional academic work.[7]

As a consequence, much Track Two work has been done outside of traditional academe, in think tanks or by NGOs. To the extent that some academics have undertaken this work it has been on top of their traditional academic functions, and often through other institutions more suited to the purpose. This may be changing, as many new programs are devoted to conflict resolution and a broader development of graduate schools occurs, which stresses practical as well as theoretical learning and research. But it remains an uphill battle. Gopin characterizes the relationship between what he calls the scholar-practitioners of "conflict resolution practice" and the more classically academic "conflict analysis research" as an "uncomfortable marriage."

On another level, too, the debate between theory and practice is not new to the field of conflict resolution generally or Track Two in particular. As we saw in Chapter 3, the field has developed a series of concerns over ripeness/readiness, theories of change, ethics, and other issues. These may not be debates over paradigms that excite more traditional scholars in international relations, but they are theoretical nevertheless. The debate between Burton and such figures as Avruch over whether Track Two can be generalized to permit the development of a widely transferable set of practices, or whether each project is so unique as to render such attempts meaningless, is an example. This was, essentially, an argument between practitioners who took different views on the best approach to practice, and it was an important one. It represented a debate within the field over fundamental principles.[8] These disputes may strike some as esoteric, but they matter. At heart, they are deliberations over how we are to understand the purpose of Track Two and assess its worth.

It is too easy to simply dismiss one side or the other in these debates. While each may have its bias, the two sides in the theory-versus-practice debate perform important functions for each other. For those oriented towards practice, it may be frustrating to be challenged to explain themselves and their activities according to criteria that may seem artificial. Yet the task of doing so forces practitioners to refine their thinking and to challenge their assumptions on an ongoing basis. As several authors have noted, many Track Two practitioners undertake projects with little if any thought given to what they are really trying to do (beyond the general goal of bringing people together to talk) and why one approach or another might be more effective; in short, they trust their gut as to how to proceed.[9] This is not good enough for a field which seeks recognition as a serious discipline. Practitioners of Track Two should have a well-developed sense of why they are pursuing a certain course—both a theory of practice and a theory of the change their project is intended to achieve—and should be able to explain and defend their actions by reference to it. This requirement is not an intrusion of mindless theory into the real world; it is a basic requirement of good social science practice. Serious Track Two practitioners, who would claim to be doing something other than uninformed trial and error, should be able to describe what they are doing in ways which provide a foundation for useful assessment. At the very least, the field needs to identify its best practices and to discuss them in order to stimulate new insights and the cross-fertilization of ideas.

Ultimately, however, the practice of Track Two is about people, not theories. Those who focus on the practice of Track Two can be forgiven for their exasperation with the requirement that they must fit their activities into theoretical paradigms if they are to be taken seriously by academe. Taken to its logical conclusion, a primarily theory-driven approach would distort practice by placing the requirements of theory-building ahead of the requirements of dealing with actual people—a situation summed up by the apocryphal theorist's question, which drives practitioners mad: "That's all very well in practice, but how does it work in theory?" If practitioners are less able or willing to develop generalizable theories about Track Two than pure academics might like, there is a reason for this which goes beyond lazy thinking.

•••

At the conclusion of this book, have we come closer to answering the basic questions? What is Track Two? What makes for successful Track Two? Much depends on what a given project seeks to achieve—there are many definitions of Track Two and each has its set of objectives and methods. By way of a set of general conclusions, I believe a number of common issues which are relevant across different cases, types, and regions are inherent in any understanding of Track Two.

First, the people involved in a Track Two dialogue must have standing in their respective communities. If the objective of the exercise is to develop ideas which can influence events, the people at the table must have the ability to make themselves, and the ideas they have developed, heard at the appropriate levels when they go home. Of course, this does not mean that all Track Two must be about elites and former senior officials. Sometimes the objective is to influence not governments but civil society. In this case, the best participants might not be officials at all. But they should be people to whom others listen—civil society, business, or religious leaders, for example. The key is influential people, matched to the audience a Track Two seeks to influence.

Second, there has to be the capacity for what might be called a sensible, informed, yet at the same time far-reaching and unconstrained discussion of the issues at hand. The people around the table need to be sufficiently connected to reality and informed to resist pie-in-the-sky thinking about solutions. Fantastical ideas, which may be perfect in theory but simply cannot be adopted in practice, don't help. And yet the discussions should not be prisoner to conventional thinking either. Track Two diplomacy must seek far-reaching ideas for transformative change which are *also* realistic enough to be adopted. That isn't easy, but progress in particularly intractable disputes requires a space for ideas which fall between well-established positions, on the one hand, and fantasy, on the other. Such ideas are hard to find, especially in situations of conflict, but they are the key to real change.

Third, Track Two is intensely collaborative. In that sense it is particularly appropriate that Track Two engagements are often called "problem-solving workshops." The objective of these discussions cannot be simply to reiterate positions; it has to be a collaborative effort to explore what lies behind those positions and then to go to the next step of working together to develop new ideas about moving forward. Track Two is about collaboration across divides in order to jointly develop new ways of seeing and doing things.

Fourth, there is no substitute for the personal commitment of those around the table. If a Track Two process is to succeed, it will require the participants to go to some uncomfortable places; they will need to revisit long-standing fears and revise long-held positions. This is not easy, particularly in cases where lives have been lost, positions are deeply held (which may verge on the self-identity of participants), and tensions are high. Those who come to the discussions must have the commitment to stick with it when the going gets tough; they must be willing to honestly confront their long-held views and positions and listen with respect and empathy as the other side does the same. And the third party must also be fully committed to the process and willing to hang in when the situation gets difficult, as it almost certainly will.

Fifth, debates over the "right" moment to commence a Track Two process, which involve discussion over such concepts as "ripeness," are interesting but often beside the point in the real world. Taken to extremes, they tend to place a discussion of when to launch a Track Two project into the context of whether and how it can produce an outcome which will have a tangible impact on official diplomacy, and within a certain timeframe. Much time is spent trying to plot out how a dialogue might take place at just the right moment (and indeed over how to identify such a moment), or how a dialogue that has already begun might be sped up or altered to take advantage of a potential development. When one is working the field, this can be a mug's game, especially at the outset of a Track Two process. Of course, these are not inconsequential matters, and considerations of how to transfer or otherwise affect Track One are important. But they should not dominate thinking about when and how to commence a dialogue; most Track Two projects cannot be so exquisitely timed as to be able to come along at just the right moment. Indeed, most often "just the right moment" will be the product of chance events and coincidences over which no one has any control. In most cases, Track Two dialogues should commence with more general objectives in mind: can a group of serious, credible people be brought together for an in-depth dialogue which will begin to

open up new thinking and new possibilities? If there are possibilities for progress on thorny issues, such dialogues can play a role in helping to open them
up by showing that new thinking is possible. Often it is the "transfer" of the
idea that serious people believe that change is possible that is the most important product of a Track Two process, especially in its early phases.

Sixth, the debate over whether the management, resolution, or transformation of conflicts is preferred is an important discussion, but it can take the
field into some rigid and not very useful places if allowed to become a dominant issue. Certainly, one should have an idea where one is going as a Track
Two dialogue begins. But these processes can also evolve; having too rigid an
understanding of the kind of process one is engaged in can obscure opportunities for such movement. Moreover, excessive debates over whether one
approach is inherently better than another can cause us to miss the fact that
multiple projects may be underway, often under different theories of change.
Sometimes this situation can lead to chaos; but it can also be fruitful when
no one really knows what the right way forward is. What is important on
the ground, then, and especially at the outset of the process, is not so much
that any one approach be favored. Rather, each project should have *unto itself*
a well-thought-out and coherent plan for what it intends to do (a theory of
change) which has been rigorously developed, ideally in collaboration with
the participants, and can be used to evaluate the process as it goes along as
well as make midcourse corrections.

Seventh, the ethical dimensions of the field require more thought. Current ethical frameworks are largely based on those which cover mediation
in domestic settings, where the interests and the number of players can be
smaller and the issues more clearly understood. Those who are engaged in
Track Two must consider these dimensions carefully and develop a strong
moral compass to guide their work. It is probably not possible to come up with
an all-encompassing ethical code which will cover all circumstances; the field
of Track Two is too broad for that. But those who would play the role of the
third party need to devote time and careful thought to ethical issues. Being
involved in a Track Two project can be an exciting, all-consuming experience.
One needs to go in with some ethical guidelines, lest the excitement of the
moment sweep one along to places which are morally precarious.

Finally, when Track Two exercises are facilitated, the role of the third party
is crucial. It is a complex role which defies easy definition, but it is the key to
providing the space where people feel sufficiently comfortable, and yet also

challenged, so that new thinking can flourish, even in the most difficult situations. The third party role is an art, like being an outstanding negotiator. But it is an art which must be informed by careful study of the process and by much experience. One of my key objectives in writing this book has been to reflect on my own experiences and to analyze the literature on Track Two in the context of what actually happens around the table. No theory can replace that kind of experience.

• • •

Each year, at the end of my course on Track Two, I pose a single question to the students: is Track Two an art, or is it a science? The question borrows from other fields of enquiry which have explored whether a particular activity, such as negotiation, can best be understood in theoretical or in artistic terms.[10] There is, of course, no right answer. Track Two is both an art and a science and it needs to be approached as both. But one may take a bias, depending on one's tastes and proclivities. I have found that most who practice Track Two lean towards the art side of the ledger, in varying degrees. But the better practitioners recognize the need to measure what they are doing against the requirements of rigorous science.

Track Two diplomacy is not a panacea for the world's ills, nor would serious proponents claim it to be. It has real and serious limitations. It cannot, in itself, "make peace" and it can never be seen as an end in itself. Track Two is, however, a tool for stimulating reflective dialogues between peoples in conflict, particularly where such dialogues might otherwise be difficult if not impossible to start at the official level. If successful, Track Two helps people develop new ways of understanding and addressing a deep-seated conflict. Sometimes it even finds a way to get new ideas onto the agendas of societies in conflict. That is no mean feat.

Notes

Preface

1. Jones, P., *Towards a Regional Security Regime for the Middle East: Issues and Options* (Stockholm: SIPRI, 1998, republished with an extensive new afterword in 2011).

2. For more on this incident, see Talbott, S., *Deadly Gambits: The Reagan Administration and the Stalemate in Nuclear Arms Control* (New York: Knopf, 1984), 116–151. The Nitze-Kvitsinski incident was the basis for the 1988 play *A Walk in the Woods* by Lee Blessing.

3. On prenegotiation, see Stein, J.G. (ed.), *Getting to the Table: The Processes of International Pre-negotiation* (Baltimore: Johns Hopkins University Press, 1989). The idea was first explored by US diplomat Harold Saunders. See his "We Need a Larger Theory of Negotiation: The Importance of Pre-Negotiation Phases," in Breslin, J.W., and Rubin, J.Z. (eds.), *Negotiation Theory and Practice* (Cambridge, MA: Program on Negotiation at Harvard Law School, 1991), 57–70.

Chapter 1

1. For more on this argument, see Saunders, H., et al., "Interactive Conflict Resolution: A View for Policy Makers on Making and Building Peace," in Druckman, D., and Stern, P.C. (eds.), *International Conflict Resolution After the Cold War* (Washington, DC: National Academy Press, 2000).

2. For more on this argument, see Rouhana, N.N., "Interactive Conflict Resolution: Issues in Theory, Methodology, and Evaluation," in Druckman and Stern, *International Conflict Resolution After the Cold War*.

3. The term was first mentioned in Davidson, W.D., and Montville, J.V., "Foreign Policy According to Freud," *Foreign Policy* 45, Winter 1981–82, but is generally attributed to Montville.

4. Montville, J.V., "Transnationalism and the Role of Track Two Diplomacy," in Thompson, W.S., and Jensen, K.M. (eds.), *Approaches to Peace: An Intellectual Map* (Washington, DC: United States Institute of Peace Press, 1991).

5. US Code: Title 18 § 953, "Private Correspondence with Foreign Governments," January 30, 1799. See also Seitzinger, M.V., "Conducting Foreign Relations Without Authority: The Logan Act" (Washington, DC: Congressional Research Service, February 1, 2006).

6. Chataway, C.J., "Track II Diplomacy from a Track I Perspective," *Negotiation Journal*, July 1998.

7. For more on this argument, see Jones, P., "Track II Diplomacy and the Gulf Weapons of Mass Destruction Free Zone," *Security and Terrorism Research Bulletin* (Gulf Research Center, Dubai) 1, October 2005, 15–17. It should be noted that there is a small literature which does believe that "unofficial diplomacy" is a legitimate term and method. See Berman, M.R., and Johnson, J.E., *Unofficial Diplomats* (New York: Columbia University Press, 1977).

8. For example, Follett, M.P., *Dynamic Administration: The Collected Papers of Mary Parker Follett*, ed. H. Metcalf and L. Urwick (New York: Harper, 1942); Lewin, K., *Resolving Social Conflicts* (New York: Harper & Bros., 1948); and Dollard, J., et al., *Frustration and Aggression* (New Haven: Yale University Press, 1939).

9. For more on the history of the field, see, for example, "Conflict Resolution: Origins, Foundations and Development of the Field," ch. 2 in Ramsbotham, O., Woodhouse, T., and Miall, H., *Contemporary Conflict Resolution*, 3rd ed. (Cambridge, UK: Polity Press, 2011), 35–62; Kriesberg, L., "The Evolution of Conflict Resolution," in Bercovitch, J., Kremenyuk, V., and Zartman, I.W. (eds.), *The Sage Handbook of Conflict Resolution* (London: Sage, 2009), 15–32; and Deutsch, M., "Introduction," in Deutsch, M., Coleman, P.T., and Marcus, E.C. (eds.), *The Handbook of Conflict Resolution: Theory and Practice, 2nd ed.* (San Francisco: Jossey-Bass, 2006), 1–20.

10. Boutros-Gali, B., *An Agenda for Peace: Preventive Diplomacy, Peacemaking and Peacekeeping*, United Nations Document A/47/277-S/24111 (New York: United Nations Organization, 1992).

11. See the website of the Program on Negotiation at the Harvard Law School at: http://www.pon.harvard.edu/tag/principled-negotiation/ (accessed August 5, 2013).

12. For a survey and analysis of developments in the field specifically after the Cold War, see Babbitt, E., "The Evolution of International Conflict Resolution: From Cold War to Peacebuilding," *Negotiation Journal* 25(4), 2009.

13. See Salem, P.E., "A Critique of Western Conflict Resolution from a Non-Western Perspective," *Negotiation Journal* 9(4), October 1993, 361–369.

14. For examples of the literature which emerged in the 1990s surrounding reconciliation as the goal of conflict resolution, see Lederach, J.P., *Building Peace: Sustainable Reconciliation in Divided Societies* (Washington, DC: United States Institute of

Peace Press, 1995); Dwyer, S., "Reconciliation for Realists," *Ethics and International Affairs* 13(1), 1999, 81–89. For a more recent study on the application of this approach, see Huyse, L., Salter, M., and Ingelaere, B., *Traditional Justice and Reconciliation After Violent Conflict: Learning From African Experiences* (Stockholm: International IDEA, 2008).

15. "Moral Rearmament" became "Initiatives of Change International" in 2001. More on its history can be found at: http://www.iofc.org/en/abt/history/. For more on this period, see Ackermann, A., "Reconciliation as a Peace-Building Process in Postwar Europe: The Franco-German Case," *Peace and Change* 19(3), 1994, 229–250.

16. The quote is from L.T. Woods, "Letters in Support of the Institute of Pacific Relations: Defending a Nongovernmental Organisation," *Pacific Affairs* 76(4), Winter 2003–2004. For more on the IPR, see Hooper, P.F. (ed.), *Rediscovering the IPR: Proceedings of the First International Research Conference on the Institute of Pacific Affairs* (Honolulu: Centre for Arts and Humanities, University of Hawaii, 1994).

17. See Evangelista, M., *Unarmed Forces: The Trans-national Movement to End the Cold War* (Ithaca, NY: Cornell University Press, 1999); Voorhees, J., *Dialogue Sustained: The Multilevel Peace Process and the Dartmouth Conference* (Washington, DC: United States Institute of Peace Press, 2002); and Schweitzer, G.E., *Scientists, Engineers and Track Two Diplomacy: A Half-Century of U.S.-Russian Inter-academy Cooperation* (Washington, DC: National Research Council of the National Academies, 2004). Pugwash was awarded a share of the 1995 Nobel Peace Prize for its work in promoting disarmament during the Cold War years.

18. See Mitchell, C., "Ending Confrontation Between Malaysia and Indonesia: A Pioneering Contribution to International Problem Solving," in Fisher, R.J. (ed.), *Paving the Way: Contributions of Interactive Conflict Resolution to Peacemaking* (New York: Lexington, 2005), 19–40; Fisher, R.J., "Historical Mapping of the Field of Interactive Conflict Resolution," in Davies, J., and Kaufman, E. (eds.), *Second Track/Citizen's Diplomacy: Concepts and Techniques for Conflict Transformation* (Lanham, MD: Rowman & Littlefield, 2002); Fisher, R.J., *Interactive Conflict Resolution* (Syracuse, NY: Syracuse University Press, 1997).

19. For more, see de Reuck, A.V.S., "Controlled Communication: Rationale and Dynamics," *The Human Context* 6(1), 1974; and Burton, J.W., *Conflict and Communication: The Use of Controlled Communication in International Relations* (London: MacMillan, 1969). For a contemporary critique of the method, which accused it of seeing conflicts as subjective rather than as objective events, see Yalem, R.J., "Controlled Communication and Conflict Resolution," *Journal of Peace Research* 8, 1971, 263–272.

20. For an overview history of the development of this field, see Fisher, "Historical Mapping of the Field of Inter-active Conflict Resolution."

21. See Kelman, H.C., "Interactive Problem-solving: Informal Mediation by the Scholar Practitioner," in Bercovitch, J. (ed.), *Studies in International Mediation: Essays in Honor of Jeffrey Z. Rubin* (New York: Palgrave Macmillan, 2002). For a comprehensive analysis of Israeli-Palestinian Track Two, see Agha, H.S., Feldman, S., Khalidi, A., and Schiff, Z., *Track II Diplomacy: Lessons from the Middle East* (Cambridge, MA:

MIT Press, 2004); and Çuhadar, E., and Dayton, B., "Oslo and Its Aftermath: Lessons Learned from Track Two Diplomacy," *Negotiation Journal*, April 2012. For more on Kelman, see Fisher, "Historical Mapping of the Field of Inter-active Conflict Resolution," 67–68; and Fisher, *Interactive Conflict Resolution*, 56–74.

22. Kelman, H.C., "The Interactive Problem-Solving Approach," in Crocker, C.A., and Kreisberg, F.O. (eds.), *Constructive Conflicts: From Escalation to Resolution* (New York: Rowman & Littlefield, 1996).

23. Kelman, H.C., "Interactive Problem Solving as a Tool for Second Track Diplomacy," in Davies and Kaufman, *Second Track/Citizens' Diplomacy*, 82.

24. The idea that the third party in a Track Two setting is not a mediator and should not act like one is further explored in Fisher, R.J., and Keashly, L., "Distinguishing Third Party Interventions in Intergroup Conflict: Consultation Is *Not* Mediation," *Negotiation Journal* 4, 1988.

25. On Doob, see among his many works, "A Cyprus Workshop: An Exercise in Intervention Methodology," *Journal of Social Psychology* 94(2), 1974; "Unofficial Intervention in Destructive Social Conflicts," in Brislin, R.W., *et al.* (eds.), *Cross Cultural Perspectives on Learning* (New York: Wiley, 1975); and *Interventions: Guides and Perils* (New Haven, CT: Yale University Press, 1993).

26. On Azar, see among his many works, "From Strategic to Humanistic International Relations," in Jamgotch, N. (ed.), *Thinking the Unthinkable: Investment in Human Survival* (Washington, DC: University Press of America, 1978); "The Theory of Protracted Social Conflicts and the Challenge of Transforming Conflict Situations," in Zinnes, D.A. (ed.), *Conflict Processes and the Breakdown of International Systems* (Denver: Graduate School of International Relations, University of Denver, 1984); "Protracted International Conflicts: Ten Propositions," *International Interactions* 12, 1985; and "Management of Protracted Conflicts in the Third World," *Ethnic Studies Report* 4(2), 1986.

27. See, for example, Volkan, V.D., "Psychological Concepts Useful in the Building of Political Foundations Between Nations: Track II Diplomacy," *Journal of the American Psychoanalytical Association* 34(4), 1987, 903–935.

28. Fisher, R.J., "Developing the Field of Interactive Conflict Resolution: Issues in Training, Funding and Institutionalisation," *Political Psychology* 14, 1993.

29. Fisher, *Interactive Conflict Resolution*, 7–8 (emphasis added).

30. Saunders, H., "Pre-negotiation and Circum-negotiation: Arenas of the Peace Process," in Crocker, C., Hampson, F.O., and Aall, P. (eds.), *Managing Global Chaos: Sources of and Responses to International Conflict* (Washington, DC: United States Institute of Peace, 1996). An example of such a process is the work that Saunders co-ran with Gennady Chufrin in Tajikistan. See Chufrin, G., and Saunders, H., "A Public Peace Process," *Negotiation Journal* 9(3), 1993, 155–177; and Slim, R., and Saunders, H., "The Inter-Tajik Dialogue: From Civil War Towards Civil Society," in Abdullaev, K., and Barnes, C. (eds.), *Politics of Compromise: The Tajikistan Peace Process* (London: Conciliation Resources, 2001).

31. Saunders, H., *A Public Peace Process: Sustained Dialogue to Transform Racial and Ethnic Conflicts* (New York: St. Martin's Press, 1999).

32. Diamond, L., and McDonald, J., *Multi-track Diplomacy: A Systems Approach to Peace*, 3rd ed. (West Hartford, CT: Kumarian Press, 1996).

33. See Chigas, D., "Unofficial Interventions with Official Actors: Parallel Negotiation Training in Violent Intrastate Conflicts," *International Negotiation* 2, 1997, 409–436.

34. See Fischer, M., "Conflict Transformation by Training in Non-violent Action: Activities of the Centre for Nonviolent Action in the Balkan Region," *Berghof Occasional Paper No. 18* (Berlin: Berghof Centre for Constructive Conflict Management, 2001); and Abu-Nimer, M., "Conflict Resolution Training in the Middle East: Lessons to Be Learned," *International Negotiation* 3, 1998, 99–116.

35. For more on this idea, see the special issue of *International Negotiation Journal*, guest edited by Ron Fisher, on "Conflict Resolution Training in Divided Societies," 2(3), 1997. See esp. Fisher's introductory article, "Training as Interactive Conflict Resolution: Characteristics and Challenges."

36. For more on Track One and a Half, see Nan, S.A., Druckman, D., and Horr, J.E., "Unofficial International Conflict Resolution: Is There a Track One and a Half? Are There Best Practices?" *Conflict Resolution Quarterly* 27(1), 2009, 65–82; Nan, A.S., "Track One and a Half Diplomacy: Contributions to Georgia-South Ossetian Peacemaking," in Fisher, *Paving the Way*; Nan, S.A., *Complementarity and Co-ordination of Conflict Resolution Efforts in the Conflicts over Abkhazia, South Ossetia and Transdniestria*, Ph.D. diss., George Mason University, 1999; and Mapendre, J., *Consequential Conflict Transformation Model, and the Complementarity of Track One, Track One and a Half and Track Two Diplomacy* (Atlanta: Carter Center, 2000).

37. For more on the Oslo process and its Track Two connections, see the collection of articles on Oslo in the special issue of the *International Negotiation Journal* 2(2), 1997.

38. For more on "back-channel" communications, see Pruitt, D.G., "Back-channel Communication in the Settlement of Conflict," *International Negotiation* 13(1), 2008, 37–54; Wanis-St. John, A., "Back-channel Negotiation: International Bargaining in the Shadows," *Negotiation Journal* 22(2), 2006, 119–144; Ó Dochartaigh, N., "Together in the Middle: Back-channel Negotiation in the Irish Peace Process," *Journal of Peace Research* 48(6), 2011; and Wanis-St. John, A., *Back-channel Negotiation: Secrecy in the Middle East Peace Process* (Syracuse, NY: Syracuse University Press, 2011).

39. See Kelman, H.C., "Contributions of an Unofficial Conflict Resolution Effort to the Israeli-Palestinian Breakthrough," *Negotiation Journal* 11(1), 1995; Kelman, H.C., "Some Determinants of the Oslo Breakthrough," *International Negotiation Journal* 2(2), 1997. See also Spillman, K.R., and Kollars, N., "Herbert Kelman's Contribution to the Methodology of Practical Conflict Resolution," *Peace and Conflict: Journal of Peace Psychology* 16(4), November 2010.

40. See Agha, H.S., Feldman, S., Khalidi, A., and Schiff, Z., *Track II Diplomacy: Lessons from the Middle East* (Cambridge, MA: MIT Press, 2003), 3–5 and *passim* for a discussion of this idea.

41. For an example of such activities, see Maoz, I., "Peacebuilding in Violent Conflict: Israeli-Palestinian Post Oslo People-to-People Activities," *International Journal of Politics, Culture and Society* 17(3), 2004, 563–574.

42. Burgess, H., and Burgess, G., *Conducting Track II Peacemaking* (Washington, DC: United States Institute of Peace Press, 2010), 5.

43. Saunders, H., et al., "Interactive Conflict Resolution: A View for Policy Makers on Making and Building Peace," in Druckman and Stern, *International Conflict Resolution After the Cold War*, 257.

44. See Lederach, J.P., *Building Peace: Sustainable Reconciliation in Divided Societies* (Washington, DC: United States Institute of Peace Press, 1997).

45. For more on the question of elicitive versus prescriptive approaches to conflict resolution, see Lederach, *Building Peace*; and Young, D.W., "Prescriptive and Elicitive Approaches to Conflict Resolution: Examples from Papua New Guinea," *Negotiation Journal* 14(3), July 1998, 211–220.

46. Kavaloski, V.C., "Transnational Citizen Peacemaking as Nonviolent Action," *Peace and Change* 15(2), April 1990.

47. Chigas, D., "Capacities and Limits of NGOs as Conflict Managers," in Crocker, C.A., Hampson, F.O., and Aall, P. (eds.), *Leashing the Dogs of War: Conflict Management in a Divided World* (Washington, DC: United States Institute of Peace Press, 2007), 553–581. A similar typology, though not represented in pyramidal form, is offered by the United States Institute of Peace on its website, in "Glossary of Terms for Conflict Management and Peacebuilding," under "Tracks of Diplomacy" at: http://glossary.usip.org/resource/tracks-diplomacy (accessed June 26, 2014).

48. For a review of the benefits and risks, see Strimling, A., "Stepping Out of the Tracks: Cooperation Between Official Diplomats and Private Facilitators," *International Negotiation* 11, 2006, 91–127.

49. Not all Track Two processes are facilitated by a third party. The Dartmouth Conferences of the Cold War were facilitated by the participants themselves. Today, the India-Pakistan dialogue known as the Chaophraya Dialogue is a contemporary example. See: http://chaophrayadialogue.net/ (accessed December 31, 2013). Most Track Two, however, features a third party.

50. The Chatham House Rule was first promulgated in 1927 at the Royal Institute of International Affairs in London, which is housed in a building called Chatham House. The rule is intended to foster open and direct discussion in an atmosphere where participants do not have to fear that their names may be revealed or otherwise publicly linked with points made. The latest refinement of the rule, issued in 2002, states, "When a meeting, or part thereof, is held under the Chatham House Rule, participants are free to use the information received, but neither the identity nor the affiliation of the speaker(s), nor that of any other participant, may be revealed."

51. For more on regional security Track Two in the Middle East, see Jones, P., "Filling a Critical Gap or Just Wasting Time? Track Two Diplomacy and Middle East Regional Security," *Disarmament Forum* (United Nations Institute for Disarmament Research), no. 2, 2008; Kaye, D.D., *Talking to the Enemy: Track Two Diplomacy in the Middle East and South Asia (Santa Monica, CA: RAND, 2007)*; Jones, "Track II Diplomacy and the Gulf Weapons of Mass Destruction Free Zone"; Agha, Feldman, Khalidi, and Schiff, *Track II Diplomacy*, ch. 8; Kaye, D.D., "Track Two Diplomacy and

Regional Security in the Middle East," *International Negotiation: A Journal of Theory and Practice* 6(1), 2001; and Jones, P., "Civil Society Dialogues and Middle East Regional Security: The Asia-Pacific Model," in Kane, C., and Murauskaite, E. (eds.), *Regional Security Dialogue in the Middle East: Changes, Challenges and Opportunities* (London: Routledge, 2014).

52. See Landau, E., "ACRS: What Worked, What Didn't and What Could Be Relevant for the Region Today," *Disarmament Forum* (United Nations Institute for Disarmament Research), no. 2, 2008; Jones, P., "Arms Control in the Middle East; Is It Time to Renew ACRS?" *Disarmament Forum (United Nations Institute for Disarmament Research)*, no. 2, 2005; Jones, P., "Negotiating Regional Security in the Middle East: The ACRS Experience and Beyond," *Journal of Strategic Studies* 26(3), September 2003.

53. "Epistemic communities" are transnational groups of experts who have together studied complex issues and come up with agreed-on understandings of what they mean. For more on their effect on international politics, see, for example, Haas, P., "Introduction: Epistemic Communities and International Policy Coordination," *International Organization* 46, Winter 1992. One attempt to sum up and assess the effectiveness of civil society processes in advocating change in international politics is the review article by Richard Price, "Transnational Civil Society and Advocacy in World Politics," *World Politics* 55, July 2003.

54. For the definitions of Track 1, Track 1.5, Track 2, and Track 3 as they apply to this region, see Capie, D., and Evans, P., *The Asia-Pacific Security Lexicon*, 2nd ed. (Singapore: Institute of Southeast Asian Studies, 2007), 229–240.

55. See Ball, D., Milner, A., and Taylor, B., "Track 2 Security Dialogue in the Asia-Pacific: Reflections and Future Directions," *Asian Security* 2(3), 2006; Job, B., "Track 2 Diplomacy: Ideational Contribution to the Evolving Asia Security Order," in Alagappa, M. (ed.), *Asian Security Order: Instrumental and Normative Features* (Stanford, CA: Stanford University Press, 2002).

56. For a history of the development of ASEAN ISIS, see Hernandez, C.G., "Track Two and Regional Policy: The ASEAN ISIS in Asian Decision-making," in Soesastro, H., Joewono, C., and Hernandez, C.G. (eds.), *Twenty Two Years of ASEAN ISIS: Origin, Evolution and Challenges of Track Two Diplomacy* (Jakarta: ASEAN ISIS and Kanisius Printing, 2006). There is an extensive literature on regional civil society dialogues. Many of the key papers are reprinted in Ball, D., and Guan, K.C. (eds.), *Assessing Track Two Diplomacy in the Asia-Pacific Region; A CSCAP Reader* (Singapore: S. Rajaratnam School of International Studies, 2010).

57. Woods, L.T., *Asia Pacific Diplomacy: Non-governmental Organizations and International Relations* (Vancouver: University of British Columbia Press, 1993), 117.

58. See, Job, B., "Track 2 Diplomacy: Ideational Contribution to the Evolving Asia Security Order," in Alagappa, M. (ed.), *Asian Security Order: Instrumental and Normative Features* (Stanford, CA: Stanford University Press, 2002).

59. See Tan, S.S., "Non-official Diplomacy in Southeast Asia: 'Civil Society' or 'Civil Service'?" *Contemporary Southeast Asia* 27(3), December 2005, 370–387; and

Kraft, H.J., "The Autonomy Dilemma of Track Two Diplomacy in Southeast Asia," *Security Dialogue* 31(3), September 2000.

60. See Evans, P., "Possibilities for Security Cooperation in the Asia-Pacific: Track 2 and Track 1," in *Multilateralism in Asia Pacific: What Role for Track Two?* (Honolulu, HI: National Defense University, Washington; U.S. Pacific Command; Asia Pacific Center for Security Studies, March, 27, 2001), at: www.ndu.edu/inss/symposia/pacific2001/evanspaper.htm

61. See the webpage on the Centre for Humanitarian Dialogue (HD Centre) website for its efforts in Aceh, at: http://www.hdcentre.org/en/our-work/peacemaking/past-activities/aceh-indonesia/.

62. See International Crisis Group, *Southern Philippines Backgrounder: Terrorism and the Peace Process*, ICG Asia Report, no. 80 (Singapore/Brussels: ICG, 2004).

63. See Goh, G., "The 'ASEAN Way': Non-intervention and ASEAN's Role in Conflict Management," *Stanford Journal of East Asian Affairs* 3(1), Spring 2003, 113–118, for a review and discussion of the ASEAN Way and the question of the policies of ASEAN states towards intervention in each other's internal conflicts. Goh maintained that this norm was changing subtly at the time of writing her article. It is not altogether clear that this has happened since.

64. One of the few to specifically study Track Two dialogues as mechanisms of regional security discussions is Dalia Dassa Kaye, who has studied regional security Track Two in the Middle East and South Asia. See her *Talking to the Enemy: Track Two Diplomacy in the Middle East and South Asia* (Santa Monica, CA: RAND, 2007).

65. The fact that it is so difficult to measure outputs is one of the criticisms of the field overall, which is made by Rouhana. Others argue that precise measurements are not possible in a subjective field. For one discussion of the debate, see d'Estrée, T.P., Fast, L.A., Weiss, J.N., and Jakobsen, M.S., "Changing the Debate About 'Success' in Conflict Resolution Efforts," *Negotiation Journal* 17(2), April 2001, 101–113.

66. See Ball, D., Milner, A., and Taylor, B., "Track 2 Security Dialogue in the Asia-Pacific: Reflections and Future Directions," *Asian Security* 2(3), 2006, 182.

67. Kaye, D.D., *Talking to the Enemy: Track Two Diplomacy in the Middle East and South Asia* (Santa Monica, CA: RAND, 2007), 21–29.

68. Jones, P., "Track II Diplomacy and the Gulf Weapons of Mass Destruction Free Zone," *Security and Terrorism Research Bulletin* (Gulf Research Center, Dubai) 1, October 2005.

Chapter 2

1. Rouhana, N.N., "Unofficial Third-Party Intervention in International Conflict: Between Legitimacy and Disarray," *Negotiation Journal*, July 1995.

2. Babbitt, E., and Hampson, F.O., "Conflict Resolution as a Field of Inquiry: Practice Informing Theory," *International Studies Review* 13, 2011, 46. As Beriker notes in her examination of this issue, conflict resolution practitioners "concentrate on the operationalization of conflict resolution approaches and activities without integrating

them with mainstream international relations literature. In other words, the conceptualization of conflict resolution practice is elaborated in isolation from theoretical and practical instruments that classical IR literature offers." See Beriker, N., "Conflict Resolution: The Missing Link Between Liberal International Relations Theory and Realistic Practice," in Sandole, J.D., Byrne, S., Sandole-Staroste, I., and Senehi, J., *Handbook of Conflict Analysis and Resolution* (Oxford, UK: Routledge, 2009), 256–271. Someone who has explored the territory where IR theory and conflict resolution meet is A.J.R. Groom. See "Paradigms in Conflict: The Strategist, the Conflict Researcher, and the Peace Researcher," *Review of International Studies* 14, 1988, 71–98.

3. For a brief review of the main theories of international relations, see Walt, S.M., "One World, Many Theories," *Foreign Policy*, Spring 1998; Jervis, R., "Theories of War in an Era of Leading Power Peace," *American Political Science Review*, March 2002; and Snyder, J., "One World, Rival Theories," *Foreign Policy*, November/December 2004.

4. A classic realist critique of the idealism of the interwar period is E.H. Carr's *The Twenty Years' Crisis 1919–1939: An Introduction to the Study of International Relations*, first published in 1939.

5. For a classic statement of this idea, see Waltz, K.N., *Theory of International Politics* (Reading, MA: Addison-Wesley, 1979).

6. See Gilpin, R., *War and Change in World Politics* (Cambridge, UK: Cambridge University Press, 1981).

7. See Brooks, S.G., "Dueling Realisms," *International Organization*, Summer 1997. For summaries of realist arguments as they relate to conflict, see Cashman, G., *What Causes War? An Introduction to Theories of International Conflict* (New York: Lexington Books, 1993).

8. On classical realism, see Morgenthau, H., *Politics Among Nations: The Struggle for Power and Peace* (New York: Knopf, 1948). On neorealism, see Waltz, *Theory of International Politics*; and Keohane, R. (ed.), *Neoclassical Realism and Its Critics* (New York: Columbia University Press, 1986).

9. Merom, G., "Realist Hypothesis on Regional Peace," *Journal of Strategic Studies* 26(1), March 2001.

10. Lemke, D., *Regions of War and Peace* (Cambridge, UK: Cambridge University Press, 2002). For more on realism as it pertains to regional security issues, see Copeland, D.C., "Realism and Neorealism in the Study of International Conflict," and Taliaferro, J.W., "Neoclassical Realism and the Study of Regional Order," both in Paul, T.V. (ed.), *International Relations Theory and Regional Transformation* (Cambridge, UK: Cambridge University Press, 2012).

11. Azar, E., "The Theory of Protracted Social Conflicts and the Challenge of Transforming Conflict Situations," in Zinnes, D.A. (ed.), *Conflict Processes and the Breakdown of International Systems* (Denver: Graduate School of International Relations, University of Denver, 1984); Azar E., "Protracted International Conflicts: Ten Propositions," *International Interactions* 12, 1985; Azar, E., "Management of Protracted Conflicts in the Third World," *Ethnic Studies Report* 4(2), 1986.

12. Posen, B.R., "The War for Kosovo: Serbia's Political-Military Strategy," *International Security* 24(4), Spring 2000.

13. See, for example, Mearsheimer, J.J., "The False Promise of International Institutions," *International Security* 19(3), Winter 1994/95.

14. Bartoli, A., "Mediating Peace in Mozambique: The Role of the Community of Sant'Egidio," in Crocker, C.A., Hampson, F.O., and Aall, P. (eds.), *Herding Cats: Multiparty Mediation in a Complex World* (Washington, DC: United States Institute of Peace Press, 2003), 250.

15. Acharya, A., *Constructing a Regional Security Community in Southeast Asia: ASEAN and the Problem of Regional Order* (London: Routledge, 2001); Acharya, A., *Whose Ideas Matters? Agency and Power in Asian Regionalism* (Ithaca, NY: Cornell University Press, 2009).

16. Lobell, S.E., Ripsman, N.M., and Taliaferro, J.W. (eds.), *Neoclassical Realism, the State and Foreign Policy* (Cambridge, UK: Cambridge University Press, 2009).

17. See Miller, B., *States, Nations and the Great Powers: The Sources of Regional War and Peace* (Cambridge, UK: Cambridge University Press, 2007).

18. See Moravschik, A., "Taking Preferences Seriously: A Liberal Theory of International Politics," *International Organization* 51(4), Autumn 1997, 513–53; and Zacher, M.W., and Matthew, R.A., "Liberal International Theory: Common Threads, Divergent Strands," in Kegley Jr., C.W. (ed.) *Controversies in International Relations Theory: Realism and the Neoliberal Challenge* (Basingstoke, UK: Macmillan, 1995), 107–150.

19. Beriker, "Conflict Resolution," *257*.

20. It was Doyle who first introduced this notion, in two articles in 1983. See Doyle, M.W., "Kant, Liberal Legacies, and Foreign Affairs," *Philosophy and Public Affairs* 12(3), Summer 1983; and "Kant, Liberal Legacies, and Foreign Affairs, Part 2," *Philosophy and Public Affairs* 12(4), Autumn 1983. See also Russet, B., and Oneal, J.R., *Triangulating Peace: Democracy, Interdependence and International Organizations* (New York: Norton, 2001); Richardson, J.L., "Contending Liberalisms: Past and Present," *European Journal of International Relations* 3(1), 1997, 5–33; and Mandelbaum, M., *The Ideas That Conquered the World* (New York: Public Affairs Book, 2002).

21. See, for example, Mattli, W., *The Logic of Regional Integration: Europe and Beyond* (Cambridge, UK: Cambridge University Press, 1999). See also Owen IV, J.M., "Economic Interdependence and Regional Peace," and Oneal, J.R., "Transforming Regional Security Through Liberal Reforms," both in Paul, *International Relations Theory and Regional Transformation*.

22. For more the democratic peace, see Brown, M.E., Lynn-Jones, S.M., and Miller, S.E., *Debating the Democratic Peace* (Cambridge, MA: MIT Press, 1996).

23. Doyle, M., *Ways of War and Peace* (New York: Norton, 1997).

24. Mansfield, E.D., and Snyder, J., *Electing to Fight: Why Emerging Democracies Go to War* (Cambridge, MA: MIT Press, 2005).

25. For more on globalization and the debates around it, see Mazlish, B., and Iriye, A. (eds.), *The Global History Reader* (Abingdon, UK: Routledge, 2005); and Held, D.,

and McGrew, A. (eds.), *The Global Transformations Reader: An Introduction to the Globalization Debate* (Cambridge, UK: Polity Press, 2003).

26. Such an admission is made in Ripsman, N.M., "Two Stages of Transition from the Region of War to a Region of Peace: Realist Transition and Liberal Endurance," *International Studies Quarterly* 49(4), December 2005. See also Ikenberry, G.J., *After Victory: Institutions, Strategic Restraint, and the Rebuilding of Order After Major Wars* (Princeton, NJ: Princeton University Press, 2001).

27. Adler, E., and Barnett, M. (eds.), *Security Communities* (Cambridge, UK: Cambridge University Press, 1998).

28. Quoted in Snyder, "One World, Rival Theories," 54. For more on the history of democracy promotion as a key theme in US foreign policy, see Cox, M., Ikenberry, G.J., and Inoguchi, T. (eds.), *American Democracy Promotion: Impulses, Strategies and Impacts* (Oxford, UK: Oxford University Press, 2000).

29. Wendt, A., *Social Theory of International Politics* (Cambridge, UK: Cambridge University Press, 1999); and Adler, E., "Constructivism," in Carlneas, W., Simmons, B., and Risse, T. (eds.), *Handbook of International Relations* (Thousand Oaks, CA: Sage, 2003). See also Acharya, A., "Ideas, Norms and Regional Orders," in Paul, *International Relations Theory and Regional Transformation*. For more on the relationship between constructivist theory and conflict resolution generally, see Jackson, R., "Constructivism and Conflict Resolution," in Bercovitch, J., Kremenyuk, V., and Zartman, I.W. (eds.), *The Sage Handbook of Conflict Resolution* (Thousand Oaks, CA: Sage, 2009), ch. 9.

30. Such communities of experts are known as "epistemic communities" and there is a literature on their effect on international politics. See, for example, Haas, P., "Introduction: Epistemic Communities and International Policy Coordination," *International Organization* 46, Winter 1992, 18. One attempt to sum up and assess the effectiveness of civil society processes in advocating change in international politics is the review article by R. Price, "Transnational Civil Society and Advocacy in World Politics," *World Politics* 55, July 2003.

31. For more on norm entrepreneurs, see Finnmore, M., *National Interests and International Society* (Ithaca, NY: Cornell University Press, 1996).

32. Job, B., "Track 2 Diplomacy: Ideational Contribution to the Evolving Asia Security Order," in Alagappa, M. (ed.), *Asian Security Order: Instrumental and Normative Features* (Stanford, CA: Stanford University Press, 2002).

33. Acharya, A., *Constructing a Regional Security Community in Southeast Asia: ASEAN and the Problem of Regional Order* (London: Routledge, 2001); and Acharya, A., *Whose Ideas Matters? Agency and Power in Asian Regionalism* (Ithaca, NY: Cornell University Press, 2009).

34. Job, B., "Track 2 Diplomacy: Ideational Contribution to the Evolving Asia Security Order," in Alagappa, *Asian Security Order*. This argument is also made by C.G. Hernandez, "Track Two and Regional Policy: The ASEAN ISIS in Asian Decision-making," in Soesastro, H., Joewono, C., and Hernandez, C.G. (eds.), *Twenty Two Years of ASEAN ISIS: Origin, Evolution and Challenges of Track Two Diplomacy*

(Jakarta: ASEAN ISIS and Kanisius Printing, 2006). There is an extensive literature on ASEAN Track Two. Many of the key papers are reprinted in Ball, D., and Guan, K.C. (eds.), *Assessing Track Two Diplomacy in the Asia-Pacific Region; A CSCAP Reader* (Singapore: S. Rajaratnam School of International Studies, 2010).

35. Khoo took the view that Acharya misunderstands ASEAN, and that it remains fundamentally a regional organization based on realist thinking; Khoo, N., "Deconstructing the ASEAN Security Community: A Review Essay," *International Relations of the Asia-Pacific* 4(1), February 2004. Peou and Ba are of the view that Khoo is wrong, and that Acharya's analysis is persuasive; Peou, S., "Merit in Security Community Studies," *International Relations of the Asia-Pacific 5(2),* August 2005; Ba, A.D., "On Norms, Rule Breaking, and Security Communities: A Constructivist Response," *International Relations of the Asia-Pacific* 5(2), August 2005. For Acharya's view on these exchanges, see Acharya, A., "Is Anyone Still Not a Constructivist?" *International Relations of the Asia-Pacific* 5(2), August 2005.

36. Barnett, M.N., *Dialogues in Arab Politics: Negotiations in Regional Order* (New York: Columbia University Press, 1998).

37. Snyder, "One World, Rival Theories," 54.

38. For example, the "decision-maker" school focuses on the processes whereby leaders, small groups of advisors, and coalitions make decisions, thereby opening up the "black box" of the nation-state and looking at what happens at the highest levels within that box. For more on this field, see Snyder, R.C., et al. (eds.), *Foreign Policy Decision Making (Revisited)* (London: Palgrave Macmillan, 2003).

39. Davidheiser, M., "Race, Worldviews, and Conflict Mediation: Black and White Styles of Conflict Revisited," *Peace and Change* 33(1), January 2008, 67–68.

40. Ibid. For an analysis of how the worldviews of the parties to a conflict (in this case, the Branch Davidians, the FBI, and the ATF at Waco, Texas) influenced the outcome, see Docherty, J.S., *Learning Lessons from Waco: When the Parties Bring Their Gods to the Negotiation Table* (Syracuse, NY: Syracuse University Press, 2001). For an analysis of how worldviews influence foreign policy analysis with respect to conflicts, see Mowle, T.S., "Worldviews in Foreign Policy: Realism, Liberalism and External Conflict," *Political Psychology* 24(3), 2003.

41. Bitter, J.N., *Les Dieux Embusqes* (Geneva: Librarie DROZ, 2003), as discussed in Mason, S.A., *Mediation and Facilitation in Peace Processes* (Zurich: Center for Security Studies, 2007), 5.

42. In addition to the sources on constructivism cited earlier in the chapter, see Lederach, J.P., *The Moral Imagination: The Art and Soul of Building Peace* (Oxford, UK: Oxford University Press, 2005), for an elaboration on this approach.

43. In addition to the work of Edward Azar that was citied in Chapter 1, see Burton, J., *Conflict: Human Needs Theory* (New York: St. Martin's Press, 1990).

44. Fisher, R.J., *Interactive Conflict Resolution* (Syracuse, NY: Syracuse University Press, 1997), 6, emphasis in original. See also his *The Social Psychology of Intergroup and International Conflict Resolution.* (New York: Springer-Verlag, 1990).

45. Fisher, R.J., *Interactive Conflict Resolution* (Syracuse, NY: Syracuse University Press, 1997), 7.

46. See Allport, G.W., "The Historical Background of Social Psychology," in Lindzey, G., and Aronson, E. (eds.), *The Handbook of Social Psychology* (New York: McGraw-Hill, 1985); and Moscovici, S., and Markova, I., *The Making of Modern Social Psychology* (Cambridge, UK: Polity Press, 2006).

47. Kelman, H.C., "A Social-psychological Approach to Conflict Analysis and Resolution," in Sandole, D., Byrne, S., and Sandole-Staroste, I. (eds.), *Handbook of Conflict Analysis and Resolution* (London: Routledge, 2008), 170.

48. For a historical review of the involvement of the field in conflict resolution, see Deutsch, M., "Social Psychology's Contributions to the Study of Conflict Resolution," *Negotiation Journal*, October 2002. Deutsch was one of the early pioneers of this work and remains one of its best known.

49. See, for example, Lewin, K., *A Dynamic Theory of Personality* (New York: McGraw-Hill, 1935); and Deutsch, M., "An Experimental Study of the Effects of Cooperation and Competition upon Group Process," *Human Relations* 2, 1949.

50. Game theory as an approach to social science was first introduced by Von Neumann and Morgenstern in their *Theory of Games and Economic Behavior*, 3rd ed. (New York: Wiley, 1964, originally published in 1944).

51. See, for example, the classic by T.C. Schelling, *The Strategy of Conflict* (Cambridge, MA: Harvard University Press, 1960).

52. Deutsch, M., "Social Psychology's Contributions to the Study of Conflict Resolution," *Negotiation Journal*, October 2002, 313.

53. Pruitt, D.G., and Kimmel, M.J., "Twenty Years of Experimental Gaming: Critique, Synthesis and Suggestions for the Future," *Annual Review of Psychology* 28, 1977.

54. See, for example, Ross, M.H., and Rothman, J., *Theory and Practice in Ethnic Conflict Management: Theorizing Success and Failure* (New York: St. Martin's Press, 1999); Coleman, P.T., and Lim, J., "A Systematic Approach to Evaluating the Effects of Collaborative Negotiation Training on Individuals and Groups," *Negotiation Journal* 17(4), 2001.

55. Çuhadar, E., and Dayton, B., "The Social Psychology of Identity and Intergroup Conflict: From Theory to Practice," *International Studies Perspectives* 12, 2011, 274.

56. One of the most famous studies on this was the so-called Robber's Cave experiment, which took a group of young boys from similar backgrounds, arbitrarily divided them into groups, and then encouraged competition between the groups for various prizes. It was found that the boys in the two groups quickly developed "in-group" and "out-group" opinions of each other which led to an intensely competitive relationship. See Sherif, M., Harvey, O.J., White, B.J., Hood, W.R., and Sherif, C.W., *Intergroup Conflict and Cooperation: The Robbers Cave Experiment (vol. 10)* (Norman, OK: University Book Exchange, 1961).

57. Crocker, C.A., Hampson, F.O., and Aall, P., "Multiparty Mediation and the Conflict Cycle," in Crocker, C.A., Hampson, F.O., and Aall, P. (eds.), *Herding Cats: Multiparty Mediation in a Complex World* (Washington, DC: United States Institute of Peace Press, 2003), 20. The authors recognize, of course, that this is a simplified characterization.

58. Ibid.

59. Ibid.

60. Touval, S., "Coercive Mediation on the Road to Dayton," *International Negotiation* 1(1), 1996. Touval used the phrase "mediator with muscle" in his *The Peace Brokers: Mediators in the Arab-Israeli Conflict, 1948–1979* (Princeton, NJ: Princeton University Press, 1982).

61. For more on the conflict cycle and conflict resolution, see Mitchell, C., "The Process and Stages of Mediation," in Smock, D.R. (ed.), *Making War and Waging Peace: Foreign Intervention in Africa* (Washington, DC: United States Institute of Peace Press, 1994); Crocker, C.A., Hampson, F.O., and Aall, P., "Multiparty Mediation and the Conflict Cycle," in Crocker, Hampson, and Aall, *Herding Cats*; and Babbitt, E., and Hampson, F.O., "Conflict Resolution as a Field of Inquiry: Practice Informing Theory," *International Studies Quarterly* 13(1), 2011, 52–53.

62. Zartman, I.W., "Ripeness: The Hurting Stalemate and Beyond," in Druckman, D., and Stern, P.C. (eds.), *International Conflict Resolution After the Cold War* (Washington, DC: National Academy Press, 2000).

63. Crocker, C.A., Hampson, F.O., and Aall, P., "Multiparty Mediation and the Conflict Cycle," in Crocker, Hampson, and Aall, *Herding Cats*, 22.

64. See Van der Stoel, M., "The Role of the OSCE High Commissioner in Conflict Prevention," in Crocker, Hampson, and Aall, *Herding Cats*.

65. See, for example, Picco, G., *Man Without a Gun: One Diplomat's Secret Struggle to Free the Hostages, Fight Terrorism, and End a War* (New York: Crown, 1999). Picco was asked by the UN Secretary General to serve on behalf of the United Nations in talks aimed at ending various conflicts in the Middle East and Afghanistan.

66. Çuhadar, E., and Dayton, B., "Oslo and Its Aftermath: Lessons Learned from Track Two Diplomacy," *Negotiation Journal*, April 2012.

67. See Pettigrew, T., "Intergroup Contact Theory," *Annual Review of Psychology* 49, 1998; Stephan, W.G., "Intergroup Relations," in Lindzey, G., and Aronson, E. (eds.), *Handbook of Social Psychology, vol. 2* (New York: Random House, 1985); and Amir, Y., "The Role of Intergroup Contact in Change of Prejudice and Ethnic Relations," in Katz, P. (ed.), *Toward the Elimination of Racism* (New York: Pergamon, 1976).

68. See Phillips, D.L., *Unsilencing the Past: Track Two Diplomacy and Turkish-Armenian Reconciliation* (New York: Berghahn, 2005).

69. See, for example, Winslade, J., and Monk, G.D., *Narrative Mediation: A New Approach to Conflict Mediation* (San Francisco: Jossey-Bass, 2000).

70. For a study of the impact of competing narratives on attempts at Israeli-Palestinian peacemaking, see Rotberg, R.J. (ed.), *Israeli and Palestinian Narratives of Conflict: History's Double Helix* (Bloomington: Indiana University Press, 2006). For

a study on the Israeli-Palestinian conflict as a contest between narratives of victim-hood, see Morris, B., *Righteous Victims: A History of the Zionist-Arab Conflict, 1881–2001* (New York: Vintage Book, 2001).

71. One such effort produced a book which if it did not succeed in providing joint narratives, at least laid out the existing narratives side by side and encouraged criti-cal analysis of them. See Scham, P., Salem, W., and Pogrund, B., *Shared Histories: A Palestinian-Israeli Dialogue* (Walnut Creek, CA: Left Coast Press, 2005).

72. An example of which would be the jointly edited and published academic jour-nal *Palestine-Israel Journal of Politics, Economics and Culture*, published by a jointly run nonprofit. The home page of the journal may be found at: http://www.pij.org/.

73. The Washington, DC–based NGO "Search for Common Ground" has run such a service for many years. "The Common Ground News Service" features "constructive articles that foster dialogue." See: http://www.commongroundnews.org/index.php.

74. According to its website, Seeds of Peace has brought together over five thou-sand youth since its founding in 1993, and "inspires and equips new generations of leaders from regions of conflict with the relationships, understanding, and skills needed to advance lasting peace." See: http://www.seedsofpeace.org/ (accessed December 31, 2013).

75. Çuhadar, E., and Dayton, B., "Oslo and Its Aftermath: Lessons Learned from Track Two Diplomacy," *Negotiation Journal*, April 2012.

76. Rouhana, N.N., "Interactive Conflict Resolution: Issues in Theory, Methodol-ogy, and Evaluation," in Druckman and Stern, *International Conflict Resolution After the Cold War*, 294–295.

Chapter 3

1. See Shapiro, I., *Extending the Framework of Inquiry: Theories of Change in Con-flict Interventions* (Berlin: Berghof Research Center for Constructive Conflict Man-agement, 2006), 2, for an elaboration of the reasons why such theories of change are important. Available at: http://www.berghof-handbook.net/documents/publications/dialogue5_shapiro_comm.pdf (accessed on August 5, 2012). See also Anderson, M., Chigas, D., and Woodrow, P., *Encouraging Effective Evaluation of Conflict Prevention and Peacebuilding Activities: Towards DAC Guidance,* DCD 2007(3) (Paris: Organisa-tion for Economic Co-operation and Development, September 2007), 74.

2. For examples of studies in the field of program evaluation, see Weiss, C., *Evalu-ation Research* (Englewood Cliffs, NJ: Prentice Hall, 1972); and Fulbright-Anderson, K., Kubisch, A., and Connell, J. (eds.), *New Approaches to Evaluating Community Ini-tiatives, vol. 2* (New York: Aspen Institute, 1998).

3. For more, see Allport, G., *The Nature of Prejudice* (Reading, MA: Addison-Wes-ley, 1954); Pettigrew, T., "Intergroup Contact Theory," *Annual Review of Psychology* 49, 1998, 65–85; and Abu-Nimer, M., *Dialogue, Conflict Resolution and Change: Arab-Jewish Encounters in Israel* (Albany: State University of New York Press, 1999).

4. Shapiro, I., "Theories of Practice and Change in Ethnic Conflict Interventions," in Fitzduff, M., and Stout, C.E. (eds.), *The Psychology of Resolving Ethnic Conflict,* vol. 3 (Santa Barbara, CA: Praeger Security International, 2006); Çuhadar, E., and Dayton, B., "The Social Psychology of Identity and Inter-group Conflict: From Theory to Practice," *International Studies Perspectives* 12, 2011, 283.

5. For examples, see Schellenberg, J., *Conflict Resolution: Theory, Research and Practice* (Albany: State University of New York Press, 1996); Pruitt, D., and Kim, S.H., *Social Conflict: Escalation, Stalemate, and Settlement, 3rd ed.* (New York: McGraw-Hill, 2004); Bush, R.B., Folger, J., *The Promise of Mediation,* new and revised edition (San Francisco: Jossey-Bass, 2005); Lederach, J.P., and Maiese, M., *Conflict Transformation,* available at: http://www.beyondintractability.org/essay/transformation/?nid=1223 (accessed on August 5, 2012).

6. Ross, M.H., "Creating the Conditions for Peacemaking: Theories of Practice in Ethnic Conflict Resolution," *Ethnic and Racial Studies* 23(6), 2000, 1002–1034.

7. From Anderson, M., Chigas, D., and Woodrow, P., *Encouraging Effective Evaluation of Conflict Prevention and Peacebuilding Activities: Towards DAC Guidance*, DCD 2007(3) (Paris: Organisation for Economic Co-operation and Development, September 2007), 86–87.

8. Shapiro, I., *Extending the Framework of Inquiry: Theories of Change in Conflict Interventions* (Berlin: Berghof Research Center for Constructive Conflict Management, 2006), 5–6. Shapiro further develops this discussion in her post on the *Beyond Intractability* site at: http://www.beyondintractability.org/essay/theories_of_change/?nid=1256.

9. Lederach, J.P., Neufeldt, R., and Culbertson, H., *Reflective Peacebuilding: A Planning, Monitoring and Learning Toolkit* (Mindanao, Philippines: Joan B. Kroc Institute for International Peace Studies and Catholic Relief Services/East Asia Regional Office, 2007), 51.

10. See, for example, Miall, H., *Conflict Transformation: A Multi-Dimensional Task* (Berlin: Berghof Research Center for Constructive Conflict Management, 2004), 3–4, available at: http://www.berghof-handbook.net/documents/publications/miall_handbook.pdf. Cordula Reimann also discusses these three, although she calls conflict *management* by the slightly different term, conflict *settlement,* in her paper *Assessing the State of the Art in Conflict Transformation* (Berlin: Berghof Research Center for Constructive Conflict Management, 2004), 7–13, available at: http://www.berghof-handbook.net/documents/publications/reimann_handbook.pdf. Babbitt and Hampson posit that the fundamental difference within the field over this subject is between the more traditional approach of "conflict settlement" and the newly emerging trend towards "conflict transformation." See Babbitt, E., and Hampson, F.O., "Conflict Resolution as a Field of Inquiry: Practice Informing Theory," *International Studies Quarterly* 13(1), 2011.

11. Bloomfield, D., and Reilly, B., "The Changing Nature of Conflict and Conflict Management," in Harris, P., and Reilly, B. (eds.), *Democracy and Deep-Rooted Conflict* (Stockholm: Institute for Democracy and Electoral Assistance, 1998), 18, quoted in Miall, *Conflict Transformation,* 3.

12. See the discussion of Burton and his work on the concept of "controlled communication" in Chapter 2. For more on his thinking, see, for example, Burton, J., *Resolving Deep-Rooted Conflicts: A Handbook* (Lanham, MD: University Press of America, 1987); and Burton, J. (ed.), *Conflict: Human Needs Theory* (London: Macmillan, 1990). Azar, also discussed in Chapter 2, was a pioneer in this field.

13. See, for example, the discussion of whether the "reconciliation" of deep-seated, identity-based animosities is "negotiable" at all, in the sense that conflict management or even resolution experts would expect, in Rosoux, V., "Is Reconciliation Negotiable?" *International Negotiation* 18, 2003, 471–493. Rosoux ultimately concludes that there is room for "negotiation" in some cases, but that it must proceed from a far less "transactional" basis than proponents of conflict management would suggest.

14. Miall, H., *Conflict Transformation: A Multi-Dimensional Task* (Berlin: Berghof Research Center for Constructive Conflict Management, 2004), 4, available at: http://www.berghof-handbook.net/documents/publications/miall_handbook.pdf.

15. Among his many works, see, for example, Lederach, J.P., *Preparing for Peace: Conflict Transformation Across Cultures* (Syracuse, NY: Syracuse University Press, 1995).

16. Among his many works, see, for example, Galtung, J., *Peace by Peaceful Means: Peace and Conflict, Development and Civilization* (London: Sage, 1996).

17. Curle, A., *Making Peace* (London: Tavistock, 1971).

18. Reimann, C., *Assessing the State of the Art in Conflict Transformation* (Berlin: Berghof Research Center for Constructive Conflict Management, 2004), 11, available at: http://www.berghof-handbook.net/documents/publications/reimann_handbook.pdf.

19. For more on advocacy in international relations, see Keck, M.E., and Sikkink, K., *Activists Beyond Borders: Advocacy Networks in International Politics* (Ithaca, NY: Cornell University Press, 1998); and Price, R., "Transnational Civil Society and Advocacy in World Politics," *World Politics*, July 2003, 579–606.

20. Sheehan, I.S., "Conflict Transformation as Counterinsurgency," *Peace Review: A Journal of Social Justice* 26, March 2014, 126.

21. See, for example, the collection of essays on this question in the context of African conflicts in Maundi, M.O., Zartman, I.W., Khadiagala, G.M., and Nuamah, K., *Getting In: Mediators' Entry into the Settlement of African Conflicts* (Washington, DC: United States Institute of Peace Press, 2006).

22. Zartman, I.W., "Ripeness: The Hurting Stalemate and Beyond," in Druckman, D., and Stern, P.C. (eds.), *International Conflict Resolution After the Cold War* (Washington, DC: National Academy Press, 2000). For more, see Zartman, I.W., *Ripe for Resolution: Conflict and Intervention in Africa* (New York: Oxford University Press, 1985); Haas, R.N., *Conflicts Unending* (New Haven, CT: Yale University Press, 1990); and Stedman, S.J., *Peacemaking in Civil War: International Mediation in Zimbabwe, 1974–1980* (Boulder, CO: Lynne Rienner, 1991).

23. See Greig, J.M., "Moments of Opportunity: Recognising Conditions of Ripeness for International Mediation Between Enduring Rivals," *Journal of Conflict Resolution* 45(6), December 2001.

24. Ibid.

25. See Kleiboer, M., "Ripeness of Conflict: A Fruitful Notion?" *Journal of Peace Research* 31(1), 1994.

26. Crocker, C.A., *High Noon in Southern Africa: Making Peace in a Rough Neighborhood* (New York: Norton, 1992), 469–472.

27. Touval, S.A., *The Peace Brokers: Mediators in the Arab-Israeli Conflict, 1948–1979* (Princeton, NJ: Princeton University Press, 1982).

28. Crocker, C.A., Hampson, F.O., and Aall, P., "Multiparty Mediation and the Conflict Cycle," in Crocker, Hampson, and Aall, *Herding Cats.*

29. Azar, E., "The Theory of Protracted Social Conflicts and the Challenge of Transforming Conflict Situations," in Zinnes, D.A. (ed.), *Conflict Processes and the Breakdown of International Systems* (Denver: Graduate School of International Relations, University of Denver, 1984); Azar, E., "Protracted International Conflicts: Ten Propositions," *International Interactions* 12, 1985; and Azar, E., "Management of Protracted Conflicts in the Third World," *Ethnic Studies Report* 4(2), 1986.

30. Pruitt, D.G., *Whither Ripeness Theory?* Working paper no. 25, Institute for Conflict Analysis and Resolution, George Mason University, 2005, 6–7. For more on readiness theory, see Pruitt's "Readiness Theory and the Northern Ireland Conflict," *American Behavioral Scientist* 50, 2007.

31. For more, see Spector, B.I., "Negotiation Readiness in the Development Context: Adding Capacity to Ripeness," in Jeong, H.W. (ed.), *Approaches to Peacebuilding* (New York: Palgrave Macmillan, 2006), 79–99. For an application of readiness theory to a specific conflict, see Schiff, A., "Reaching a Mutual Agreement: Readiness Theory and Coalition Building in the Aceh Peace Process," *Negotiation and Conflict Management Research* 7(1), 2014, 57–82.

32. See Stimec, A., Poitras, J., and Campbell, J.J., "Ripeness, Readiness and Grief in Conflict Analysis," in Matyok, T., Senehi, J., and Byrne, S. (eds.), *Critical Issues in Peace and Conflict Studies: Theory, Practice and Pedagogy* (Blue Ridge Summit, PA: Lexington Books, 2011), 143–157.

33. Pruitt, D.G., *Whither Ripeness Theory?* Working paper no. 25, Institute for Conflict Analysis and Resolution, George Mason University, 2005, 6–7.

34. Bartoli, A., "Mediating Peace in Mozambique: The Role of the Community of Sant'Egidio," in Crocker, Hampson, and Aall, *Herding Cats*, 250.

35. See Fisher, R.J., "The Contingency Model for Third Party Interventions," in Nan, S.A., Mamphilly, Z.C., and Bartoli, A. (eds.), *Peacemaking: From Practice to Theory*, vol. 2 (Santa Barbara, CA: Praeger, 2012), 683–700; and Fisher, R.J., and Keashly, L., "The Potential Complementarity of Mediation and Consultation Within a Contingency Model of Third Party Intervention," *Journal of Peace Research* 28, 1991. Others who speak of the need to utilize different approaches at different points in the cycle of conflict include Crocker, C.A., Hampson, F.O., and Aall, P., "Multiparty Mediation and the Conflict Cycle," in Crocker, Hampson, and Aall, *Herding Cats;* and Jessop, M., Aljets, D., and Chacko, B., "The Ripe Moment for Civil Society," *International Negotiation* 13, 2008, 93–109.

36. For a small sample of these writings, see Docherty, J.S., "Culture and Negotiation: Symmetrical Anthropology for Negotiators," *Marquette Law Review* 87(4), 2004; Moore, C.W., and Woodrow, P., "Mapping Cultures: Strategies for Effective Intercultural Negotiations," in Davies, J., and Kaufman, E. (eds.), *Second Track/Citizen's Diplomacy: Concepts and Techniques for Conflict Transformation* (Lanham, MD: Rowman & Littlefield, 2002); Kimmel, P.R., "Culture and Conflict," in Deutsch, M., Coleman, P.T., and Marcus, E.C. (eds.), *The Handbook of Conflict Resolution: Theory and Practice, 2nd ed.* (San Francisco: Jossey-Bass, 2006), 625–648; and Cohen, R., "Negotiating Across Cultures," in Crocker, C., Hampson, F.O., and Aall, P. (eds.), *Managing Global Chaos: Sources of and Responses to International Conflict* (Washington, DC: United States Institute of Peace Press, 1996).

37. For more on "low context"/"high context" communication, see, for example, Kim, D., Pan, Y., and Soo Park, H., "High-Versus Low-Context Culture: A Comparison of Chinese, Korean, and American Cultures," *Psychology and Marketing* 15(6), September 1998, 505–521; Chua, E.G., Gudykunst, W.B., "Conflict Resolution Styles in Low- and High-context Cultures," *Communication Research Reports* 4(1), June 1987, 32–37; and Korac-Kakabadse, N., Kouzmin, A., Korac-Kakabadse, A., and Savery, L., "Low- and High-context Communication Patterns: Towards Mapping Cross-Cultural Encounters," *Cross Cultural Management: An International Journal* 8(2), 2001, 3–24.

38. Hall, E.T., *Beyond Culture* (Garden City, NY: Anchor Books, 1976). Similarly, Bernstein's work on "linguistic codes" makes many of the same points. See Bernstein, B., *Classes, Codes and Control* (London: Routledge, 1975).

39. See Stewart, E.C., "An Intercultural Interpretation of the Persian Gulf Crisis," *International Communication Studies* 4, 1991, 1–47; and Kimmel, P.R., "Cultural Perspectives on International Negotiation," *Journal of Social Issues* 50(1), 1994, 179–196.

40. For more on how the question of culture has had an impact on Iran-US discussions over the years, see Limbert, J.K, *Negotiating with Iran: Wrestling with the Ghosts of History* (Washington, DC: United States Institute of Peace Press, 2009); and Jones, P., "How to Negotiate with Iran," *Foreign Policy*, April 7, 2009. For an examination of US-Iran Track Two, which includes a consideration of how the culture issue affected these discussions, see Jones, P., "U.S.–Iran Nuclear Track Two from 2005 to 2011: What Have We Learned? Where Are We Going?" *Negotiation Journal*, October 2014, 347–366.

41. Another scholar who has explored the idea that people can belong to multiple cultures simultaneously, and that this can significantly influence how they respond to various conflict situations, is T.A. Northrup, "The Dynamic Identity in Personal and Social Conflict," in Kriesberg, L., Northrup, T.A., and Thorson, S.J. (eds.), *Intractable Conflicts and Their Transformation* (Syracuse, NY: Syracuse University Press, 1989).

42. Davidheiser, M., "Race, Worldviews, and Conflict Mediation: Black and White Styles of Conflict Revisited," *Peace and Change* 33(1), January 2008. Davidheiser applies the insights from his research to conflict resolution in West Africa in this same article. He also acknowledges that he is building on the earlier work of T. Kochman, *Black and White Styles of Conflict* (Chicago: University of Chicago Press, 1981).

43. See Burton, J.W., and Sandole, D., "Generic Theory: The Basis of Conflict Resolution," *Negotiation Journal* 2, 1986.

44. Zartman, I.W., and Berman, M.R., *The Practical Negotiator* (New Haven, CT: Yale University Press, 1982), 226. For other expressions of this idea, see Rubin, J.Z., and Sander, F.E.A., "Culture, Negotiation, and the Eye of the Beholder," *Negotiation Journal* 7, 1991, 249–254; Zartman, I.W., "A Skeptic's View," in Faure, G., and Rubin, J. (eds.), *Culture and Negotiation* (Newbury Park, CA: Sage, 1993); and Senger, J.M., "Tales of the Bazaar: Interest-based Negotiation Across Cultures," *Negotiation Journal*, July 2002, 233–250.

45. See, for example, the responses to Burton and Sandole by Avruch and Black: Avruch, K., and Black, P.W., "A Generic Theory of Conflict Resolution, A Critique," *Negotiation Journal* 3, 1987; Avruch, K., and Black, P.W., "The Culture Question and Conflict Resolution," *Peace and Change* 16, 1991. Avruch later expanded on the arguments made in these papers in his *Culture and Conflict Resolution* (Washington, DC: United States Institute of Peace Press, 1998). For a more recent critical response to Burton's ideas on culture in negotiation and mediation, see Vayrynen, T., *Culture and International Conflict Resolution: A Critical Analysis of the Work of John Burton* (Manchester, UK: University of Manchester Press, 2001).

46. Cohen, R., "Negotiating Across Cultures," in Crocker, Hampson, and Aall, *Managing Global Chaos*, 488.

47. Mitchell, C.R., and Banks, M., *Handbook of Conflict Resolution: The Analytical Problem-Solving Approach* (New York: Continuum, 1996), 86.

48. See Doob, L.W., and Foltz, W.J., "The Belfast Workshop: An Application of Group Techniques to a Destructive Conflict," *Journal of Conflict Resolution* 17, 1973; and Doob, L.W., "A Cyprus Workshop: An Exercise in Intervention Methodology," *Journal of Social Psychology* 94, 1974. Years later, Doob reflected on these experiences in his *Interventions: Guides and Perils* (New Haven, CT: Yale University Press, 1993).

49. Rouhana, N.N., "Unofficial Third-Party Intervention in International Conflict: Between Legitimacy and Disarray," *Negotiation Journal*, July 1995, 261.

50. See, for example, Fast, L.A., Neufeldt, R.C., Schirch, L., "Toward Ethically Grounded Conflict Interventions: Reevaluating Challenges in the 21st Century," *International Negotiation* 7(2), 2002; Barry, B., and Robinson, R.J., "Ethics in Conflict Resolution: The Ties That Bind," *International Negotiation* 7(2), 2002; and "Conflict Resolution and the Ethics of Intervention," ch. 14 in Ramsbotham, O., Woodhouse, T., and Miall, H., *Contemporary Conflict Resolution, 3rd ed.* (Cambridge, UK: Polity Press, 2011), 317–331.

51. For an early example, see Laue, J., and Cormick, C., "The Ethics of Intervention in Community Disputes," in Bermant, G., et al. (eds.), *The Ethics of Social Intervention* (New York: Halstead Press, 1978).

52. See Forsythe, D., *Humanitarian Politics: The International Committee of the Red Cross* (Baltimore: Johns Hopkins University Press, 1977).

53. See the discussion in Ramsbotham, O., Woodhouse, T., and Miall, H., *Contemporary Conflict Resolution, 3rd ed.* (Cambridge, UK: Polity Press, 2011), 320–321.

54. For an example of such a piece, see, Kydd, A., "Which Side Are You On? Bias, Credibility and Mediation," *American Journal of Political Science* 47(4), 2007, 597–611.

55. Kleiboer, M., "Understanding the Success or Failure of International Mediation," *Journal of Conflict Resolution* 40(2), 1996, 369.

56. Gent, S.E., and Shannon, M., "Bias and Effectiveness of Third Party Conflict Management Mechanisms," *Conflict Management and Peace Science* 28(2), 2011, 124–144.

57. For more on these arguments, see, for example, Kydd, A., "Which Side Are You On? Bias, Credibility and Mediation," *American Journal of Political Science* 47(4), 2007, 597–611; Wehr, P., and Lederach, J.P., "Mediating Conflict in Central America," *Journal of Conflict Resolution* 53(3), 2009, 446–469; and Savun, B., "Information, Bias and Mediation Success," *International Studies Quarterly* 52, 2008.

58. See Svensson, I., "Who Brings Peace? Neutral Versus Biased Mediation and Institutional Peace Arrangements in Civil Wars," *Journal of Conflict Resolution* 53(3), 2009, 446–469. For others who challenge the traditional notion that mediators should be "neutral," see Mayer, B., *Beyond Neutrality: Confronting the Crisis in Conflict Resolution* (San Francisco: Jossey-Bass, 2004); Cobb, S., and Rifkin, J., "Practice and Paradox: Deconstructing Neutrality in Mediation," *Law and Social Inquiry* 16(1), 1991, 35–62; and Princen, T., *Intermediaries in International Conflict* (Princeton, NJ: Princeton University Press, 1992).

59. For a discussion of these questions as they relate to an actual process, see Aspinall, E., *Peace Without Justice? The Helsinki Peace Process in Aceh*, HD Report (Geneva: Centre for Humanitarian Dialogue, April 2008). This report was commissioned by the HD Centre to reflect on whether efforts that it had been much involved in to end the fighting in the Indonesian region of Aceh had given too much priority to stopping the fighting and not enough to justice for the victims.

60. Ramsbotham, O., Woodhouse, T., and Miall, H., *Contemporary Conflict Resolution, 3rd ed.* (Cambridge, UK: Polity Press, 2011), 210. See also the collection of essays in Abu-Nimer, M. (ed.), *Reconciliation, Justice, and Coexistence: Theory and Practice* (Lanham, MD: Lexington, 2001); and Deutsch, M., "Justice and Conflict," in Deutsch, Coleman, and Marcus, *Handbook of Conflict Resolution*, 43–68.

61. Baker, P., "Conflict Resolution Versus Democratic Governance: Divergent Paths to Peace," in Crocker, Hampson, and Aall, *Managing Global Chaos*, 564.

62. Babbitt, E.F., "Conflict Resolution and Human Rights: The State of the Art," in Bercovitch, J., Kremenyuk, V., and Zartman, I.W. (eds.), *The Sage Handbook of Conflict Resolution* (Thousand Oaks, CA: Sage, 2009), 619.

63. The idea that individual dialogues are part of a much larger process of building peace, which must ultimately include questions of reconciliation, is fundamental to Saunders's concept of "circum-negotiation." See Saunders, H., "Pre-negotiation and Circum-negotiation: Arenas of the Peace Process," in Crocker, Hampson, and Aall, *Managing Global Chaos*.

64. A discussion of the ways in which reconciliation can be affected through such means as truth and reconciliation bodies, policies of official forgetting, restorative

justice, trials, and other means may be found in Ramsbotham, O., Woodhouse, T., and Miall, H., *Contemporary Conflict Resolution, 3rd ed.* (Cambridge, UK: Polity Press, 2011), 250–258. See also, Clark, P., and Kaufman, Z., *After Genocide: Transnational Justice, Post-Conflict Reconstruction, and Reconciliation in Rwanda and Beyond* (New York: Columbia University Press, 2009). For the views of one who lived through a situation of great harshness but saw the need to press forward with peace and then develop a reconciliation mechanism, see Tutu, Desmond, *No Peace Without Forgiveness* (London: Rider, 1999). See also Huyse, L., Salter, M., and Ingelaere, B., *Traditional Justice and Reconciliation After Violent Conflict: Learning from African Experiences* (Stockholm: International IDEA, 2008). Deutsch, M., "Justice and Conflict," in Deutsch, Coleman, and Marcus, *Handbook of Conflict Resolution*, 43–68, gives a good overview of the different *kinds* of justice that can be sought in a conflict reconciliation exercise.

65. Hara, F., "Burundi: A Case of Parallel Diplomacy," in Crocker, Hampson, and Aall, *Herding Cats*, 151.

66. See Fast, L.A., Neufeldt, R.C., Schirch, L., "Toward Ethically Grounded Conflict Interventions: Reevaluating Challenges in the 21st Century," *International Negotiation* 7(2), 2002, for an elaboration of these ideas.

67. First published in Jones, P., *Canada and Track Two Diplomacy* (Toronto: Canadian International Council, 2008). A similar set of codes, though different in some respects, may be found in Ramsbotham, O., Woodhouse, T., and Miall, H., *Contemporary Conflict Resolution, 3rd ed.* (Cambridge, UK: Polity Press, 2011), 320–324.

Chapter 4

1. Chataway, C., "The Problem of Transfer from Confidential Interactive Problem-Solving: What Is the Role of the Facilitator?" *Political Psychology* 23(1), 2002, 166. In making this point, Chataway was drawing on the work of J. Rubin, D. Pruitt, and S. Kim, *Social Conflict, Escalation, Stalemate and Settlement* (New York: McGraw-Hill, 1994).

2. See Keashly, L., and Fisher, R., "A Contingency Perspective on Conflict Interventions: Theoretical and Practical Considerations," in Bercovitch, J. (ed.), *Resolving International Conflicts* (London: Lynne Rienner, 1996); and Cross, S., and Rosenthal, R., "Three Models of Conflict Resolution: Effects on Intergroup Expectancies and Attitudes," *Journal of Social Issues* 55, 1999.

3. See Keashly, L., Fisher, R., and Grant, P., "The Comparative Utility of Third Party Consultation and Mediation Within a Complex Simulation of Intergroup Conflict," *Human Relations* 46, 1993.

4. See Jones, P., "U.S.–Iran Nuclear Track Two from 2005 to 2011: What Have We Learned? Where Are We Going?" *Negotiation Journal*, October 2014, 347–366.

5. Chataway, C., "Track II Diplomacy from a Track I Perspective," *Negotiation Journal*, July 1998.

6. See Doob, L.W., and Foltz, W.J., "The Belfast Workshop: An Application of Group Techniques to a Destructive Conflict," *Journal of Conflict Resolution* 17, 1973;

and Doob, L.W., "A Cyprus Workshop: An Exercise in Intervention Methodology," *Journal of Social Psychology* 94, 1974. Years later, Doob reflected on these experiences in his "Adieu to Private Intervention in Political Conflicts?" *International Journal of Group Tensions* 17(1), 15–27; and his *Interventions: Guides and Perils* (New Haven, CT: Yale University Press, 1993).

7. Burton, J.W., *Resolving Deep-Rooted Conflict: A Handbook* (Lanham, MD: University Press of America, 1987), 24.

8. Crocker, C.A., "Thoughts on the Conflict Management Field After 30 Years," *International Negotiation* 16, 2011, 3.

9. See, for example, the humorous, but rather sarcastic op-ed of Brigadier Gurmeet Kanwal of India on the seemingly never-ending India-Pakistan Track Two world, "India-Pakistan Track II Peace-making Efforts," posted on US-INPAC on December 22, 2011, at: http://blog.usinpac.com/gurmeet-kanwal/india-pakistan-track-ii-peace-making-efforts/ (accessed August 1, 2012). See also the much more caustic piece by former Israeli senior official and frequent participant in Israeli-Palestinian Track Two Jossi Alpher, "Time to Hang Up My Track (II) Shoes," posted on the website Jewish Daily Forward on June 16, 2006, at: http://forward.com/articles/782/time-to-hang-up-my-track-ii-shoes/ (accessed August 1, 2012). Despite these articles, both Kanwal and Alpher remain active and highly valued participants in Track Two in their respective regions.

10. Rouhana, N.N., "Unofficial Third-Party Intervention in International Conflict: Between Legitimacy and Disarray," *Negotiation Journal*, July 1995, 260–261.

11. For example, the Global Directory of Peace Studies and Conflict Resolution Programs contains profiles of over 450 undergraduate, masters, and doctoral programs in the field in over forty countries. It is available at: http://www.peacejusticestudies.org/globaldirectory/ (accessed August 2, 2012).

12. According to one recent survey, there have been at least 350 articles on mediation published in scholarly journals in English over the past decade, to say nothing of many books and nonscholarly papers. See Wall, J.A., and Dunne, T.C., "State of the Art—Mediation Research: A Current Review," *Negotiation Journal*, April 2012, 234. See also Crocker, C.A., "Thoughts on the Conflict Management Field After 30 Years," *International Negotiation* 16, 2011.

13. See, for example, Burgess, H., and Burgess, G., *Conducting Track II Peacemaking* (Washington, DC: United States Institute of Peace Press, 2010); Burton, J.W., *Resolving Deep-rooted Conflict: A Handbook* (Lanham, MD: University Press of America, 1987); and Mitchell, C.R., and Banks, M., *Handbook of Conflict Resolution: The Analytical Problem-Solving Approach* (New York: Continuum, 1996).

14. Mandell, B.S., and Fisher, R.J., "Training Third-Party Consultants in International Conflict Resolution," *Negotiation Journal* 8, July 1992.

15. One of the most respected of these is *Beyond Intractability*, which is maintained by the Conflict Information Consortium at the University of Colorado, Boulder. It may be found at: http://www.beyondintractability.org/ (accessed August 2, 2012).

16. Rouhana, N.N., "Interactive Conflict Resolution: Issues in Theory, Methodology, and Evaluation," in Druckman, D., and Stern, P.C. (eds.), *International Conflict*

Resolution After the Cold War (Washington, DC: National Academy Press, 2000), 318–324.

17. Ibid., 319.

18. Saunders, H., et al., "Interactive Conflict Resolution: A View for Policy Makers on Making and Building Peace," in *Druckman and Stern, International Conflict Resolution After the Cold War*, 257 and 291.

19. Ibid., 261. For a consideration of third party qualities organized around a "levels of analysis" approach, see Fisher, R.J., "Intergroup Conflict," in Deutsch, M., Coleman, P.T., and Marcus, E.C. (eds.), *The Handbook of Conflict Resolution: Theory and Practice, 2nd ed.* (San Francisco: Jossey-Bass, 2006), 176–196.

20. Fisher, R.J., "Introduction: Analyzing Successful Transfer Effects in Interactive Conflict Resolution," in Fisher, R.J. (ed.), *Paving the Way: Contributions of Interactive Conflict Resolution to Peacemaking* (New York: Lexington, 2005).

21. See, for example, the discussion of the qualities of the panel in Mitchell, C.R., and Banks, M., *Handbook of Conflict Resolution: The Analytical Problem-Solving Approach* (New York: Continuum, 1996), 84–86.

22. Lederach, J.P., *The Moral Imagination: The Art and Soul of Building Peace* (Oxford, UK: Oxford University Press, 2005), esp. 34–39.

23. Fisher, R.J., "Historical Mapping of the Field of Inter-active Conflict Resolution," in Davies, J., and Kaufman, E. (eds.), *Second Track/Citizen's Diplomacy: Concepts and Techniques for Conflict Transformation* (Lanham, MD: Rowman & Littlefield, 2002), 62.

24. Kelman, H.C., "Interactive Problem Solving as a Tool for Second Track Diplomacy," in Davies and Kaufman, *Second Track/Citizens' Diplomacy*, 82. See also his "Interactive Problem-solving: Informal Mediation by the Scholar Practitioner," in Bercovitch, J. (ed.), *Studies in International Mediation: Essays in Honor of Jeffrey Z. Rubin* (New York: Palgrave MacMillan, 2002), 168.

25. How much expertise in the specifics of the conflict is necessary for the third party is debated, as seen in the debate between Burton/Sandole and Avruch/Black in Chapter 2.

26. Kelman, H.C., "Interactive Problem Solving as a Tool for Second Track Diplomacy," in Davies and Kaufman, *Second Track/Citizens' Diplomacy*.

27. For an overview, see Lewicki, R.J., "Trust, Trust Development and Trust Repair," in Deutsch, Coleman, and Marcus, *Handbook of Conflict Resolution*, 92–119; Kramer, R., and Tyler, T.R. (eds.), *Trust in Organizations: Frontiers of Theory and Research* (Thousand Oaks, CA: Sage, 1996); Sitkin, S.B., Rousseau, D.M., Burt, R.S., and Camerer, C. (eds.), "Special Topic Forum on Trust in and Between Organizations," *Academy of Management Review* 23(3, entire issue), 1998.

28. For one of the first but still highly regarded discussions of how the concept of trust can be aggregated into different groupings, see Worchel, P., "Trust and Distrust," in Austin, W.G., and Worchel, S. (eds.), *The Social Psychology of Intergroup Relations* (Belmont, CA: Wadsworth, 1979). Others have built on Worchel's groupings, including Sitkin, S.B., Rousseau, D.M., Burt, R.S., and Camerer, C. (eds.), "Special Topic Forum on Trust in and Between Organizations," *Academy of Management Review*

23(3, entire issue), 1998; Lewicki, R.J., "Trust, Trust Development and Trust Repair," in Deutsch, Coleman, and Marcus, *Handbook of Conflict Resolution*, 92–119; and Dirks, K., and Ferrin, D., "The Role of Trust in Organizational Settings," *Organization Science* 12(4), 2001, 450–467.

29. Lewicki, R.J., "Trust, Trust Development and Trust Repair," in Deutsch, Coleman, and Marcus, *Handbook of Conflict Resolution*, 92–119.

30. Lewicki, R.J., and Bunker, B.B., "Developing and Maintaining Trust in Work Relationships," in Kramer, R., and Tyler, T.R. (eds.), *Trust in Organizations: Frontiers of Theory and Research* (Thousand Oaks, CA: Sage, 1996).

31. Miller, P.J., and Rempel, J.K., "Trust and Partner-Enhancing Attributions in Close Relationships," *Personality and Social Psychology Bulletin* 30(6), 2004, 695–705.

32. Goldberg, S.B., "The Secrets of Successful Mediators," *Negotiation Journal*, July 2005, 366. See also Bowling, D., and Hoffman, D., "Bringing Peace into the Room: The Personal Qualities of the Mediator and the Impact on Mediation," *Negotiation Journal*, January 2000.

33. Ross, W., and Wieland C., "Effects of Interpersonal Trust and Time Pressure on Managerial Mediation Strategy in a Simulated Organizational Dispute," *Journal of Applied Psychology* 81, 1996. For more on the importance of trust in mediation, see Rousseau, D., Sitkin, S., Burt, R., and Camerer, C., "Not so Different After All: A Cross-Discipline View of Trust," *Academy of Management Review* 23(3), 1998; and Salem R., "Trust in Mediation," in *Beyond Intractability*, at: http://www.beyondintractability.org/essay/trust_mediation/.

34. Ó Dochartaigh, N., "Together in the Middle: Back-channel Negotiation in the Irish Peace Process," *Journal of Peace Research* 48(6), 2011, 769.

35. The question of the "ground rules" of these meetings will be discussed in the next chapter.

36. Burgess, H., and Burgess, G., *Conducting Track II Peacemaking* (Washington, DC: United States Institute of Peace Press, 2010), 50. Another set of ideas as to how trust can be built may be found in Lewicki, R.J., "Trust, Trust Development and Trust Repair," in Deutsch, Coleman, and Marcus, *Handbook of Conflict Resolution*, 103–107.

37. See Mitchell, C.R., and Banks, M., *Handbook of Conflict Resolution: The Analytical Problem-Solving Approach* (New York: Continuum, 1996), 84: "However eminent a person may be . . . he or she will frequently damage a workshop if he has seen recent government service. . . . His or her neutrality would be in question."

38. See, for example, Svensson, I., "Who Brings Peace? Neutral Versus Biased Mediation and Institutional Peace Arrangements in Civil Wars," *Journal of Conflict Resolution* 53(3), 2009; and, Mason, S.A., *Mediation and Facilitation in Peace Processes* (Zurich: Center for Security Studies, 2007), 6.

39. Burgess, H., and Burgess, G., *Conducting Track II Peacemaking* (Washington, DC: United States Institute of Peace Press, 2010), 50.

40. Kelman, H.C., and Cohen, S.P., "The Problem-Solving Workshop: A Social-Psychological Contribution to the Resolution of International Conflicts," *Journal of Peace Research* 13(2), 1976, 86–88.

41. Ibid., 86.

42. Burton, J.W., *Conflict and Communication: The Use of Controlled Communication in International Relations* (London: Macmillan, 1969).

43. Kelman, H.C., and Cohen, S.P., "The Problem-Solving Workshop: A Social-Psychological Contribution to the Resolution of International Conflicts," *Journal of Peace Research* 13(2), 1976, 86.

44. For more on the question of how culture and history affect Iranian negotiating behavior, see Limbert, J.W., *Negotiating with Iran: Wrestling the Ghosts of History* (Washington, DC: United States Institute of Peace Press, 2009); and Jones, P., "How to Negotiate with Iran," *Foreign Policy*, 2009, online edition at: http://www.foreignpolicy.com/story/cms.php?story_id=4801. For more on the impact of culture and history on negotiations generally, see Cohen, R., "Negotiating Across Cultures," in Crocker, C., Hampson, F.O., and Aall, P. (eds.), *Managing Global Chaos: Sources of and Responses to International Conflict* (Washington, DC: United States Institute of Peace Press, 1996); and Moore, C.W., and Woodrow, P., "Mapping Cultures: Strategies for Effective Intercultural Negotiations," in Davies and Kaufman, *Second Track/Citizen's Diplomacy.*

45. Aall, P., "The Power of Nonofficial Actors in Conflict Management," in Crocker, C.A., Hampson, F.O., and Aall, P. (eds.), *Leashing the Dogs of War: Conflict Management in a Divided World* (Washington, DC: United States Institute of Peace Press, 2007), 480.

46. Touval, S., "Coercive Mediation on the Road to Dayton," *International Negotiation* 1(1), 1996. Touval used the phrase "mediator with muscle" in his *The Peace Brokers: Mediators in the Arab-Israeli Conflict, 1948–1979* (Princeton, NJ: Princeton University Press, 1982). For a more general discussion of the way in which the concept of power affects conflict situations, and therefore the environment in which mediators work, see Coleman, P.T., "Power and Conflict," in Deutsch, Coleman, and Marcus, *Handbook of Conflict Resolution,* 120–143; Blalock, H.M., *Power and Conflict: Toward a General Theory* (Thousand Oaks, CA: Sage, 1989); and Davidson, J.A., McElwee, G., and Hannan, G., "Trust and Power as Determinants of Conflict Resolution Strategy and Outcome Satisfaction," *Peace and Conflict: Journal of Peace Psychology* 10, 2004, 275–292.

47. Rubin, J.Z., "International Mediation in Context," in Bercovitch. J., and Rubin, J.Z. (eds.), *Mediation in International Relations* (New York: St. Martin's Press, 1992), 254–256, quoted in Aall, "Power of Nonofficial Actors in Conflict Management," who also discusses these different kinds of power and their implications for mediators. This typology is based on groundbreaking research into the nature of power in relationships done in the 1950s by French and Raven. See French Jr., J.R.P., and Raven, B., "The Bases of Social Power," in Cartwright, D. (ed.), *Studies in Social Power* (Ann Arbor: University of Michigan Press, 1959), 150–167.

Chapter 5

1. This history of the evolution of the problem-solving approach is taken from Mitchell, C.R., "From Controlled Communication to Problem Solving: The Origins

of Facilitated Conflict Resolution," *International Journal of Peace Studies* 6(1), Spring 2001. Another author who has written about the origins of the field is Hill, B.J., "An Analysis of Conflict Resolution Techniques: From Problem-Solving Workshops to Theory," *Journal of Conflict Resolution* 26(1), March 1982, 109–138.

2. Hollis, F., "Personality Diagnosis in Casework," in Farad, H. (ed.), *Ego Psychology and Dynamic Case Work* (New York: Family Service Association of America, 1958).

3. Emery, F.E., and Trist, E.L., "The Causal Texture of Organizational Environments," *Human Relations* 18(1), 1964, 21–32.

4. Blake, R.R., Shepherd, H.A., and Mouton, J.S., *Managing Inter-Group Conflict in Industry* (Houston: Gulf, 1964).

5. Mitchell, C.R., "From Controlled Communication to Problem Solving: The Origins of Facilitated Conflict Resolution," *International Journal of Peace Studies* 6(1), Spring 2001, 3.

6. Chataway, C., "The Problem of Transfer from Confidential Interactive Problem-Solving: What Is the Role of the Facilitator?" *Political Psychology* 23(1), 2002, 166. Chataway was drawing on the work of Rubin, J., Pruitt, D., and Kim, S., *Social Conflict, Escalation, Stalemate and Settlement* (New York: McGraw-Hill, 1994).

7. See Keashly, L., and Fisher, R., "A Contingency Perspective on Conflict Interventions: Theoretical and Practical Considerations," in Bercovitch, J. (ed.), *Resolving International Conflicts* (London: Lynne Rienner, 1996); and Cross, S., and Rosenthal, R., "Three Models of Conflict Resolution: Effects on Intergroup Expectancies and Attitudes," *Journal of Social Issues* 55, 1999.

8. See Keashly, L., Fisher, R., and Grant, P., "The Comparative Utility of Third Party Consultation and Mediation Within a Complex Simulation of Intergroup Conflict," *Human Relations* 46, 1993. See also Babbitt, E., and d'Estrée, T.P., "An Israeli-Palestinian Women's Workshop: Application of the Interactive Problem-solving Approach," in Crocker, C.A., Hampson, F.O., and Aall, P. (eds.), *Managing Global Chaos: Sources of an Responses to International Conflict* (Washington, DC: United States Institute of Peace Press, 1996).

9. Çuhadar, E., and Dayton, B., "The Social Psychology of Identity and Inter-group Conflict: From Theory to Practice," *International Studies Perspectives* 12, 2011, 277. For a sampling of the studies that have looked at contact theory and how it works, see Allport, G., *The Nature of Prejudice* (Cambridge, MA: Perseus Books, 1954); Pettigrew, T., "Advancing Racial Justice: Past Lessons for Future Use," in Knopke, H.J., Norrell, R.J., and Rogers, R.W. (eds.), *Opening Doors: Perspectives on Race Relations in Contemporary America* (Tuscaloosa: University of Alabama Press, 1991); Cook, S.W., "Interpersonal and Attitudinal Outcomes in Cooperating Interracial Groups," *Journal of Research and Development in Education* 12(1), 1978, 97–113; Amir, Y., "The Role of Inter-group Contact in Change of Prejudice and Ethnic Relations," in Katz, P.A. (ed.), *Towards the Elimination of Racism* (New York: Pergamon, 1976); Smith, C.B., "Back and to the Future: The Inter-Group Contact Hypothesis Revisited," *Sociological Inquiry* 64, 1994, 438–455; Powers, D.A., and Ellison, C.G., "Interracial Contact and

Black Racial Attitudes: The Contact Hypothesis and Selectivity Bias," *Social Forces* 74, 1995, 205–226; and Bercovitch, J., and Chalfin, J., "Contact and Conflict Resolution: Examining the Extent to Which Interpersonal Contact and Cooperation Can Affect the Management of International Conflicts," *International Negotiation* 16, 2011, 11–37.

10. Authors who have written outlines of what a "hypothetical" PSW looks like include Kelman, H.C., and Cohen, S.P., "The Problem-Solving Workshop: A Social-Psychological Contribution to the Resolution of International Conflicts," *Journal of Peace Research* 13(2), 1976; and Mitchell, C.R., and Banks, M., *Handbook of Conflict Resolution: The Analytical Problem-Solving Approach* (New York: Continuum, 1996), esp. ch. 8, "The Conduct of a Workshop." See also Çuhadar, E., "Problem Solving Workshops," in Young, N.J. (ed.), *The Oxford International Encyclopedia of Peace* (Oxford, UK: Oxford University Press, 2010), vol. 3, 574–578.

11. Rouhana, N.N., "Interactive Conflict Resolution: Issues in Theory, Methodology, and Evaluation," in Druckman, D., and Stern, P.C. (eds.), *International Conflict Resolution After the Cold War* (Washington, DC: National Academy Press, 2000).

12. This discussion draws on Rouhana, "Interactive Conflict Resolution," 306–318.

13. Linville, P.W., Salovy, P., and Fisher, G.W., "Stereotyping and Perceived Distribution of Social Characteristics: An Application to Inter-group Perception," in Dovidio, J.F. and Gartner, S.L., eds., *Prejudice, Discrimination and Racism* (Orlando, FL: Academic press, 1986), 165–208.

14. Rouhana, N.N., "Interactive Conflict Resolution: Issues in Theory, Methodology, and Evaluation," in Druckman and Stern, *International Conflict Resolution After the Cold War*, 324–326.

15. This point is made in Shapiro, I., "Theories of Practice and Change in Ethnic Conflict Interventions," in Fitzduff, M., and Stout, C.E. (eds.), *The Psychology of Resolving Ethnic Conflict*, vol. 3 (Santa Barbara, CA: Praeger Security International, 2006). See also Çuhadar, E., and Dayton, B., "The Social Psychology of Identity and Inter-group Conflict: From Theory to Practice," *International Studies Perspectives* 12, 2011, 283: "We observed that an important number of practitioners have been undertaking their activities without formulating a theory of change."

16. Cross, S., and Rosenthal, R., "Three Models of Conflict Resolution: Effects on Intergroup Expectancies and Attitudes," *Journal of Social Issues* 55(3), 1999, 577.

17. Çuhadar, E., and Dayton, B., "The Social Psychology of Identity and Inter-group Conflict: From Theory to Practice," *International Studies Perspectives* 12, 2011, 277.

18. Saunders, H., et al., "Interactive Conflict Resolution: A View for Policy Makers on Making and Building Peace," in Druckman and Stern, *International Conflict Resolution After the Cold War*, 259–260.

19. Kochman, T., *Black and White Styles of Conflict* (Chicago: University of Chicago Press, 1981).

20. Davidheiser, M. "Race, Worldviews, and Conflict Mediation: Black and White Styles of Conflict Revisited," *Peace and Change* 33(1), January 2008, 63–64.

21. Rothman, J., *Resolving Identity-based Conflict in Nations, Organizations and Communities* (San Francisco: Jossey Bass, 1997); and Rothman, J. (ed.), *From*

Identity-Based Conflict to Identity-Based Cooperation: The ARIA Approach in Theory and Practice (New York: Springer, 2012). See esp. the chapter by Kaufman, E., Davies, J., and Patel, H., "Experimenting with ARIA Globally: Best Practices and Lessons Learned," for an analysis of how the ARIA method has worked in real-world cases.

22. For more on recruitment, see Burgess, H., and Burgess, G., *Conducting Track II Peacemaking* (Washington, DC: United States Institute of Peace Press, 2010), 41–43.

23. For a discussion of the dangers of the easy coalition, see Kellen, D., Bekerman, Z., and Maoz, I., "An Easy Coalition: The Peacecamp Identity and Israeli-Palestinian Track Two Diplomacy," *Journal of Conflict Resolution* 57(4), 2012, 543–569.

24. Volkan has probed the relationships between what he calls "large group identities" (the ways in which individuals identify with, and conceive of themselves as being members of large groups), and the individual identities of the people who are around a table. See his post, Volkan, V., "Large-group Identity and Post-Traumatic Flocking," on the *Psychology Tomorrow* blog at: http://www.psychologytomorrowmagazine.com/large-group-identity-and-post-traumatic-flocking/ (accessed June 27, 2014). See also Volkan, V., "Large-group Identity: Border Psychology and Other Related Issues," *Mind and Human Interaction* 13, 2003, 49–75.

25. Agha, H.S., Feldman, S., Khalidi, A., and Schiff, Z., *Track II Diplomacy: Lessons from the Middle East* (Cambridge, MA: MIT Press, 2003), 2. See also Burgess, H., and Burgess, G., *Conducting Track II Peacemaking* (Washington, DC: United States Institute of Peace Press, 2010), 40–41.

26. Gibb, J.R., "Defensive Communication," *Journal of Communications* 11(3), 1961, 141–148.

27. Quotes from Chaitin, J., "Creating Safe Spaces for Communication," in Burgess, G., and Burgess, H. (eds.), *Beyond Intractability*, Conflict Information Consortium, University of Colorado, Boulder. Posted July 2003 at: http://www.beyondintractability.org/bi-essay/safe-spaces.

28. See Maoz, I., "Power Relations in Inter-group Encounters: A Case Study of Jewish-Arab Encounters in Israel," *International Journal of Intercultural Relations* 24, 2002, 259–277. See also Maoz, I., "Evaluating the Communication Between Groups in Dispute: Equality on Contact Interventions Between Jews and Arabs in Israel," *Negotiation Journal* 21(1), 2005, 131–146.

29. See Tieku, T.K., "Perks Diplomacy: The Role of Perquisites in Mediation," *International Negotiation* 18, 2013, 245–263, for an analysis of how overly generous perks for participants in mediation exercises can delay progress because the participants do not wish to give up their perks. In most cases the kinds of perks Tieku is talking about in this article are being offered by governments within official mediation processes and are far beyond the resources and capabilities of Track Two projects, but the point is a valid one.

30. Rouhana, N.N., "Interactive Conflict Resolution: Issues in Theory, Methodology, and Evaluation," in Druckman and Stern, *International Conflict Resolution After the Cold War*, 297.

31. Çuhadar, E., and Dayton, B., "The Social Psychology of Identity and Inter-group Conflict: From Theory to Practice," *International Studies Perspectives* 12, 2011, 286.

32. Fisher, R.J., *Interactive Conflict Resolution* (Syracuse, NY: Syracuse University Press, 1997), 219.

33. Mitchell, C.R., and Banks, M., *Handbook of Conflict Resolution: The Analytical Problem-Solving Approach* (New York: Continuum, 1996), 83.

34. Burgess, H., and Burgess, G., *Conducting Track II Peacemaking* (Washington, DC: United States Institute of Peace Press, 2010), 46.

35. Egeland, J., "The Oslo Accord: Multiparty Facilitation Through the Norwegian Channel," in Crocker, C.A., Hampson, F.O., and Aall, P. (eds.), *Herding Cats: Multiparty Mediation in a Complex World* (Washington, DC: United States Institute of Peace Press, 2003), 543.

36. Ibid.

37. The Ottawa Dialogue website is at: http://socialsciences.uottawa.ca/dialogue/eng/.

38. Walton, R.E., and McKersie, R.B., *A Behavioral Theory of Labor Negotiations: An Analysis of a Social Interaction System* (Ithaca, NY: School of Industrial Labor Relations, Cornell University, 1991).

39. Ó Dochartaigh, N., "Together in the Middle: Back-channel Negotiation in the Irish Peace Process," *Journal of Peace Research* 48(6), 2011, 773. Of course, these discussions were necessarily "secret," as opposed to most Track Two, which is certainly done quietly but is not completely secret.

40. Çuhadar, E., and Dayton, B., "The Social Psychology of Identity and Inter-group Conflict: From Theory to Practice," *International Studies Perspectives* 12, 2011, 289.

Chapter 6

1. The succeeding paragraphs draw on Fisher, R.J., "Introduction: Analysing Successful Transfer Effects in Interactive Conflict Resolution," in Fisher, R.J. (ed.), *Paving the Way: Contributions of Interactive Conflict Resolution to Peacemaking* (New York: Lexington, 2005); *hereafter cited as* Fisher, "Introduction." See also Jones, P., *Canada and Track Two Diplomacy* (Toronto: Canadian International Council, 2008).

2. Fisher, "Introduction," 3.

3. Burton, J., *Conflict: Resolution and Prevention* (New York: St. Martin's Press, 1990).

4. For a contemporaneous paper questioning whether Burton's model might have been influenced by a situation in which the parties were looking for a solution anyway, see de Reuck, A., "A Note on Techniques and Procedures" (London: CIBA Foundation, 1966). For a later analysis which raises these same points, see Mitchell, C., "Ending Confrontation Between Indonesia and Malaysia: A Pioneering Contribution to International Problem Solving," in Fisher, *Paving the Way*, 19–40.

5. Çuhadar, E., "Assessing Transfer from Track Two Diplomacy: The Cases of Water and Jerusalem," *Journal of Peace Research* 46(5), 2009, 642.

6. Kelman, H.C., "The Problem Solving Workshop in Conflict Resolution," in Merritt, R.L. (ed.), *Communication in International Politics* (Urbana: University of Illinois Press, 1972). See also Fisher, "Introduction," 5.

7. Kelman, H.C., "Contributions of an Unofficial Conflict Resolution Effort to the Israeli-Palestinian Breakthrough," *Negotiation Journal* 11(1), January 1995. Fisher outlines three similar categories: "Preparing the ground for negotiations and improving the current negotiating process; . . . creat[ing] new ideas and insights, including options for solutions to be fed into the political process; [and] transforming relations among the parties at all levels." Fisher, R.J., "Conclusion," in Fisher, R.J. (ed.), *Paving the Way: Contributions of Interactive Conflict Resolution to Peacemaking* (New York: Lexington, 2005), 223–224; *hereafter cited as* Fisher, "Conclusion."

8. One of the first to mention the idea of "re-entry" as a problem in this context was Walton, R., "A Problem-solving Workshop on Border Conflicts in Eastern Africa," *Journal of Applied Behavioral Science* 6, 1970, 453–489.

9. Mitchell, C.R., *Peacemaking and the Consultant's Role* (Westmead, UK: Gower, 1981). See also Fisher, "Introduction," 5.

10. Mitchell, C.R., *Peacemaking and the Consultant's Role* (Westmead, UK: Gower, 1981).

11. See, for example, Kelman, H., "Evaluating the Contributions of Interactive Problem Solving to the Resolution of Ethnonational Conflicts," *Peace and Conflict* 14, 2008, 33; and Fisher, R.J., *Interactive Conflict Resolution* (Syracuse, NY: Syracuse University Press, 1997), 202–204.

12. Kraft, H. J., "The Autonomy Dilemma of Track Two Diplomacy in Southeast Asia," *Security Dialogue* 31(3), September 2000, 346.

13. Lederach, J.P., *The Moral Imagination: The Art and Soul of Building Peace* (Oxford, UK: Oxford University Press, 2005), 34–39.

14. Keashly, L., and Fisher, R., "A Contingency Perspective on Conflict Interventions: Theoretical and Practical Considerations," in Bercovitch, J. (ed.), *Resolving International Conflicts* (London: Lynne Rienner, 1996), 255.

15. Fisher, R.J., *Interactive Conflict Resolution* (Syracuse, NY: Syracuse University Press, 1997), 202.

16. See Nan, S.A., Druckman, D., and Horr, J.E., "Unofficial International Conflict Resolution: Is There a Track One and a Half? Are There Best Practices?" *Conflict Resolution Quarterly* 27(1), 2009, 65–82.

17. See Agha, H.S., Feldman, S., Khalidi, A., and Schiff, Z., *Track II Diplomacy: Lessons from the Middle East* (Cambridge, MA: MIT Press, 2003), 3–5 and *passim* for a discussion of this idea.

18. Fisher, "Conclusion," 207–209.

19. Ibid., 225.

20. Fitzduff, M., and Church, C. (eds.), *NGOs at the Table: Strategies for Influencing Policies in Areas of Conflict* (New York: Rowman & Littlefield, 2004).

21. See, for example, Goodhand, J., *Aiding Peace: The Role of NGOs in Armed Conflict* (Boulder, CO: Lynne Rienner, 2006); and Wanis-St. John, A., and Kew, D., "Civil Society and Peace Negotiations: Confronting Exclusion," *International Negotiation* 13(1), 2009, 11–36.

22. For example, in their broad assessment of seventy-nine Track Two projects that have taken place in the Israeli-Palestinian case, Çuhadar and Dayton specifically use Fitzduff and Church's typology of "insider" and "outsider" strategies to assess the transfer effects of these projects. See Çuhadar, E., and Dayton, B., "Oslo and Its Aftermath: Lessons Learned from Track Two Diplomacy," *Negotiation Journal*, April 2012, 170–174.

23. See Agha, H.S., Feldman, S., Khalidi, A., and Schiff, Z., *Track II Diplomacy: Lessons from the Middle East* (Cambridge, MA: MIT Press, 2003).

24. Ibid., 4.

25. Ibid., 4–5.

26. Çuhadar, E., "Assessing Transfer from Track Two Diplomacy: The Cases of Water and Jerusalem," *Journal of Peace Research* 46(5), 2009, 642.

27. Ibid., 643.

28. The home page of the Geneva Initiative may be found at: http://www.geneva-accord.org/.

29. Çuhadar, E., "Assessing Transfer from Track Two Diplomacy: The Cases of Water and Jerusalem," *Journal of Peace Research* 46(5), 2009, 654.

30. Capie, D., "When Does Track Two Matter? Structure, Agency and Asian Regionalism," *Review of International Political Economy* 17(2), May 2010.

31. Job, B., "Track 2 Diplomacy: Ideational Contribution to the Evolving Asia Security Order," in Alagappa, M. (ed.), *Asian Security Order: Instrumental and Normative Features* (Stanford, CA: Stanford University Press, 2002).

32. Acharya, A., *Constructing a Regional Security Community in Southeast Asia: ASEAN and the Problem of Regional Order* (London: Routledge, 2001); and Acharya, A., *Whose Ideas Matters? Agency and Power in Asian Regionalism* (Ithaca, NY: Cornell University Press, 2009).

33. Chataway, C., "The Problem of Transfer from Confidential Interactive Problem-Solving: What Is the Role of the Facilitator?" *Political Psychology* 23(1), 2002.

34. For examples of this, see ibid., 175–176.

35. Ibid., 181.

36. Mitchell, C.R., "Persuading Lions: Problems of Transferring Insights from Track-Two Exercises Undertaken in Conditions of Asymmetry," *Dynamics of Asymmetric Conflict* 2(1), 2009, 32–50.

37. Çuhadar, E., "Assessing Transfer from Track Two Diplomacy: The Cases of Water and Jerusalem," *Journal of Peace Research* 46(5), 2009, 647 and 650.

38. See, for example, Stern, P.C., and Druckman, D., "Evaluating Interventions in History: The Case of International Conflict Resolution," *International Studies Review* 2(1), Spring 2000, 33–63; Church, C., and Shouldice, J., *The Evaluation of Conflict Resolution Interventions: Framing the State of Play* (Letterkenny, Ireland: Browne, 2002);

Church, C., and Shouldice, J., *The Evaluation of Conflict Resolution Intervention, Part II: Emerging Practice and Theory* (Letterkenny, Ireland: Browne, 2003); Deutsch, M., and Goldman, J.S., "A Framework for Thinking About Research on Conflict Resolution Initiatives," in Deutsch, M., Coleman, P.T., and Marcus, E.C. (eds.), *The Handbook of Conflict Resolution: Theory and Practice, 2nd ed.* (San Francisco: Jossey-Bass, 2006), 825–848; Kelman, H., "Evaluating the Contributions of Interactive Problem Solving to the Resolution of Ethnonational Conflicts," *Peace and Conflict* 14, 2008, 29–60; and Çuhadar, E., Dayton, B., and Paffenholz, T., "Evaluation in Conflict Resolution and Peacebuilding," in Sandole, D.J., Byrne, S., Sandole-Staroste, I., and Senehi, J. (eds.), *Handbook of Conflict Analysis and Resolution* (New York: Routledge, 2009), 286–299.

39. See Bush, K., and Duggan, C., "Evaluation in Conflict Zones: Methodological and Ethical Challenges," *Journal of Peacebuilding and Development* 8(2), 2013, 5–25.

40. See Elliott, M., d'Estrée, T.P., and Kaufman, S., "Evaluation as a Tool for Reflection, " in Burgess, G., and Burgess, H. (eds.), *Beyond Intractability*, Conflict Information Consortium, University of Colorado, Boulder. Posted September 2003 at: http://www.beyondintractability.org/bi-essay/evaluation-reflection.

41. Malhotra, D., and Liyanage, S., "Long-Term Effects of Peace Workshops in Protracted Conflicts," *Journal of Conflict Resolution* 49(6), 2005, 908–924.

42. Maoz, I., "An Experiment in Peace: Reconciliation-Aimed Dialogues of Israeli and Palestinian Youth," *Journal of Peace Research* 37, 2000, 721–736. More recently, J. Schroeder and L. Risen have come up with similar findings. See their "Peace Through Friendship," *New York Times*, August 24, 2014, Focus section, 9; journal article forthcoming.

43. For a discussion of the difficulties of assessing the relationship between short- and long-term contributions made by mediation exercises, see Beardly, K., "Agreements Without Peace? International Mediation and Time Inconsistency Problems," *American Journal of Political Science* 52(4), 2008, 723–740.

44. Kaye, D.D., *Talking to the Enemy: Track Two Diplomacy in the Middle East and South Asia (Santa Monica, CA: RAND, 2007),* 105–106, emphasis in original.

45. See, for example, the assessment of seventy-nine very different Track Two projects that have taken place in the Israeli-Palestinian case between the signing of the Oslo Accord and 2010, in Çuhadar, E., and Dayton, B., "Oslo and Its Aftermath: Lessons Learned from Track Two Diplomacy," *Negotiation Journal*, April 2012.

46. For a discussion of the implications of multiple projects involving many of the same people, see Jones, P., "U.S.–Iran Nuclear Track Two from 2005 to 2011: What Have We Learned? Where Are We Going?" *Negotiation Journal*, October 2014, 347–366.

47. Çuhadar, E., Dayton, B., and Paffenholz, T., "Evaluation in Conflict Resolution and Peacebuilding," in Sandole, Byrne, Sandole-Staroste, and Senehi, *Handbook of Conflict Analysis and Resolution*, 289–293.

48. See d'Estrée, T.P., Fast, L.A., Weiss, J.N., and Jakobsen, M.S., "Changing the Debate About 'Success' in Conflict Resolution Efforts," *Negotiation Journal*, April 2001, 103.

49. Elliott, M., d'Estrée, T.P., and Kaufman, S., "Evaluation as a Tool for Reflection," in Burgess and Burgess, *Beyond Intractability.*

50. Deutsch, M., and Goldman, J.S., "A Framework for Thinking About Research on Conflict Resolution Initiatives," in Deutsch, Coleman, and Marcus, *Handbook of Conflict Resolution,* 838–841. They also identify other evaluation tools more suited to conflict resolution activities in other settings, such as schools and workplaces, on 841–845 in the same book.

51. d'Estrée, T.P., Fast, L.A., Weiss, J.N., and Jakobsen, M.S., "Changing the Debate About 'Success' in Conflict Resolution Efforts," *Negotiation Journal,* April 2001.

52. For more on "action evaluation research," see Ross, M.H., "Action Evaluation in the Theory and Practice of Conflict Resolution," *Peace and Conflict Studies* 8(1), 2001; and Rothman, J., "Action Evaluation," in Burgess and Burgess, *Beyond Intractability.* Posted October 2003 at: http://www.beyondintractability.org/bi-essay/action-evaluation.

53. Deutsch and Goldman, "A Framework for Thinking About . . . " op cit.

54. Kelman, H., "Evaluating the Contributions of Interactive Problem Solving to the Resolution of Ethnonational Conflicts," *Peace and Conflict* 14, 2008, 44–51. Kelman also discusses the utility of using students to run mock PSWs as a method of testing and evaluating hypotheses, on 51–56 of the same article, but he is generally lukewarm on this method.

55. Saunders, H.H., *Sustained Dialogue in Conflicts: Transformation and Change* (New York: Palgrave Macmillan, 2011).

56. Fisher, R.J., "Transfer Effects from Track Two Diplomacy: Toward a Process and Outcome Model," paper presented at workshop "Transfer and Track Two Diplomacy" at Stanford University, March 20–21, 2014; edited volume forthcoming.

57. For a discussion of other possible means, see Church, C., and Shouldice, J., *The Evaluation of Conflict Resolution Interventions: Framing the State of Play* (Letterkenny, Ireland: Browne, 2002); and Church, C., and Shouldice, J., *The Evaluation of Conflict Resolution Intervention, Part II: Emerging Practice and Theory* (Letterkenny, Ireland: Browne, 2003).

58. See the website of the Canadian International Development Agency (CIDA) for webpage "Results-Based Management Tools at CIDA: A How-to Guide" at: http://www.acdi-cida.gc.ca/acdi-cida/acdi-cida.nsf/eng/NAT-92213444-N2H (accessed on August 11, 2013).

59. For a discussion of the impact of all this on the management of Canada's public service, see Clark, I.D., and Swain, H., "Distinguishing the Real from the Surreal in Management Reform: Suggestions for Beleaguered Administrators in the Government of Canada," *Canadian Public Administration* 48(4), Winter 2005, 453–476.

60. The exact Performance Measurement Framework Template may be found at: http://www.acdi-cida.gc.ca/INET/IMAGES.NSF/vLUImages/Form/$file/4033–02E.pdf (accessed on August 11, 2013).

61. For more on how bureaucratic rigidity is hampering Canada's ability to support Track Two, see Jones, P., *Canada and Track Two Diplomacy* (Toronto:

Canadian International Council, 2008). For more on how Canadian diplomats feel it has impacted Canada's ability to be a mediator at the Track One level, see Jones, P., "Canada and International Conflict Mediation," *International Negotiation* 18, 2013.

62. A study which supports the notion that changes within the attitudes of group members and their willingness to advocate for those changes outside the group are among the most tangible things that can be measured from Track Two is De Vries, M., and Maoz, I., "Tracking for Peace: Assessing the Effectiveness of Track Two Diplomacy in the Israeli-Palestinian Conflict," *Dynamics of Asymmetric Conflict* 6(1-3), 2013, 62-74.

Conclusion

1. One study reports that some 350 NGOs were engaged in peacemaking and peacebuilding in 2007, compared with some 83 ten years before. Though the definitions between the two datasets were slightly different, the trend line is clear. See Dayton, B.W., "Useful but Insufficient: Intermediaries in Peacebuilding," in Dayton, B.W., and Kriesberg, L. (eds.), *Conflict Transformation and Peacebuilding* (New York: Routledge, 2009), 61-73.

2. For more on the changing face of diplomacy, see Sending, O.J., Pouliot, V., and Neumann, I.B., "The Future of Diplomacy: Changing Practices, Evolving Relationships," *International Journal*, Summer 2011, 527-542.

3. *International Studies Review* 13(1), 2011. A discussion of this special issue and its implications for conflict resolution may also be found in Avruch, K., and Nan, S.A., "Introduction: The Constraints of Practicing Conflict Resolution from Academic Settings," *Negotiation Journal*, April 2013.

4. Weiss, T.G., and Kittikhoun, A., "Theory vs. Practice: A Symposium," *International Studies Review* 13(1), 2011, 1.

5. See, for example, George, A.L., "The Two Cultures of Academia and Policy-Making: Bridging the Gap," *Political Psychology* 15(1), 1994, 143-172; Girard, M., Wolf-Dieter, E., and Webb, K. (eds.), *Theory and Practice in Foreign Policy Making: National Perspectives on Academics and Professionals in International Relations* (London: Pinter, 1994); Hill, C., and Beshoff, P. (eds.), *Two Worlds of International Relations: Academics, Practitioners and the Trade in Ideas (London: Routledge, 1994)*; Jentleson, B.W., "The Need for Praxis: Bringing Policy Relevance Back In," *International Security* 4, 2002, 169-183; Nincic, M., and Lepgold, J. (eds.), *Being Useful: Policy Relevance and International Relations Theory* (Ann Arbor: University of Michigan Press, 2000); and Nye Jr., J.S., "International Relations: The Relevance of Theory to Practice," in Reus-Smit, C., and Snidal, D. (eds.), *The Oxford Handbook of International Relations* (Oxford, UK: Oxford University Press, 2008), 648-660.

6. Babbitt, E., and Hampson, F.O., "Conflict Resolution as a Field of Inquiry: Practice Informing Theory," *International Studies Review* 13, 2011, 46.

7. Avruch, K., and Nan, S.A., "Introduction: The Constraints of Practicing Conflict Resolution from Academic Settings," *Negotiation Journal*, April 2013. See also the

articles by Mitchell, "Institutional Models for Track Two Interventions"; Docherty, "What Can We Learn from a University That Rewards Faculty Practice?"; and Gopin, "Conflict Analysis and Conflict Resolution: Divorce or Friendly Mediation?" in the same issue.

8. On one side of this debate, see Burton, J.W., and Sandole, D., "Generic Theory: The Basis of Conflict Resolution," *Negotiation Journal* 2, 1986. On the other, see Avruch, K., and Black, P.W., "A Generic Theory of Conflict Resolution: A Critique," *Negotiation Journal* 3, 1987; and more recently, and indeed retrospectively, Vayrynen, T., *Culture and International Conflict Resolution: A Critical Analysis of the Work of John Burton* (Manchester, UK: University of Manchester Press, 2001).

9. Shapiro, I., "Theories of Practice and Change in Ethnic Conflict Interventions," in Fitzduff, M., and Stout, C.E. (eds.), *The Psychology of Resolving Ethnic Conflict,* vol. 3 (Santa Barbara, CA: Praeger Security International, 2006); Çuhadar, E., and Dayton, B., "The Social Psychology of Identity and Inter-group Conflict: From Theory to Practice," *International Studies Perspectives* 12, 2011, 283.

10. Notably explored in Raffia, H., *The Art and Science of Negotiation* (Cambridge, MA: Harvard University Press, 1982).

Bibliography

Aall, P. "The Power of Nonofficial Actors in Conflict Management." In Crocker, C.A., Hampson, F.O., and Aall, P. (eds.), *Leashing the Dogs of War: Conflict Management in a Divided World* (Washington, DC: United States Institute of Peace Press, 2007).

Abu-Nimer, M. "Conflict Resolution Training in the Middle East: Lessons to Be Learned." *International Negotiation* 3, 1998, 99–116.

———. *Dialogue, Conflict Resolution and Change: Arab-Jewish Encounters in Israel* (Albany: State University of New York Press, 1999).

———. (ed.). *Reconciliation, Justice, and Coexistence: Theory and Practice* (Lanham, MD: Lexington, 2001).

Acharya, A. *Constructing a Regional Security Community in Southeast Asia: ASEAN and the Problem of Regional Order* (London: Routledge, 2001).

———. "Is Anyone Still Not a Constructivist?" *International Relations of the Asia-Pacific* 5(2), August 2005.

———. *Whose Ideas Matters? Agency and Power in Asian Regionalism* (Ithaca, NY: Cornell University Press, 2009).

Ackermann, A. "Reconciliation as a Peace-Building Process in Postwar Europe: The Franco-German Case." *Peace and Change* 19(3), 1994, 229–250.

Adler, E. "Constructivism." In Carlneas, W., Simmons, B., and Risse, T. (eds.), *Handbook of International Relations* (Thousand Oaks, CA: Sage, 2003).

Adler, E., and Barnett, M. (eds.). *Security Communities* (Cambridge, UK: Cambridge University Press, 1998).

Agha, H.S., Feldman, S., Khalidi, A., and Schiff, Z. *Track II Diplomacy: Lessons from the Middle East* (Cambridge, MA: MIT Press, 2003).

Allport, G.W. "The Historical Background of Social Psychology." In Lindzey, G., and Aronson, E. (eds.), *The Handbook of Social Psychology* (New York: McGraw-Hill, 1985).

———. *The Nature of Prejudice* (Cambridge, MA: Perseus Books, 1954).

Alpher, J. "Time to Hang Up My Track (II) Shoes." Posted on "Jewish Daily Forward" website, June 16, 2006, at: http://forward.com/articles/782/time-to-hang-up-my-track-ii-shoes/ (accessed August 1, 2012).

Amir, Y. "The Role of Inter-group Contact in Change of Prejudice and Ethnic Relations." In Katz, P.A. (ed.), *Towards the Elimination of Racism* (New York: Pergamon, 1976).

Anderson, M., Chigas, D., and Woodrow, P. *Encouraging Effective Evaluation of Conflict Prevention and Peacebuilding Activities; Towards DAC Guidance,* DCD 2007(3) (Paris: Organisation for Economic Co-operation and Development, September 2007).

Avruch, K., and Nan, S.A. "Introduction: The Constraints of Practicing Conflict Resolution from Academic Settings." *Negotiation Journal* 13(1), April 2013.

Azar, E. "From Strategic to Humanistic International Relations." In Jamgotch, N. (ed.), *Thinking the Unthinkable: Investment in Human Survival* (Washington, DC: University Press of America, 1978).

———. "Management of Protracted Conflicts in the Third World." *Ethnic Studies Report* 4(2), 1986.

———. "Protracted International Conflicts: Ten Propositions." *International Interactions* 12, 1985.

———. "The Theory of Protracted Social Conflicts and the Challenge of Transforming Conflict Situations." In Zinnes, D.A. (ed.), *Conflict Processes and the Breakdown of International Systems* (Denver: Graduate School of International Relations, University of Denver, 1984).

Ba, A.D. "On Norms, Rule Breaking, and Security Communities: A Constructivist Response," *International Relations of the Asia-Pacific* 5(2), August 2005.

Babbitt, E. "Conflict Resolution and Human Rights: The State of the Art." In Bercovitch, J., Kremenyuk, V., and Zartman, I.W. (eds.), *The Sage Handbook of Conflict Resolution* (Thousand Oaks, CA: Sage, 2009).

———. "The Evolution of International Conflict Resolution: From Cold War to Peacebuilding." *Negotiation Journal* 25(4), 2009.

Babbitt, E., and d'Estrée, T.P. "An Israeli-Palestinian Women's Workshop: Application of the Interactive Problem-solving Approach." In Crocker, C.A., Hampson, F.O., and Aall, P. (eds.), *Managing Global Chaos: Sources of and Responses to International Conflict* (Washington, DC: United States Institute of Peace Press, 1996).

Babbitt, E., and Hampson, F.O. "Conflict Resolution as a Field of Inquiry: Practice Informing Theory." *International Studies Quarterly* 13(1), 2011.

Baker, P. "Conflict Resolution Versus Democratic Governance: Divergent Paths to Peace." In Crocker, C.A., Hampson, F.O., and Aall., P. (eds.), *Managing Global Chaos: Sources of and Responses to International Conflict* (Washington, DC: United States Institute of Peace Press, 1996).

Ball, D., and Guan, K.C. (eds.). *Assessing Track Two Diplomacy in the Asia-Pacific*

Region; A CSCAP Reader (Singapore: S. Rajaratnam School of International Studies, 2010).

Ball, D., Milner, A., and Taylor, B. "Track 2 Security Dialogue in the Asia-Pacific: Reflections and Future Directions." *Asian Security* 2(3), 2006.

Barnett, M.N. *Dialogues in Arab Politics: Negotiations in Regional Order* (New York: Columbia University Press, 1998).

Barry, B., and Robinson, R.J. "Ethics in Conflict Resolution: The Ties That Bind." *International Negotiation* 7(2), 2002.

Bartoli, A. "Mediating Peace in Mozambique: The Role of the Community of Sant'Egidio." In Crocker, C.A, Hampson, F.O., and Aall, P. (eds.), *Herding Cats: Multiparty Mediation in a Complex World* (Washington, DC: United States Institute of Peace Press, 2003).

Beardly, K. "Agreements Without Peace? International Mediation and Time Inconsistency Problems." *American Journal of Political Science* 52(4), 2008, 723–740.

Bercovitch, J., and Chalfin, J. "Contact and Conflict Resolution: Examining the Extent to Which Interpersonal Contact and Cooperation Can Affect the Management of International Conflicts." *International Negotiation* 16, 2011, 11–37.

Beriker, N. "Conflict Resolution: The Missing Link Between Liberal International Relations Theory and Realistic Practice." In Sandole, J.D., Byrne, S., Sandole-Staroste, I., and Senehi, J. (eds.), *Handbook of Conflict Analysis and Resolution* (Oxford, UK: Routledge, 2009).

Berman, M.R., and Johnson, J.E. *Unofficial Diplomats* (New York: Columbia University Press, 1977).

Bernstein, B. *Classes, Codes and Control* (London: Routledge, 1975).

Bitter, J.N. *Les Dieux Embusqes* (Geneva: Librarie DROZ, 2003). In Mason, S.A., *Mediation and Facilitation in Peace Processes* (Zurich: Center for Security Studies, 2007).

Blake, R.R., Shepherd, H.A., and Mouton, J.S. *Managing Inter-group Conflict in Industry* (Houston: Gulf, 1964).

Blalock, H.M. *Power and Conflict: Toward a General Theory* (Thousand Oaks, CA: Sage, 1989).

Bloomfield, D., and Reilly, B. "The Changing Nature of Conflict and Conflict Management." In Harris, P., and Reilly, B. (eds.), *Democracy and Deep-Rooted Conflict* (Stockholm: Institute for Democracy and Electoral Assistance, 1998).

Boutros-Gali, B. *An Agenda for Peace: Preventive Diplomacy, Peacemaking and Peace-keeping*, United Nations Document A/47/277-S/24111 (New York: United Nations Organization, 1992).

Bowling, D., and Hoffman, D. "Bringing Peace into the Room: The Personal Qualities of the Mediator and the Impact on Mediation." *Negotiation Journal* 16(1), January 2000.

Brooks, S.G. "Dueling Realisms." *International Organization* 51(3), Summer 1997.

Brown, M.E., Lynn-Jones, S.M., and Miller, S.E. *Debating the Democratic Peace* (Cambridge, MA: MIT Press, 1996).

Burgess, H., and Burgess, G. *Conducting Track II Peacemaking* (Washington, DC: United States Institute of Peace Press, 2010).

Burton, J.W. *Conflict: Human Needs Theory* (New York: St. Martin's Press, 1990).

———. *Conflict: Resolution and Prevention* (New York: St. Martin's Press, 1990).

———. *Conflict and Communication: The Use of Controlled Communication in International Relations* (London: Macmillan, 1969).

———. *Resolving Deep-rooted Conflict: A Handbook* (Lanham, MD: University Press of America, 1987).

Burton, J.W., and Sandole, D. "Generic Theory: The Basis of Conflict Resolution." *Negotiation Journal* 2, 1986.

Bush, K., and Duggan, C. "Evaluation in Conflict Zones: Methodological and Ethical Challenges." *Journal of Peacebuilding and Development* 8(2), 2013, 5–25.

Bush, R.B., and Folger, J. *The Promise of Mediation,* rev. ed. (San Francisco: Jossey-Bass, 2005).

Canadian International Development Agency. "Results-Based Management Tools at CIDA: A How-to Guide." http://www.acdi-cida.gc.ca/acdi-cida/acdi-cida.nsf/eng/NAT-92213444-N2H (accessed August 11, 2013).

Capie, D. "When Does Track Two Matter? Structure, Agency and Asian Regionalism." *Review of International Political Economy* 17(2), May 2010.

Capie, D., and Evans, P. *The Asia-Pacific Security Lexicon, 2nd ed.* (Singapore: Institute of Southeast Asian Studies, 2007), 229–240.

Carr, E.H. *The Twenty Years' Crisis 1919–1939: An Introduction to the Study of International Relations,* first published in 1939.

Cashman, G. *What Causes War? An Introduction to Theories of International Conflict* (New York: Lexington Books, 1993).

Centre for Humanitarian Dialogue (HD Centre). "Aceh, Indonesia." http://www.hdcentre.org/en/our-work/peacemaking/past-activities/aceh-indonesia/ (accessed December 31, 2013).

Chaitin, J. "Creating Safe Spaces for Communication." In Burgess, G., and Burgess, H. (eds.), *Beyond Intractability*. Conflict Information Consortium, University of Colorado, Boulder. Posted July 2003 at: http://www.beyondintractability.org/bi-essay/safe-spaces.

Chataway, C.J. "The Problem of Transfer from Confidential Interactive Problem-Solving: What Is the Role of the Facilitator?" *Political Psychology* 23(1), 2002.

———. "Track II Diplomacy from a Track I Perspective." *Negotiation Journal* 14(3), July 1998.

Chigas, D. "Capacities and Limits of NGOs as Conflict Managers." In Crocker, C.A., Hampson, F.O., and Aall, P. (eds.), *Leashing the Dogs of War: Conflict Management in a Divided World* (Washington, DC: United States Institute of Peace Press, 2007).

———. "Unofficial Interventions with Official Actors: Parallel Negotiation Training in Violent Intrastate Conflicts." *International Negotiation* 2, 1997, 409–436.

Chua, E.G., and Gudykunst, W.B. "Conflict Resolution Styles in Low- and High-context Cultures." *Communication Research Reports* 4(1), June 1987.

Chufrin, G., and Saunders, H. "A Public Peace Process." *Negotiation Journal* 9(3), 1993, 155–177.

Church, C., and Shouldice, J. *The Evaluation of Conflict Resolution Interventions: Framing the State of Play* (Letterkenny, Ireland: Browne, 2002).

Church, C., and Shouldice, J. *The Evaluation of Conflict Resolution Intervention, Part 2: Emerging Practice and Theory* (Letterkenny, Ireland: Browne, 2003).

Clark, I.D., and Swain, H. "Distinguishing the Real from the Surreal in Management Reform: Suggestions for Beleaguered Administrators in the Government of Canada." *Canadian Public Administration* 48(4), Winter 2005, 453–476.

Clark, P., and Kaufman, Z. *After Genocide: Transnational Justice, Post-Conflict Reconstruction, and Reconciliation in Rwanda and Beyond* (New York: Columbia University Press, 2009).

Cobb, S., and Rifkin, J. "Practice and Paradox: Deconstructing Neutrality in Mediation." *Law and Social Inquiry* 16(1), 1991.

Cohen, R. "Negotiating Across Cultures." In Crocker, C.A., Hampson, F.O., and Aall, P. (eds.), *Managing Global Chaos: Sources of and Responses to International Conflict* (Washington, DC: United States Institute of Peace Press, 1996).

Coleman, P.T. "Power and Conflict." In Deutsch, M., Coleman, P.T., and Marcus, E.C. (eds.), *The Handbook of Conflict Resolution: Theory and Practice, 2nd ed.* (San Francisco: Jossey-Bass, 2006), 120–143.

Coleman, P.T., and Lim, J. "A Systematic Approach to Evaluating the Effects of Collaborative Negotiation Training on Individuals and Groups." *Negotiation Journal* 17(4), 2001.

Common Ground News Service. "Search for Common Ground." http://www.commongroundnews.org/index.php (accessed December 31, 2013).

Conflict Information Consortium, University of Colorado. "Beyond Intractability." http://www.beyondintractability.org/ (accessed August 2, 2012).

Cook, S.W. "Interpersonal and Attitudinal Outcomes in Cooperating Interracial Groups." *Journal of Research and Development in Education* 12(1), 1978, 97–113.

Cox, M., Ikenberry, G.J., and Inoguchi, T. (eds.). *American Democracy Promotion: Impulses, Strategies and Impacts* (Oxford, UK: Oxford University Press, 2000).

Crocker, C.A. *High Noon in Southern Africa: Making Peace in a Rough Neighborhood* (New York: Norton, 1992).

———. "Thoughts on the Conflict Management Field After 30 Years." *International Negotiation* 16, 2011.

Crocker, C.A., Hampson, F.O., and Aall, P. "Multiparty Mediation and the Conflict Cycle." In Crocker, C.A., Hampson, F.O., and Aall, P. (eds.), *Herding Cats: Multiparty Mediation in a Complex World* (Washington, DC: United States Institute of Peace Press, 2003).

Cross, S., and Rosenthal, R. "Three Models of Conflict Resolution: Effects on Intergroup Expectancies and Attitudes." *Journal of Social Issues* 55(1), 1999, 561–580.

Çuhadar, E. "Assessing Transfer from Track Two Diplomacy: The Cases of Water and Jerusalem." *Journal of Peace Research*, 46(5), 2009.

———. "Problem Solving Workshops." In Young, N.J. (ed.), *The Oxford International Encyclopedia of Peace* (Oxford, UK: Oxford University Press, 2010), vol. 3, 574–578.

Çuhadar, E., and Dayton, B. "Oslo and Its Aftermath: Lessons Learned from Track Two Diplomacy." *Negotiation Journal 28(2)*, April 2012.

Çuhadar, E., and Dayton, B. "The Social Psychology of Identity and Inter-group Conflict: From Theory to Practice." *International Studies Perspectives* 12, 2011.

Çuhadar, E., Dayton, B., and Paffenholz, T. "Evaluation in Conflict Resolution and Peacebuilding." In Sandole, D.J., Byrne, S., Sandole-Staroste, I., and Senehi, J. (eds.), *Handbook of Conflict Analysis and Resolution* (New York: Routledge, 2009), 286–299.

Curle, A. *Making Peace* (London: Tavistock, 1971).

Davidheiser, M. "Race, Worldviews, and Conflict Mediation: Black and White Styles of Conflict Revisited." *Peace and Change* 33(1), January 2008.

Davidson, J.A., McElwee, G., and Hannan, G. "Trust and Power as Determinants of Conflict Resolution Strategy and Outcome Satisfaction." *Peace and Conflict: Journal of Peace Psychology* 10, 2004, 275–292.

Davidson, W.D., and Montville, J.V. "Foreign Policy According to Freud." *Foreign Policy* 45, Winter 1981–82.

Dayton, B.W. "Useful but Insufficient: Intermediaries in Peacebuilding." In Dayton, B.W., and Kriesberg, L. (eds.), *Conflict Transformation and Peacebuilding* (New York: Routledge, 2009), 61–73.

de Reuck, A.V.S. "Controlled Communication: Rationale and Dynamics." *The Human Context* 6(1), 1974.

———. "A Note on Techniques and Procedures" (London: CIBA Foundation, 1966).

De Vries, M., and Maoz, I. "Tracking for Peace: Assessing the Effectiveness of Track Two Diplomacy in the Israeli-Palestinian Conflict." *Dynamics of Asymmetric Conflict* 6(1–3), 2013, 62–74.

d'Estrée, T.P., Fast, L.A., Weiss, J.N., and Jakobsen, M.S. "Changing the Debate About 'Success' in Conflict Resolution Efforts." *Negotiation Journal* 17(2), April 2001, 101–113.

Deutsch, M. "An Experimental Study of the Effects of Cooperation and Competition upon Group Process." *Human Relations* 2, 1949.

———. "Introduction." In Deutsch, M., Coleman, P.T., and Marcus, E.C. (eds.), *The Handbook of Conflict Resolution: Theory and Practice, 2nd ed.* (San Francisco: Jossey-Bass, 2006), 1–20.

———. "Justice and Conflict." In Deutsch, M., Coleman, P.T., and Marcus, E.C. (eds.), *The Handbook of Conflict Resolution: Theory and Practice, 2nd ed.* (San Francisco: Jossey-Bass, 2006).

———. "Social Psychology's Contributions to the Study of Conflict Resolution." *Negotiation Journal*, October 2002.

Deutsch, M., and Goldman, J.S. "A Framework for Thinking About Research on Conflict Resolution Initiatives." In Deutsch, M., Coleman, P.T., and Marcus, E.C. (eds.), *The Handbook of Conflict Resolution: Theory and Practice, 2nd ed.* (San Francisco: Jossey-Bass, 2006).

Diamond, L., and McDonald, J. *Multi-track Diplomacy: A Systems Approach to Peace, 3rd ed.* (West Hartford, CT: Kumarian Press, 1996).

Dirks, K., and Ferrin, D. "The Role of Trust in Organizational Settings." *Organization Science* 12(4), 2001, 450–467.

Docherty, J.S. "Culture and Negotiation: Symmetrical Anthropology for Negotiators." *Marquette Law Review* 87(4), 2004.

———. *Learning Lessons from Waco: When the Parties Bring Their Gods to the Negotiation Table* (Syracuse, NY: Syracuse University Press, 2001).

Dollard, J., *et al. Frustration and Aggression* (New Haven, CT: Yale University Press, 1939).

Doob, L.W. "Adieu to Private Intervention in Political Conflicts?" *International Journal of Group Tensions* 17(1), 1987, 15–27.

———. "A Cyprus Workshop: An Exercise in Intervention Methodology." *Journal of Social Psychology* 94(2), 1974.

———. *Interventions: Guides and Perils* (New Haven, CT: Yale University Press, 1993).

———. "Unofficial Intervention in Destructive Social Conflicts." In Brislin, R.W., *et al.* (eds.), *Cross Cultural Perspectives on Learning* (New York: Wiley, 1975).

Doob, L.W., and Foltz, W.J. "The Belfast Workshop: An Application of Group Techniques to a Destructive Conflict." *Journal of Conflict Resolution* 17, 1973.

Doyle, M.W. "Kant, Liberal Legacies, and Foreign Affairs, Part 2." *Philosophy and Public Affairs* 12(4), Autumn 1983.

———. *Ways of War and Peace* (New York: Norton, 1997).

Dwyer, S. "Reconciliation for Realists." *Ethics and International Affairs* 13(1), 1999, 81–89.

Egeland, J. "The Oslo Accord: Multiparty Facilitation Through the Norwegian Channel." In Crocker, C.A, Hampson, F.O., and Aall, P. (eds.), *Herding Cats: Multiparty Mediation in a Complex World* (Washington, DC: United States Institute of Peace Press, 2003).

Elliott, M., d'Estrée, T.P., and Kaufman, S. "Evaluation as a Tool for Reflection." In Burgess, G., and Burgess, H. (eds.), *Beyond Intractability.* Conflict Information Consortium, University of Colorado, Boulder. Posted September 2003 at: http://www.beyondintractability.org/bi-essay/evaluation-reflection.

Emery, F.E., and Trist, E.L. "The Causal Texture of Organizational Environments." *Human Relations* 18(1), 1964, 21–32.

Evangelista, M. *Unarmed Forces: The Trans-national Movement to End the Cold War* (Ithaca, NY: Cornell University Press, 1999).

Evans, P. "Possibilities for Security Cooperation in the Asia-Pacific: Track 2 and Track 1." In *Multilateralism in Asia Pacific: What Role for Track Two?* (Honolulu, HI: National Defense University, Washington; U.S. Pacific Command; Asia Pacific Center for Security Studies, March 27, 2001). www.ndu.edu/inss/symposia/pacific2001/evanspaper.htm.

Fast, L.A., Neufeldt, R.C., and Schirch, L. "Toward Ethically Grounded Conflict Interventions: Reevaluating Challenges in the 21st Century." *International Negotiation* 7(2), 2002.

Finnmore, M. *National Interests and International Society* (Ithaca, NY: Cornell University Press, 1996).

Fischer, M. "Conflict Transformation by Training in Non-violent Action: Activities of the Centre for Nonviolent Action in the Balkan Region." *Berghof Occasional Paper No. 18* (Berlin: Berghof Centre for Constructive Conflict Management, 2001).

Fisher, R.J. "The Contingency Model for Third Party Interventions." In Nan, S.A., Mamphilly, Z.C., and Bartoli, A. (eds.), *Peacemaking: From Practice to Theory, vol. 2* (Santa Barbara, CA: Praeger, 2012).

———. "Developing the Field of Interactive Conflict Resolution: Issues in Training, Funding and Institutionalisation." *Political Psychology* 14, 1993.

———. "Historical Mapping of the Field of Inter-active Conflict Resolution." In Davies, J., and Kaufman, E. (eds.), *Second Track/Citizen's Diplomacy: Concepts and Techniques for Conflict Transformation* (Lanham, MD: Rowman & Littlefield, 2002).

———. *Interactive Conflict Resolution* (Syracuse, NY: Syracuse University Press, 1997).

———. "Intergroup Conflict." In Deutsch, M., Coleman, P.T., and Marcus, E.C. (eds.), *The Handbook of Conflict Resolution: Theory and Practice, 2nd ed.* (San Francisco: Jossey-Bass, 2006), 176–196.

———. "Introduction: Analysing Successful Transfer Effects in Interactive Conflict Resolution." In Fisher, R.J. (ed.), *Paving the Way: Contributions of Interactive Conflict Resolution to Peacemaking* (New York: Lexington, 2005).

———. *The Social Psychology of Intergroup and International Conflict Resolution* (New York: Springer-Verlag, 1990).

———. "Training as Interactive Conflict Resolution: Characteristics and Challenges." *International Negotiation* 2(3), 1997, special issue, "Conflict Resolution Training in Divided Societies," guest edited by Fisher.

———. "Transfer Effects from Track Two Diplomacy: Toward a Process and Outcome Model." paper presented at workshop "Transfer and Track Two Diplomacy," Stanford University, March 20–21, 2014, edited volume forthcoming.

Fisher, R., and Keashly, L. "Distinguishing Third Party Interventions in Intergroup Conflict: Consultation Is *Not* Mediation." *Negotiation Journal* 4, 1988.

Fisher, R.J., and Keashly, L. "The Potential Complementarity of Mediation and Consultation Within a Contingency Model of Third Party Intervention." *Journal of Peace Research* 28, 1991.

Fisher, R., Ury, W., and Patton, B. *Getting to Yes: Negotiating Agreement Without Giving In* (New York: Penguin, 1991).

Fitzduff, M., and Church, C. (eds.). *NGOs at the Table: Strategies for Influencing Policies in Areas of Conflict* (New York: Rowman & Littlefield, 2004).

Follett, M.P. *Dynamic Administration: The Collected Papers of Mary Parker Follett*, ed. H. Metcalf and L. Urwick (New York: Harper, 1942).

Forsythe, D. *Humanitarian Politics: The International Committee of the Red Cross* (Baltimore: Johns Hopkins University Press, 1977).

French, J.R.P., Jr., and Raven, B. "The Bases of Social Power." In Cartwright, D. (ed.), *Studies in Social Power* (Ann Arbor: University of Michigan Press, 1959), 150–167.

Fulbright-Anderson, K., Kubisch, A., and Connell, J. (eds.). *New Approaches to Evaluating Community Initiatives, vol. 2* (New York: Aspen Institute, 1998).

Galtung, J. *Peace by Peaceful Means: Peace and Conflict, Development and Civilization* (London: Sage, 1996).

Gent, S.E., and Shannon, M. "Bias and Effectiveness of Third Party Conflict Management Mechanisms." *Conflict Management and Peace Science* 28(2), 2011.

George, A.L. "The Two Cultures of Academia and Policy-Making: Bridging the Gap." *Political Psychology* 15(1), 1994, 143–172.

Gibb, J.R. "Defensive Communication." *Journal of Communications* 11(3), 1961, 141–148.

Gilpin, R. *War and Change in World Politics* (Cambridge, UK: Cambridge University Press, 1981).

Girard, M., Wolf-Dieter, E., and Webb, K. (eds.). *Theory and Practice in Foreign Policy Making: National Perspectives on Academics and Professionals in International Relations* (London: Pinter, 1994).

Goh, G. "The 'ASEAN Way': Non-intervention and ASEAN's Role in Conflict Management." *Stanford Journal of East Asian Affairs* 3(1), Spring 2003, 113–118.

Goldberg, S.B. "The Secrets of Successful Mediators." *Negotiation Journal 21(3)*, July 2005, 366.

Goodhand, J. *Aiding Peace: The Role of NGOs in Armed Conflict* (Boulder, CO: Lynne Rienner, 2006).

Greig, J.M. "Moments of Opportunity: Recognising Conditions of Ripeness for International Mediation Between Enduring Rivals." *Journal of Conflict Resolution* 45(6), December 2001.

Groom, A.J.R. "Paradigms in Conflict: The Strategist, the Conflict Researcher, and the Peace Researcher." *Review of International Studies* 14, 1988.

Haas, P. "Introduction: Epistemic Communities and International Policy Coordination." *International Organization* 46, Winter 1992.

Haas, R.N. *Conflicts Unending* (New Haven, CT: Yale University Press, 1990).

Hall, E.T. *Beyond Culture* (Garden City, NY: Anchor Books, 1976).

Hara, F. "Burundi: A Case of Parallel Diplomacy." In Crocker, C.A, Hampson, F.O., and Aall, P. (eds.), *Herding Cats: Multiparty Mediation in a Complex World* (Washington, DC: United States Institute of Peace Press, 2003).

Held, D., and McGrew, A. (eds.). *The Global Transformations Reader: An Introduction to the Globalization Debate* (Cambridge, UK: Polity Press, 2003).

Hernandez, C.G. "Track Two and Regional Policy: The ASEAN ISIS in Asian Decision-making." In Soesastro, H., Joewono, C., and Hernandez, C.G. (eds.), *Twenty Two Years of ASEAN ISIS: Origin, Evolution and Challenges of Track Two Diplomacy* (Jakarta: ASEAN ISIS; Kanisius Printing, 2006).

Hill, B.J. "An Analysis of Conflict Resolution Techniques: From Problem-Solving Workshops to Theory." *Journal of Conflict Resolution* 26(1), March 1982, 109–138.

Hill, C., and Beshoff, P. (eds.). *Two Worlds of International Relations: Academics, Practitioners and the Trade in Ideas* (London: Routledge, 1994).

Hircshfeld, Y. *Track Two Diplomacy Toward an Israeli-Palestinian Solution, 1978–2014* (Washington, DC: Woodrow Wilson Center Press, 2014).

Hollis, F. "Personality Diagnosis in Casework." In Farad, H. (ed.), *Ego Psychology and Dynamic Case Work* (New York: Family Service Association of America, 1958).

Hooper, P.F. (ed.). *Rediscovering the IPR: Proceedings of the First International Research Conference on the Institute of Pacific Affairs* (Honolulu: Centre for Arts and Humanities, University of Hawaii, 1994).

Huyse, L., Salter, M., and Ingelaere, B. *Traditional Justice and Reconciliation After Violent Conflict: Learning from African Experiences* (Stockholm: International IDEA, 2008).

Ikenberry, G.J. *After Victory: Institutions, Strategic Restraint, and the Rebuilding of Order After Major Wars* (Princeton, NJ: Princeton University Press, 2001).

Initiatives of Change. "A Brief History." http://www.iofc.org/history (accessed December 31, 2013).

International Crisis Group. *Southern Philippines Backgrounder: Terrorism and the Peace Process*, ICG Asia Report, no. 80 (Singapore/Brussels: International Crisis Group, 2004).

Jackson, R. "Constructivism and Conflict Resolution." In Bercovitch, J., Kremenyuk, V., and Zartman, I.W. (eds.), *The Sage Handbook of Conflict Resolution* (Thousand Oaks, CA: Sage, 2009), ch. 9.

Jentleson, B.W. "The Need for Praxis: Bringing Policy Relevance Back In." *International Security* 4, 2002, 169–183.

Jervis, R. "Theories of War in an Era of Leading Power Peace." *American Political Science Review 96(1)*, March 2002.

Jessop, M., Aljets, D., and Chacko, B. "The Ripe Moment for Civil Society." *International Negotiation* 13, 2008, 93–109.

Job, B. "Track 2 Diplomacy: Ideational Contribution to the Evolving Asia Security Order." In Alagappa, M. (ed.), *Asian Security Order: Instrumental and Normative Features* (Stanford, CA: Stanford University Press, 2002).

Jones, P. "Arms Control in the Middle East; Is It Time to Renew ACRS?" *Disarmament Forum (United Nations Institute for Disarmament Research), no. 2*, 2005.

——. "Canada and International Conflict Mediation." *International Negotiation* 18, 2013.

——. *Canada and Track Two Diplomacy* (Toronto: Canadian International Council, 2008).

——. "Civil Society Dialogues and Middle East Regional Security: The Asia-Pacific Model." In Kane, C., and Murauskaite, E. (eds.), *Regional Security Dialogue in the Middle East: Changes, Challenges and Opportunities* (London: Routledge, 2014).

——. "Filling a Critical Gap or Just Wasting Time? Track Two Diplomacy and

Middle East Regional Security." *Disarmament Forum (United Nations Institute for Disarmament Research), no.* 2, 2008.

——. "How to Negotiate with Iran." *Foreign Policy (online ed.),* April 7, 2009.

——. "Negotiating Regional Security in the Middle East: The ACRS Experience and Beyond." *Journal of Strategic Studies* 26(3), September 2003.

——. "Talking with Al Qaeda: Is There a Role for Track Two?" *International Negotiation* 20(2), Summer 2015.

——. *Towards a Regional Security Regime for the Middle East: Issues and Options* (Stockholm: Stockholm International Peace Research Institute, 1998; reprinted with an extensive new afterword in 2011).

——. "Track II Diplomacy and the Gulf Weapons of Mass Destruction Free Zone." *Security and Terrorism Research Bulletin* (Gulf Research Center, Dubai) 1, October 2005.

——. "U.S.–Iran Nuclear Track Two from 2005 to 2011: What Have We Learned? Where Are We Going?" *Negotiation Journal 30(4),* October 2014, 347–366.

Kanwal, G. "India-Pakistan Track II Peace-making Efforts." Posted on US-INPAC website, December 22, 2011, at: http://blog.usinpac.com/gurmeet-kanwal/india-pakistan-track-ii-peace-making-efforts/ (accessed August 1, 2012).

Kavaloski, V.C. "Transnational Citizen Peacemaking as Nonviolent Action." *Peace and Change* 1(2), April 1990.

Kaye, D.D. *Talking to the Enemy: Track Two Diplomacy in the Middle East and South Asia* (Santa Monica, CA: RAND, 2007).

——. "Track Two Diplomacy and Regional Security in the Middle East." *International Negotiation* 6(1), 2001.

Keashly, L., and Fisher, R. "A Contingency Perspective on Conflict Interventions: Theoretical and Practical Considerations." In Bercovitch, J. (ed.), *Resolving International Conflicts* (London: Lynne Rienner, 1996).

Keashly, L., Fisher, R., and Grant, P. "The Comparative Utility of Third Party Consultation and Mediation Within a Complex Simulation of Intergroup Conflict." *Human Relations* 46, 1993.

Keck, M.E., and Sikkink, K. *Activists Beyond Borders: Advocacy Networks in International Politics* (Ithaca, NY: Cornell University Press, 1998).

Kellen, D., Bekerman, Z., and Maoz, I. "An Easy Coalition: The Peacecamp Identity and Israeli-Palestinian Track Two Diplomacy." *Journal of Conflict Resolution* 57(4), 2012, 543–569.

Kelman, H.C. "Contributions of an Unofficial Conflict Resolution Effort to the Israeli-Palestinian Breakthrough." *Negotiation Journal* 11(1), January 1995.

——. "Evaluating the Contributions of Interactive Problem Solving to the Resolution of Ethnonational Conflicts." *Peace and Conflict* 14, 2008, 29–60.

——. "Interactive Problem-solving: Informal Mediation by the Scholar Practitioner." In Bercovitch, J. (ed.), *Studies in International Mediation: Essays in Honor of Jeffrey Z. Rubin* (New York: Palgrave Macmillan, 2002).

——. "The Interactive Problem-Solving Approach." In Crocker, C.A., and Kreisberg,

F.O. (eds.), *Constructive Conflicts: From Escalation to Resolution* (New York: Rowman & Littlefield, 1996).

——. "Interactive Problem Solving as a Tool for Second Track Diplomacy." In Davies, J., and Kaufman, E. (eds.), *Second Track/Citizen's Diplomacy: Concepts and Techniques for Conflict Transformation* (Lanham, MD: Rowman & Littlefield, 2002).

——. "The Problem Solving Workshop in Conflict Resolution." In Merritt, R.L. (ed.), *Communication in International Politics* (Urbana: University of Illinois Press, 1972).

——. "A Social-Psychological Approach to Conflict Analysis and Resolution." In Sandole, D., Byrne, S., and Sandole-Staroste, I. (eds.), *Handbook of Conflict Analysis and Resolution* (London: Routledge, 2008).

——. "Some Determinants of the Oslo Breakthrough." *International Negotiation* 2(2), 1997.

Kelman, H.C., and Cohen, S.P. "The Problem-Solving Workshop: A Social-Psychological Contribution to the Resolution of International Conflicts." *Journal of Peace Research* 13(2), 1976.

Keohane, R. (ed.). *Neoclassical Realism and Its Critics* (New York: Columbia University Press, 1986).

Khoo, N. "Deconstructing the ASEAN Security Community: A Review Essay." *International Relations of the Asia-Pacific* 4(1), February 2004.

Kim, D., Pan, Y., and Soo Park, H. "High- Versus Low-Context Culture: A Comparison of Chinese, Korean, and American Cultures." *Psychology and Marketing* 15(6), September 1998.

Kimmel, P.R. "Cultural Perspectives on International Negotiation." *Journal of Social Issues* 50(1), 1994, 179–196.

——. "Culture and Conflict." In Deutsch, M., Coleman, P.T., and Marcus, E.C. (eds.), *The Handbook of Conflict Resolution: Theory and Practice, 2nd ed.* (San Francisco: Jossey-Bass, 2006).

Kleiboer, M. "Ripeness of Conflict: A Fruitful Notion?" *Journal of Peace Research* 31(1), 1994.

——. "Understanding the Success or Failure of International Mediation." *Journal of Conflict Resolution* 40(2), 1996.

Kochman, T. *Black and White Styles of Conflict* (Chicago: University of Chicago Press, 1981).

Korac-Kakabadse, N., Kouzmin, A., Korac-Kakabadse, A., and Savery, L. "Low- and High-Context Communication Patterns: Towards Mapping Cross-cultural Encounters." *Cross Cultural Management: An International Journal* 8(2), 2001.

Kraft, H.J. "The Autonomy Dilemma of Track Two Diplomacy in Southeast Asia." *Security Dialogue* 31(3), September 2000.

Kramer, R., and Tyler, T.R. (eds.). *Trust in Organizations: Frontiers of Theory and Research* (Thousand Oaks, CA: Sage, 1996).

Kriesberg, L. "The Evolution of Conflict Resolution." In Bercovitch, J., Kremenyuk,

V., and Zartman, I.W. (eds.), *The Sage Handbook of Conflict Resolution* (London: Sage, 2009), 15–32.

Kydd, A. "Which Side Are You On? Bias, Credibility and Mediation." *American Journal of Political Science* 47(4), 2007.

Kydd, A., Wehr, P., and Lederach, J.P. "Mediating Conflict in Central America." *Journal of Conflict Resolution* 53(3), 2009.

Landau, E. "ACRS: What Worked, What Didn't and What Could Be Relevant for the Region Today." *Disarmament Forum (United Nations Institute for Disarmament Research), no. 2,* 2008.

Laue, J., and Cormick, C. "The Ethics of Intervention in Community Disputes." In Bermant, G., *et al.* (eds.), *The Ethics of Social Intervention* (New York: Halstead Press, 1978).

Lederach, J.P. *Building Peace: Sustainable Reconciliation in Divided Societies* (Washington, DC: United States Institute of Peace Press, 1995).

———. *Preparing for Peace: Conflict Transformation Across Cultures* (Syracuse, NY: Syracuse University Press, 1995).

———. *The Moral Imagination: The Art and Soul of Building Peace* (Oxford, UK: Oxford University Press, 2005).

Lederach, J.P., and Maiese, M. *Conflict Transformation.* http://www.beyondintractability.org/essay/transformation/?nid=1223 (accessed August 5, 2012).

Lederach, J.P., Neufeldt, R., and Culbertson, H. *Reflective Peacebuilding: A Planning, Monitoring and Learning Toolkit* (Mindanao, Philippines: Joan B. Kroc Institute for International Peace Studies; Catholic Relief Services/East Asia Regional Office, 2007).

Lemke, D. *Regions of War and Peace* (Cambridge, UK: Cambridge University Press, 2002).

Lewicki, R.J. "Trust, Trust Development and Trust Repair." In Deutsch, M., Coleman, P.T., and Marcus, E.C. (eds.), *The Handbook of Conflict Resolution: Theory and Practice, 2nd ed.* (San Francisco: Jossey-Bass, 2006), 92–119.

Lewicki, R.J., and Bunker, B.B. "Developing and Maintaining Trust in Work Relationships." In Kramer, R., and Tyler, T.R. (eds.), *Trust in Organizations: Frontiers of Theory and Research* (Thousand Oaks, CA: Sage, 1996).

Lewin, K. *A Dynamic Theory of Personality* (New York: McGraw-Hill, 1935).

———. *Resolving Social Conflicts* (New York: Harper & Bros., 1948).

Limbert, J.W. *Negotiating with Iran: Wrestling with the Ghosts of History* (Washington, DC: United States Institute of Peace Press, 2009).

Linville, P.W., Salovy, P., and Fisher, G.W. "Stereotyping and Perceived Distribution of Social Characteristics: An Application to Inter-group Perception." In Dovidio, J.F., and Gartner, S.L. (eds.), *Prejudice, Discrimination and Racism* (Orlando, FL: Academic Press, 1986), 165–208.

Lobell, S.E., Ripsman, N.M., and Taliaferro, J.W. (eds.). *Neoclassical Realism, the State and Foreign Policy* (Cambridge, UK: Cambridge University Press, 2009).

Malhotra, D., and Liyanage, S. "Long-Term Effects of Peace Workshops in Protracted Conflicts." *Journal of Conflict Resolution* 49(6), 2005, 908–924.

Mandelbaum, M. *The Ideas That Conquered the World* (New York: Public Affairs, 2002).

Mandell, B.S., and Fisher, R.J. "Training Third-Party Consultants in International Conflict Resolution." *Negotiation Journal* 8, July 1992.

Mansfield, E.D., and Snyder, J. *Electing to Fight: Why Emerging Democracies Go to War* (Cambridge, MA: MIT Press, 2005).

Maoz, I. "Evaluating the Communication Between Groups in Dispute: Equality on Contact Interventions Between Jews and Arabs in Israel." *Negotiation Journal* 21(1), 2005, 131–146.

———. "An Experiment in Peace: Reconciliation-aimed Dialogues of Israeli and Palestinian Youth." *Journal of Peace Research* 37, 2000, 721–736.

———. "Peacebuilding in Violent Conflict: Israeli-Palestinian Post Oslo People-to-People Activities." *International Journal of Politics, Culture and Society* 17(3), 2004, 563–574.

———. "Power Relations in Inter-group Encounters: A Case Study of Jewish-Arab Encounters in Israel." *International Journal of Intercultural Relations* 24, 2002, 259–277.

Mapendre, J. *Consequential Conflict Transformation Model, and the Complementarity of Track One, Track One and a Half and Track Two Diplomacy* (Atlanta, GA: Carter Center, 2000).

Mason, S.A. *Mediation and Facilitation in Peace Processes* (Zurich, Switzerland: Center for Security Studies, 2007).

Mattli, W. *The Logic of Regional Integration: Europe and Beyond* (Cambridge, UK: Cambridge University Press, 1999).

Maundi, M.O., Zartman, I.W., Khadiagala, G.M., and Nuamah, K. *Getting In: Mediators' Entry into the Settlement of African Conflicts* (Washington, DC: United States Institute of Peace Press, 2006).

Mayer, B. *Beyond Neutrality: Confronting the Crisis in Conflict Resolution* (San Francisco: Jossey-Bass, 2004).

Mazlish, B., and Iriye, A. (eds.). *The Global History Reader* (Abingdon, UK: Routledge, 2005).

Mearsheimer, J.J. "The False Promise of International Institutions." *International Security* 19(3), Winter 1994/95.

Merom, G. "Realist Hypothesis on Regional Peace." *Journal of Strategic Studies* 26(1), March 2001.

Miall, H. *Conflict Transformation: A Multi-Dimensional Task* (Berlin: Berghof Research Center for Constructive Conflict Management, 2004), available at: http://www.berghof-handbook.net/documents/publications/miall_handbook.pdf.

Miller, B. *States, Nations and the Great Powers: The Sources of Regional War and Peace* (Cambridge, UK: Cambridge University Press, 2007).

Miller, P.J., and Rempel, J.K. "Trust and Partner-Enhancing Attributions in Close Relationships." *Personality and Social Psychology Bulletin* 30(6), 2004, 695–705.

Mitchell, C.R. "Ending Confrontation Between Malaysia and Indonesia: A Pioneering Contribution to International Problem Solving." In Fisher, R.J. (ed.), *Paving the Way: Contributions of Interactive Conflict Resolution to Peacemaking* (New York: Lexington, 2005), 19–40.

———. "From Controlled Communication to Problem Solving: The Origins of Facilitated Conflict Resolution." *International Journal of Peace Studies* 6(1), Spring 2001.

———. *Peacemaking and the Consultant's Role* (Westmead, UK: Gower, 1981).

———. "Persuading Lions: Problems of Transferring Insights from Track-Two Exercises Undertaken in Conditions of Asymmetry." *Dynamics of Asymmetric Conflict* 2(1), 2009, 32–50.

———. "The Process and Stages of Mediation." In Smock, D.R. (ed.), *Making War and Waging Peace: Foreign Intervention in Africa* (Washington, DC: United States Institute of Peace Press, 1994).

Mitchell, C.R., and Banks, M. *Handbook of Conflict Resolution: The Analytical Problem-Solving Approach* (New York: Continuum, 1996).

Montville, J.V. "Transnationalism and the Role of Track Two Diplomacy." In Thompson, W.S., and Jensen, K.M. (eds.), *Approaches to Peace: An Intellectual Map* (Washington, DC: United States Institute of Peace Press, 1991).

Moore, C.W., and Woodrow, P. "Mapping Cultures: Strategies for Effective Intercultural Negotiations." In Davies, J., and Kaufman, E. (eds.), *Second Track/Citizen's Diplomacy: Concepts and Techniques for Conflict Transformation* (Lanham, MD: Rowman & Littlefield, 2002).

Moravschik, A. "Taking Preferences Seriously: A Liberal Theory of International Politics." *International Organization* 51(4), Autumn 1997, 513–53.

Morgenthau, H. *Politics Among Nations: The Struggle for Power and Peace* (New York: Knopf, 1948).

Morris, B. *Righteous Victims: A History of the Zionist-Arab Conflict, 1881–2001* (New York: Vintage Books, 2001).

Moscovici, S., and Markova, I. *The Making of Modern Social Psychology* (Cambridge, UK: Polity Press, 2006).

Mowle, T.S. "Worldviews in Foreign Policy: Realism, Liberalism and External Conflict." *Political Psychology* 24(3), 2003.

Nan, S.A. "*Complementarity and Co-ordination of Conflict Resolution Efforts in the Conflicts over Abkhazia, South Ossetia and Transdniestria.*" Ph.D. diss., George Mason University, 1999.

———. "Track One and a Half Diplomacy: Contributions to Georgia-South Ossetian Peacemaking." In Fisher, R.J. (ed.), *Paving the Way: Contributions of Interactive Conflict Resolution to Peacemaking* (New York: Lexington, 2005).

Nan, S.A., Druckman, D., and Horr, J.E. "Unofficial International Conflict Resolution: Is There a Track One and a Half? Are There Best Practices?" *Conflict Resolution Quarterly* 27(1), 2009, 65–82.

Nincic, M., and Lepgold, J. (eds.). *Being Useful: Policy Relevance and International Relations Theory* (Ann Arbor: University of Michigan Press, 2000).

Northrup, T.A. "The Dynamic Identity in Personal and Social Conflict." In Kriesberg, L., Northrup, T.A., and Thorson, S.J. (eds.), *Intractable Conflicts and Their Transformation* (Syracuse, NY: Syracuse University Press, 1989).

Nye, J.S., Jr. "International Relations: The Relevance of Theory to Practice." In Reus-Smit, C., and Snidal, D. (eds.), *Oxford Handbook of International Relations* (Oxford, UK: Oxford University Press, 2008), 648–660.

Ó Dochartaigh, N. "Together in the Middle: Back-channel Negotiation in the Irish Peace Process." *Journal of Peace Research* 48(6), 2011.

Paul, T.V. (ed.). *International Relations Theory and Regional Transformation* (Cambridge, UK: Cambridge University Press, 2012).

Peace and Justice Studies Association; International Peace Research Association Foundation. "Global Directory of Peace Studies and Conflict Resolution Programs." http://www.peacejusticestudies.org/globaldirectory (accessed August 2, 2012).

Peou, S. "Merit in Security Community Studies." *International Relations of the Asia-Pacific* 5(2), August 2005.

Pettigrew, T. "Advancing Racial Justice: Past Lessons for Future Use." In Knopke, H.J., Norrell, R.J., and Rogers, R.W. (eds.), *Opening Doors: Perspectives on Race Relations in Contemporary America* (Tuscaloosa: University of Alabama Press, 1991).

———. "Intergroup Contact Theory." *Annual Review of Psychology* 49, 1998, 65–85.

Phillips, D.L. *Unsilencing the Past: Track Two Diplomacy and Turkish-Armenian Reconciliation* (New York: Berghahn, 2005).

Picco, G. *Man Without a Gun: One Diplomat's Secret Struggle to Free the Hostages, Fight Terrorism, and End a War* (New York: Crown, 1999).

Posen, B.R. "The War for Kosovo: Serbia's Political-Military Strategy." *International Security* 24(4), Spring 2000.

Powers, D.A., and Ellison, C.G. "Interracial Contact and Black Racial Attitudes: The Contact Hypothesis and Selectivity Bias." *Social Forces* 74, 1995, 205–226.

Price, R. "Transnational Civil Society and Advocacy in World Politics." *World Politics* 55(4), July 2003.

Princen, T. *Intermediaries in International Conflict* (Princeton, NJ: Princeton University Press, 1992).

Program on Negotiation, Harvard Law School. "Principled Negotiation." http://www.pon.harvard.edu/tag/principled-negotiation/ (accessed August 5, 2013).

Pruitt, D.G. "Back-channel Communication in the Settlement of Conflict." *International Negotiation* 13(1), 2008, 37–54.

———. "Readiness Theory and the Northern Ireland Conflict." *American Behavioral Scientist* 50, 2007.

———. *Whither Ripeness Theory?* Working paper no. 25, Institute for Conflict Analysis and Resolution, George Mason University, 2005.

Pruitt, D.G., and Sung Hee Kim. *Social Conflict: Escalation, Stalemate, and Settlement*, 3rd. ed. (New York: McGraw-Hill, 2004).

Pruitt, D.G., and Kimmel, M.J. "Twenty Years of Experimental Gaming: Critique, Synthesis and Suggestions for the Future." *Annual Review of Psychology* 28, 1977.

Raffia, H. *The Art and Science of Negotiation* (Cambridge, MA: Harvard University Press, 1982).

Ramsbotham, O., Woodhouse, T., and Miall, H. *Contemporary Conflict Resolution, 3rd ed.* (Cambridge, UK: Polity Press, 2011).

Reimann, C. *Assessing the State of the Art in Conflict Transformation* (Berlin: Berghof Research Center for Constructive Conflict Management, 2004), 7–13, available at: http://www.berghof-handbook.net/documents/publications/reimann_handbook.pdf.

Ripsman, N.M. "Two Stages of Transition from the Region of War to a Region of Peace: Realist Transition and Liberal Endurance." *International Studies Quarterly* 49(4), December 2005.

Rosoux, V. "Is Reconciliation Negotiable?" *International Negotiation* 18, 2003, 471–493.

Ross, M.H. "Action Evaluation in the Theory and Practice of Conflict Resolution." *Peace and Conflict Studies* 8(1), 2001.

———. "Creating the Conditions for Peacemaking: Theories of Practice in Ethnic Conflict Resolution." *Ethnic and Racial Studies* 23(6), 2000, 1002–1034.

Ross, M.H., and Rothman, J. *Theory and Practice in Ethnic Conflict Management: Theorizing Success and Failure* (New York: St. Martin's Press, 1999).

Ross, W., and Wieland, C. "Effects of Interpersonal Trust and Time Pressure on Managerial Mediation Strategy in a Simulated Organizational Dispute." *Journal of Applied Psychology* 81, 1996.

Rotberg, R.J. (ed.). *Israeli and Palestinian Narratives of Conflict: History's Double Helix* (Bloomington: Indiana University Press, 2006).

Rothman, J. "Action Evaluation." In Burgess, G., and Burgess, H. (eds.), *Beyond Intractability*. Conflict Information Consortium, University of Colorado, Boulder. Posted October 2003 at: http://www.beyondintractability.org/bi-essay/action-evaluation.

———. (ed.). *From Identity-Based Conflict to Identity-Based Cooperation: The ARIA Approach in Theory and Practice* (New York: Springer, 2012).

———. *Resolving Identity-Based Conflict in Nations, Organizations and Communities* (San Francisco: Jossey-Bass, 1997).

Rouhana, N.N. "Interactive Conflict Resolution: Issues in Theory, Methodology, and Evaluation." In Druckman, D., and Stern, P.C. (eds.), *International Conflict Resolution After the Cold War* (Washington, DC: National Academy Press, 2000).

———. "Unofficial Third-Party Intervention in International Conflict: Between Legitimacy and Disarray." *Negotiation Journal* 11(3), July 1995.

Rousseau, D., Sitkin, S., Burt, R., and Camerer, C. "Not so Different After All: A Cross-discipline View of Trust." *Academy of Management Review* 23(3), 1998.

Rubin, J.Z. "International Mediation in Context." In Bercovitch, J., and Rubin, J.Z. (eds.), *Mediation in International Relations* (New York: St. Martin's Press, 1992).

Rubin, J., Pruitt, D., and Kim, S. *Social Conflict, Escalation, Stalemate and Settlement* (New York: McGraw-Hill, 1994).

Rubin, J.Z., and Sander, F.E.A. "Culture, Negotiation, and the Eye of the Beholder." *Negotiation Journal* 7, 1991.

Russet, B., and Oneal, J.R. *Triangulating Peace: Democracy, Interdependence and International Organizations* (New York: Norton, 2001).

Salem, P.E. "A Critique of Western Conflict Resolution from a Non-Western Perspective." *Negotiation Journal* 9(4), October 1993, 361–369.

Salem R. "Trust in Mediation." In *Beyond Intractability.* http://www.beyondintractability.org/essay/trust_mediation/ (accessed July 7, 2014).

Saunders, H.H. "Pre-negotiation and Circum-negotiation: Arenas of the Peace Process." In Crocker, C., Hampson, F.O., and Aall, P. (eds.), *Managing Global Chaos: Sources of and Responses to International Conflict* (Washington, DC: United States Institute of Peace Press, 1996).

———. *A Public Peace Process: Sustained Dialogue to Transform Racial and Ethnic Conflicts* (New York: St. Martin's Press, 1999).

———. *Sustained Dialogue in Conflicts: Transformation and Change* (New York: Palgrave Macmillan, 2011).

———. "We Need a Larger Theory of Negotiation: The Importance of Pre-Negotiation Phases." In Breslin, J.W., and Rubin, J.Z. (eds.), *Negotiation Theory and Practice* (Cambridge, MA: Program on Negotiation at Harvard Law School, 1991), 57–70.

Saunders, H.H., et al. "Interactive Conflict Resolution: A View for Policy Makers on Making and Building Peace." In Druckman, D., and Stern, P.C. (eds.), *International Conflict Resolution After the Cold War* (Washington, DC: National Academy Press, 2000).

Savun, B. "Information, Bias and Mediation Success." *International Studies Quarterly* 52, 2008.

Scham, P., Salem, W., and Pogrund, B. *Shared Histories: A Palestinian-Israeli Dialogue* (Walnut Creek, CA: Left Coast Press, 2005).

Schellenberg, J. *Conflict Resolution: Theory, Research and Practice* (Albany: State University of New York Press, 1996).

Schelling, T.C. *The Strategy of Conflict* (Cambridge, MA: Harvard University Press, 1960).

Schiff, A. "Reaching a Mutual Agreement: Readiness Theory and Coalition Building in the Aceh Peace Process." *Negotiation and Conflict Management Research* 7(1), 2014, 57–82.

Schroeder, J., and Risen, L. "Peace Through Friendship." *New York Times*, August 24, 2014, Focus section, p. 9.

Schweitzer, G.E. *Scientists, Engineers and Track Two Diplomacy: A Half-Century of*

U.S.-Russian Inter-academy Cooperation (Washington, DC: National Research Council of the National Academies, 2004).

Seitzinger, M.V. "Conducting Foreign Relations Without Authority: The Logan Act" (Washington, DC: Congressional Research Service, February 1, 2006), available at: https://www.fas.org/sgp/crs/misc/RL33265.pdf.

Sending, O.J., Pouliot, V., and Neumann, I.B. "The Future of Diplomacy: Changing Practices, Evolving Relationships." *International Journal 66(3)*, Summer 2011, 527–542.

Senger, J.M. "Tales of the Bazaar: Interest-based Negotiation Across Cultures." *Negotiation Journal* 18(3), July 2002.

Shapiro, I. *Extending the Framework of Inquiry: Theories of Change in Conflict Interventions* (Berlin: Berghof Research Center for Constructive Conflict Management, 2006), available at: http://www.berghof-handbook.net/documents/publications/dialogue5_shapiro_comm.pdf (accessed August 5, 2012).

———. "Theories of Practice and Change in Ethnic Conflict Interventions." In Fitzduff, M., and Stout, C.E. (eds.), *The Psychology of Resolving Ethnic Conflict, vol. 3* (Santa Barbara, CA: Praeger Security International, 2006).

Sheehan, I.S. "Conflict Transformation as Counterinsurgency." *Peace Review: A Journal of Social Justice* 26, March 2014, 121–128.

Sherif, M., Harvey, O.J., White, B.J., Hood, W.R., and Sherif, C.W. *Intergroup Conflict and Cooperation: The Robbers Cave Experiment (vol. 10)* (Norman, OK: University Book Exchange, 1961).

Sitkin, S.B., Rousseau, D.M., Burt, R.S., and Camerer, C. (eds.). "Special Topic Forum on Trust in and Between Organizations." *Academy of Management Review* 23(3), 1998.

Slim, R., and Saunders, H. "The Inter-Tajik Dialogue: From Civil War Towards Civil Society." In Abdullaev, K., and Barnes, C. (eds.), *Politics of Compromise: The Tajikistan Peace Process* (London: Conciliation Resources, 2001).

Smith, C.B. "Back and to the Future: The Inter-group Contact Hypothesis Revisited." *Sociological Inquiry* 64, 1994, 438–455.

Snyder, J. "One World, Rival Theories." *Foreign Policy* 145, November/December 2004.

Snyder, R.C., et al. (eds.). *Foreign Policy Decision Making (Revisited)* (London: Palgrave Macmillan, 2003).

Spector, B.I. "Negotiation Readiness in the Development Context: Adding Capacity to Ripeness." In Jeong, H.W. (ed.), *Approaches to Peacebuilding* (New York: Palgrave Macmillan, 2006), 79–99.

Spillman, K.R., and Kollars, N. "Herbert Kelman's Contribution to the Methodology of Practical Conflict Resolution." *Peace and Conflict: Journal of Peace Psychology* 16(4), November 2010.

Stedman, S.J. *Peacemaking in Civil War: International Mediation in Zimbabwe, 1974–1980* (Boulder, CO: Lynne Rienner, 1991).

Stein, J.G. (ed.). *Getting to the Table: The Processes of International Pre-negotiation* (Baltimore: Johns Hopkins University Press, 1989).

Stephan, W.G. "Intergroup Relations." In Lindzey, G., and Aronson, E. (eds.), *Handbook of Social Psychology, vol. 2* (New York: Random House, 1985).

Stern, P.C., and Druckman, D. "Evaluating Interventions in History: The Case of International Conflict Resolution." *International Studies Review* 2(1), Spring 2000, 33–63.

Stewart, E.C. "An Intercultural Interpretation of the Persian Gulf Crisis." *International Communication Studies* 4, 1991.

Stimec, A., Poitras, J., and Campbell, J.J. "Ripeness, Readiness and Grief in Conflict Analysis." In Matyok, T., Senehi, J., and Byrne, S. (eds.), *Critical Issues in Peace and Conflict Studies: Theory, Practice and Pedagogy* (Blue Ridge Summit, PA: Lexington Books, 2011), 143–157.

Strimling, A. "Stepping Out of the Tracks: Cooperation Between Official Diplomats and Private Facilitators." *International Negotiation* 11, 2006, 91–127.

Svensson, I. "Who Brings Peace? Neutral Versus Biased Mediation and Institutional Peace Arrangements in Civil Wars." *Journal of Conflict Resolution* 53(3), 2009.

Talbott, S. *Deadly Gambits; The Reagan Administration and the Stalemate in Nuclear Arms Control* (New York: Knopf, 1984), 116–151.

Tan, S.S. "Non-official Diplomacy in Southeast Asia: 'Civil Society' or 'Civil Service'?" *Contemporary Southeast Asia* 27(3), December 2005, 370–387.

Tieku, T.K. "Perks Diplomacy: The Role of Perquisites in Mediation." *International Negotiation* 18, 2013, 245–263.

Touval, S. "Coercive Mediation on the Road to Dayton." *International Negotiation* 1(1), 1996.

———. *The Peace Brokers: Mediators in the Arab-Israeli Conflict, 1948–1979* (Princeton, NJ: Princeton University Press, 1982).

Tutu, D. *No Peace Without Forgiveness* (London: Rider, 1999).

University of Ottawa, Faculty of Social Sciences. "Ottawa Dialogue." http://socialsciences.uottawa.ca/dialogue/eng/ (accessed December 31, 2013).

Van der Stoel, M. "The Role of the OSCE High Commissioner in Conflict Prevention." In Crocker, C.A., Hampson, F.O., and Aall, P. (eds.), *Herding Cats: Multiparty Mediation in a Complex World* (Washington, DC: United States Institute of Peace Press, 2003).

Vayrynen, T. *Culture and International Conflict Resolution: A Critical Analysis of the Work of John Burton* (Manchester, UK: University of Manchester Press, 2001).

Volkan, V.D. "Large-group Identity: Border Psychology and Other Related Issues." *Mind and Human Interaction* 13, 2003, 49–75.

———. "Large-group Identity and Post-Traumatic Flocking." *Psychology Tomorrow* blog at: http://www.psychologytomorrowmagazine.com/large-group-identity-and-post-traumatic-flocking/ (accessed June 27, 2014).

———. "Psychological Concepts Useful in the Building of Political Foundations Between Nations: Track II Diplomacy." *Journal of the American Psychoanalytical Association* 34(4), 1987, 903–935.

Von Neumann, J., and Morgenstern, O. *Theory of Games and Economic Behavior, 3rd ed.* (New York: Wiley, 1964, originally published in 1944).

Voorhees, J. *Dialogue Sustained: The Multilevel Peace Process and the Dartmouth Conference* (Washington, DC: United States Institute of Peace Press, 2002).

Wall, J.A., and Dunne, T.C. "State of the Art—Mediation Research: A Current Review." *Negotiation Journal* 28(2), April 2012.

Walt, S.M. "One World, Many Theories." *Foreign Policy* 110, Spring 1998.

Walton, R.E. "A Problem-solving Workshop on Border Conflicts in Eastern Africa." *Journal of Applied Behavioral Science* 6, 1970, 453–489.

Walton, R.E., and McKersie, R.B., *A Behavioral Theory of Labor Negotiations: An Analysis of a Social Interaction System* (Ithaca, NY: School of Industrial Labor Relations, Cornell University, 1991).

Waltz, K.N. *Theory of International Politics* (Reading, MA: Addison-Wesley, 1979).

Wanis-St. John, A. "Back-channel Negotiation: International Bargaining in the Shadows." *Negotiation Journal* 22(2), 2006, 119–144.

———. *Back-channel Negotiation: Secrecy in the Middle East Peace Process* (Syracuse, NY: Syracuse University Press, 2011).

Wanis-St. John, A., and Kew, D. "Civil Society and Peace Negotiations: Confronting Exclusion." *International Negotiation* 13(1), 2009, 11–36.

Weiss, C. *Evaluation Research* (Englewood Cliffs, NJ: Prentice Hall, 1972).

Weiss, T.G., and Kittikhoun, A. "Theory vs. Practice: A Symposium." *International Studies Review* 13(1), 2011.

Wendt, A. *Social Theory of International Politics* (Cambridge, UK: Cambridge University Press, 1999).

Winslade, J., and Monk, G.D. *Narrative Mediation: A New Approach to Conflict Mediation* (San Francisco: Jossey-Bass, 2000).

Woods, L.T. *Asia Pacific Diplomacy: Non-governmental Organizations and International Relations* (Vancouver: University of British Columbia Press, 1993).

———. "Letters in Support of the Institute of Pacific Relations: Defending a Nongovernmental Organisation." *Pacific Affairs* 76(4), Winter 2003–2004.

Worchel, P. "Trust and Distrust." In Austin, W.G., and Worchel, S. (eds.), *The Social Psychology of Intergroup Relations* (Belmont, CA: Wadsworth, 1979).

Yalem, R.J. "Controlled Communication and Conflict Resolution." *Journal of Peace Research* 8, 1971, 263–272.

Young, D.W. "Prescriptive and Elicitive Approaches to Conflict Resolution: Examples from Papua New Guinea." *Negotiation Journal* 14(3), July 1998, 211–220.

Zacher, M.W., and Matthew, R.A. "Liberal International Theory: Common Threads, Divergent Strands." In Kegley, C.W., Jr. (ed.), *Controversies in International Relations Theory: Realism and the Neoliberal Challenge* (Basingstoke, UK: Macmillan, 1995), 107–50.

Zartman, I.W. *Ripe for Resolution: Conflict and Intervention in Africa* (New York: Oxford University Press, 1985).

———. "Ripeness: The Hurting Stalemate and Beyond." In Druckman, D., and Stern, P.C. (eds.), *International Conflict Resolution After the Cold War* (Washington, DC: National Academy Press, 2000).

———. "A Skeptic's View." In Faure, G., and Rubin, J. (eds.), *Culture and Negotiation* (Newbury Park, CA: Sage, 1993).

Zartman, I.W., and Berman, M.R. *The Practical Negotiator* (New Haven, CT: Yale University Press, 1982).

Index

CPSIA information can be obtained
at www.ICGtesting.com
Printed in the USA
LVHW041053151219
640579LV00004B/673/P